PENGUIN

SELECTED POEMS:

JULES LAFORGUE was born in 1860 in Montevideo, where his father taught French. Educated at Tarbes, in the Pyrenees, he moved to Paris in 1876. Here he lived a life of restricted means until 1881 when he secured the comfortable, if unexciting, post of reader to the German Empress Augusta. In 1886 he married Leah Lee, an English governess, and they left Berlin for Paris and a return to poverty. He died of tuberculosis in 1887, seven months after his return to France.

A poet of considerable influence despite his short life, Laforgue was a symbolist, a master of irony and the originator of *vers libre*, and has been claimed as one of the most important innovators of modern poetry. His main poetic works were *Les Complaintes* (1885), *L'Imitation de Notre-Dame la Lune* (1886), *Le Concile Féerique* (1886), and, posthumously, *Derniers Vers* (1886–7) and *Des Fleurs de Bonne Volonté* (1890). His prose work, *Moralités légendaires* (1887), a collection of six retellings of old tales, was also published after his death.

GRAHAM DUNSTAN MARTIN was born in 1932 in Leeds, Yorkshire, has been twice married, with five children, and taught French and English in schools for several years. Since 1965 he has lectured in French literature at Edinburgh University. Besides writing and translating poetry he has written a number of prose works, including two children's books and several novels with fantastic, futuristic or mystical elements. He has also published *Language, Truth and Poetry* and *The Architecture of Experience* – primarily books about poetry and the philosophy of literature – and *Shadows in the Cave* (Penguin 1990), which calls upon modern science to support a non-materialist view of the universe.

JULES LAFORGUE

Selected Poems

*With a plain prose translation, introduction
and notes by* GRAHAM DUNSTAN MARTIN

PENGUIN BOOKS

PENGUIN BOOKS

Published by the Penguin Group
Penguin Books Ltd, 27 Wrights Lane, London w8 5TZ, England
Penguin Putnam Inc., 375 Hudson Street, New York, New York 10014, USA
Penguin Books Australia Ltd, Ringwood, Victoria, Australia
Penguin Books Canada Ltd, 10 Alcorn Avenue, Toronto, Ontario, Canada M4V 3B2
Penguin Books (NZ) Ltd, Private Bag 102902, NSMC, Auckland, New Zealand

Penguin Books Ltd, Registered Offices: Harmondsworth, Middlesex, England

This translation first published 1998
10 9 8 7 6 5 4 3 2 1

Copyright © Graham Dunstan Martin, 1998
All rights reserved

The moral right of the translator has been asserted

Set in 10.5/12.5 pt Monotype Bembo
Typeset by Rowland Phototypesetting Ltd, Bury St Edmunds, Suffolk
Printed in England by Clays Ltd, St Ives plc

CONTENTS

INTRODUCTION

Jules Laforgue is one of the founders of modernism, a major innovator in the language of poetry, and influenced most notably the Americans, Eliot, Pound and Hart Crane. Yet (except for his fellow-Montevidean, Supervielle) his own countrymen have rarely acknowledged him at his true worth. He is one of those artists of huge promise – Chatterton, Arriaga, Keats, Wilfred Owen – whose lives were tragically cut short. He had time, however, for one acknowledged masterpiece, *Derniers Vers*, published posthumously in 1890.

Had the poet foreseen his life, it would not have surprised him, for his philosophy was learnt from Schopenhauer and Hartmann, and he took the universe to be an irony practised against its own inhabitants. He was born on 16 August 1860 at Montevideo. His parents were both members of the little French 'colony' in Uruguay. In 1866, Jules's father Charles sent the family back to France, where they settled in Tarbes, while Charles stayed behind in Montevideo, continuing his job at the Duplessis Bank.

Jules was thus separated from his father at the age of six. At the age of eight he was parted from his mother and from his beloved sister Marie, when Laforgue *père* took the whole family back to Montevideo, except for Jules and his elder brother Emile, who were put to board in the lycée in Tarbes. The emotional rejection must have been appalling. It was not till Jules was fifteen that the family returned, father included, to settle permanently in France. In 1876, they moved to Paris, where Jules attended the famous Lycée Fontanes. (Its name was later changed to the Lycée Condorcet.) It was in Paris, on 6 April 1877, that his mother Pauline, weakened by a miscarriage earlier in the year, died of pneumonia. It would have been her twelfth child. We need look no further. This tragedy was a question put to Jules by life itself. And that question was perfectly fitted to the melancholy answer he would find in Hartmann.

Brought up in a boarding school on the other side of the ocean from his parents, Laforgue was an orphan even before they began to die. But now he had been orphaned *literally*. The image of the orphan recurs throughout his poetry, marking not only his own grief, but his equal sympathy for the young girls who, exiled to their nunnery schools, suffer a similar abandonment. But there is a metaphysical dimension, too. We are all orphans, for God, our Father in Heaven, does not exist.

His father Charles died of *angina pectoris* in 1881, on the very day that Laforgue's literary and artistic friends – Paul Bourget (who called him '*mon petit pessimiste*') and the rich and kindly art expert Charles Ephrussi – announced to him the great stroke of lucky generosity which they had just pulled off. Jules was offered an appointment in Berlin, as official French Reader to Augusta, Empress of Germany, a Russian aristocrat who had great contempt for the Germans among whom she lived. The saddest day of her year was the anniversary of Sedan (1870), when her German husband had defeated the French!

Laforgue performed his duties well. He had a luxurious apartment, an excellent salary of 9000 francs a year, and much leisure to read and write. But he felt frustrated at the German Court, and longed to return to the literary life of Paris. Besides, during the year 1886 he was slowly resolving to get married; but if he did so he could not remain in the Empress's employ. He had saved no money for, though the Empress paid him well, he liked to live beyond his means, and on his return to Paris he found himself penniless.

During 1883, in Germany, he had had a brief but stormy relationship with a mysterious 'R', who has been (long after) identified as a Lady of the Bedchamber, twenty years older than the young poet. Early in 1886, he began to have English lessons from the young Leah Lee. Laforgue said, '*Il y a trois sexes – l'homme, la femme et l'anglaise*' ('There are three sexes – the man, the woman and the Englishwoman'), and he meant it as a compliment. This English girl was the origin, perhaps, of some of the references to coffee-coloured

eyes in his poetry, and his friend Gustave Kahn said she was the
model for the delightful Andromède in Laforgue's facetious story
'Persée et Andromède'.

He left Germany late in 1886, and married Leah in London on
New Year's Eve, in freezing weather. At some point, somehow, he
had caught tuberculosis. Poverty-stricken and exhausted, he died
in Paris on 20 August 1887. Leah did not survive him long. She
died, also of TB, on 6 June 1888.

LAFORGUE AND THE ANGLO-SAXONS

It is hard to believe in a Symbolist Movement, for all the major
Symbolists – Verlaine, Rimbaud, Mallarmé, Laforgue – were indi-
viduals markedly different in style from each other. In Anglo-Saxon
countries the influence of Rimbaud and Laforgue has probably been
strongest. Eliot and Pound admitted Laforgue's influence to be
crucial.

Peter Dale (one of his major translators) notes that, after submerg-
ing oneself in Laforgue for months, one is astonished by returning
to early Eliot. I have just had the same experience. 'Conversation
Galante' reads like one of Laforgue's poems transcribed into English.
In 'The Love Song of J. Alfred Prufrock', wandering through the
streets resembles Laforgue's most depressing stage-settings – followed
by the very Laforguian send-up, hand-in-hand with the deliberately
silly rhyme:

Oh, do not ask, 'What is it?'
Let us go and make our visit.

There are familiar Laforguian references – to Hamlet, to St John
the Baptist's head on its platter – there is the protestation that 'It is
impossible to say just what I mean!', there is exacerbated self-irony
and agonized indecision. In the 'Portrait of a Lady' we have a
self-conscious awareness of scene-setting (as in Laforgue's most
tragic 'Dimanches' piece), and the plot of the Eliot poem seems

quintessential Laforgue. The conversation is full of false notes, the young man cannot make up his mind, he loses contact with the lady, he imagines her dying unexpectedly like the young woman in Laforgue's 'Autre Complainte de Lord Pierrot'. But the woman is pretentiously aesthetic, and, unlike Laforgue's women, the poet's persona appears to feel little for her. We have none of the desperation hidden behind the flirtatious poses of Laforgue's young women – their awful loneliness (these orphanesses) – none of the 'misery of wanting to be our wife' (*DV* XII). Eliot's is a less sympathetic view; his persona turns in on itself, his young women are seen condescendingly or with distaste.

Laforgue's persona is more various than Prufrock – resembling perhaps the Hamlet whom he guyed admiringly in one of his *Moralités Légendaires*. He mourns, rants and weeps, at the same time as he contemptuously views himself doing so. Illness and death are close. His self-pity is more tearful than Eliot's, his sense of his own absurdity is more shameful, he is more compassionate (while also being ruder) towards women.

It is true that if we turn to others of Eliot's early poems, we will find some of these features too: 'The Hippopotamus' – also Eliot's excellent pieces in French, particularly 'Mélange adultère de tout'. Savagery bursts out in 'Burbank with a Baedeker' and 'Sweeney Erect'. And, of course, Eliot will in time develop his own qualities – the hypnotic near-biblical rhythms, the ability to raise us almost to the poetic level of *Ecclesiastes*.

None the less, Laforgue's young man, more acrimonious, rebellious and intractable than Eliot's, is also more touching. His emotions seem more undisciplined, his appreciation of women warmer. Laforgue is certainly as much our contemporary as Eliot and Pound – more so, perhaps, for there is no hint of racism or fascism in him, and his metaphysics may be gloomy, but at least it asserts no false positives.

Moreover, his influence persists. We may find his disenchanted tone in many places – in Larkin's overquoted line:

They fuck you up, your mum and dad . . .

– but Larkin is not properly wretched like Laforgue – just grouchy and petty bourgeois. We can find him in the irony of Peter Redgrove:

I know conic sections also because of the fall of her skirt (*Poems 1954–87*, p. 84)

and across the Atlantic, in Lowell's 'Hawthorne':

Follow its lazy main street [. . .] / along a flat, unvaried surface / covered with wooden houses / aged by yellow drain / like the unhealthy hair of an old dog.

One could quote on endlessly, for Laforgue has become pervasive and inescapable. He it was who *enabled* this sort of shifting, relaxed, aware tone, this ability to register the immediate sensation, with downcast irony, with conscious pain, shrugging off pretension.

LAFORGUE, FRANCE AND WOMEN

So why, in his native country, has he never had a secure reputation? Is it because of (a) his squeamish 'Will I? Won't she?' attitude to sex, (b) his blackly ironic world-view, (c) his facetiousness, his taste for gaudy and strident clashes of emotion? Jacques Rivière, a great literary opinion-former, responded to his friend Alain-Fournier's enthusiasm for Laforgue by saying he was 'pleurard et pédant' (snivelling and over-learned). He admits his sensitivity and his verbal skill. On the other hand, Rivière goes on, he suffers from

une trop grande richesse verbale. Dirai-je du bagout? Il se répète [. . .] sous les formes les plus hétérogènes [. . .] A ce propos, je lance mon blasphème [. . .]: quel bonheur pour lui d'être mort si jeune! Car, qu'eût-il pu ajouter après les Derniers Vers, où il s'est définitivement expliqué? (3) Je lui reproche de réduire perpétuellement toute l'histoire, toute la littérature, toute la fantaisie à sa vision. C'est agaçant. Car enfin le malentendu entre les sexes, c'est très joli, mais c'est connu et peu intéressant.'[1]

[too great a verbal richness. Shall I say blether? He repeats himself under the most heterogeneous forms. While on this subject, I shall utter my blasphemy: how lucky he was to die so young! For what could he have added after the Last Poems, in which he finally explained himself? (3) I reproach him with reducing all history, all literature and all imagination to his own vision. It's exasperating. For after all, the misunderstanding between the sexes is great fun, but it's old hat and a bit of a bore.]

In a sense this is a strange objection. Critics have never jibbed at whole books full of love sonnets. Why then complain that, in Laforgue, there's only one problem, the sexual one? Yes, but burning with passion is more interesting than melting with compassion. Passion carries you away, Laforguian self-doubt is a cooler thing! Besides, the French have always claimed to understand 'l'amour'. Their attitude, of course, is partly cynical, partly idealist-romantic. Laforgue's cynicism and idealism about love are equally intense, but they are, as it were, orientated quite differently.

It is true of course that lines such as

Aimer, uniquement, ces jupes éphémères? ('Complainte du sage de Paris')

[To love nothing but these ephemeral skirts?]

sound, in modern terms, sexist. But we must put Laforgue into the context of his philosophy, and the society he lived in. He was the victim of the locked-down morals of his time, and so were the young women he tried so unsuccessfully to court, or perhaps to court and *not* to court in his own special way. But he understands what the problem is, and he is a feminist *avant la lettre*. In *Mélanges posthumes* his views are quite explicit:

Non, la femme n'est pas notre frère; par la paresse et la corruption nous en avons fait un être à part, inconnu, n'ayant d'autre arme que son sexe, ce qui est non seulement la guerre perpétuelle, mais encore une arme pas de bonne guerre – adorant ou haïssant mais pas compagnon franc, un être qui forme légion avec esprit de corps, franc-maçonnerie – des défiances d'éternel petit esclave. O jeunes filles, quand serez-vous nos frères, nos frères intimes sans arrière-pensée d'exploitation! Quand nous donnerons-nous la vraie poignée de main! (*MP*, 47)

[No, woman is not our brother; by forcing her into idleness and corrupting her, we have made her a being unknown and apart, possessing no weapon except her sex – which not only leads to perpetual warfare, but is also an unfair weapon – in adoration or in hatred, but never our frank companions, closing their ranks with *esprit de corps* in the freemasonry of their sex – but with the mistrustfulness of the eternal little slave. O young ladies, when will you be our brothers, our bosom friends, with no ulterior motive of exploitation! When shall we exchange an honest handshake!]

The poems make this equally clear.

Arkell claims that Rivière's later views are different. I am not so sure – he is simply more forgiving of his friend's sensibility:

Comme Laforgue, [Fournier] avait un immense besoin de la Femme, mais avant tout comme d'un calmant pour sa susceptibilité frémissante [. . .] Il lui fallut l'union des âmes avant celle des corps et un certain absolu d'affection où se plonger [. . .][2]

[Like Laforgue [Fournier] had a great longing for women, but above all as a sort of tranquillizer for his quivering susceptibility [. . .] The union of souls was more urgent to him than the union of bodies, he needed to be surrounded by an unconditional affection[. . .]]

The second objection is to Laforgue's pessimistic world-view, and to the fact that it pervades his poetry.

LAFORGUE AND THE PESSIMISTIC UNIVERSE

There was a time when everyone was discussing Schopenhauer. This German philosopher was deeply imbued with Buddhism. The Universe consists of inner Will – an immanent unitary Force which creates and drives the Universe – and of outer Appearance (Maya) – a delusive veil upon ultimate reality. Maya appears to offer us happiness, but actually delivers suffering. Compassion, the noblest of emotions, demands an answer to this greatest of problems. Schopenhauer (echoing Buddhism) says that the only way to avoid suffering is to detach ourselves from the seductions of Maya, and seek a state of wisdom in which we renounce our 'will to live', so as to enter the serene detachment of Nirvana. The main things which assist us in this are Art and Pure Reason – for both are perfectly disinterested. Our efforts towards detachment are however continually opposed by Maya. Principal among her attractions are Women, who are Maya's paid temptresses – it is above all through them that the Will of the Universe distracts us from Nirvana, and ensures the survival of the race.

Eduard von Hartmann's philosophy has a similar starting-point. His *Philosophy of the Unconscious* had been translated into French in 1877.[3] The inner being of the Universe is here called 'The Unconscious'. (Both Freud and Jung were directly influenced by Hartmann.) It is so termed because *we* are unconscious of it, though *it* drives our actions and is in fact purposive, clairvoyant and all-seeing. It is a superconscious World-Spirit.

In Hartmann, 'the escape from suffering is not by our individual detachment from the World, one by one, but by the collective decision of mankind. When we reach a sufficiently lofty state of enlightenment, Hartmann predicts, then, by a collective decision of the human race, the Will to Live will be reduced to nothing, and the Universe will be redeemed – i.e. abolished, swallowed up in nothingness. The Universe will sacrifice itself to itself, like Jesus. 'If this result appears to the reader [...] a cheerless one,' writes Hartmann, 'I must assure him that he was in error if he sought to find consolation and hope in philosophy.' (*PU* III, 118

Nietzsche called this 'a philosophical joke'. But we must see why Laforgue was so attracted to Hartmann. Suffering is a genuine philosophical problem, and there is no solution to it, least of all in Christianity. Moreover, though he was often dismissive about science, Laforgue had devoured the latest medical and scientific textbooks in the libraries of Paris, and it was easy to see life as a set of murderous arrangements. Think of the human reproductive process, in which millions of spermatozoa swim frantically towards the ovum. One succeeds, millions perish. Or think of the thousands of newly born turtles, hatching on the beach, as gigantic flocks of birds of prey gather, to feast on the young turtles as they race towards the safety of the sea. The observations of science bore out the implications of Darwin's 'Survival of the Fittest', namely that the Universe is built on pain and death. Nature is an unending massacre – a holocaust, Laforgue calls it. It provides no place for purpose – though there is plenty of room for desire, and plenty of desire for purpose.

Nietzsche, an older contemporary of Laforgue, accepted struggle and violence as a part of life. But Laforgue, like Schopenhauer and Hartmann, like *classic* Buddhism (for this is not an argument of Germans against Frenchmen!), is horrified by pain. He agrees with Schopenhauer and Hartmann that the Universe is a dreadful mistake, and the purpose of all rational people must be to escape from it.

THE POETRY OF LAFORGUE

Laforgue was so taken by Hartmann that he carried his book around with him like a Bible. But this was also because of what Hartmann says about the function of art. All artistic production is the result of inspiration by the Unconscious, but, since the Unconscious is the ground of all being, art is – excitingly – a direct reflection of it. So when the poet observes his own passing moods and inner impulses, he is observing fundamental reality:

Épier des instincts avec autant que possible absence de calcul, de volonté, de peur de les faire dévier de leur naturel, de les influencer. (*Entretiens politiques et littéraires*, IV, Feb. 1892, p. 49)

[To spy out the instincts with the greatest possible absence of calculation and will-power, for fear of making them deviate from their natural direction, of influencing them.]

And if it is complained that what is dredged up from the Unconscious is in part valuable, in part worthless, Laforgue might have replied by quoting Hartmann:

[. . .] all that happens happens with absolute wisdom, with absolute fitness, i.e. as means to the foreseen end, by the never-erring Unconscious [. . .] (*EPL*, II, 27)'

It logically follows from this view that the liberty of the artist must be total. All schools and tendencies in art must be accepted (*MP*, 206), for all reflect a necessary part of the Unconscious's great purpose. Hartmann's philosophy is most flattering to the artist, as when Laforgue writes:

Le génie, lui, n'a pas de sens, il est prêtre immédiat de l'Inconscient. (*MP*, 207).

[The genius has no [rational] meaning, he is the immediate priest of the Unconscious.]

We must, however, distinguish Laforgue's attitude from that (forty years later) of Breton and the Surrealists. Not only did the latter have a different definition of the Unconscious, one which was influenced by the post-Hartmann work of Freud, but also they believed in the abandonment of conscious control over the productions of the Unconscious, as seen for example in their practice of Automatic Writing. Now, there is no automatic writing in Laforgue, and he says:

[l'artiste] travaille avant tout, il variationne sur la création en avant vers la conscience. [*ibid.*]

[[the artist] is above all a worker, he writes variations on creation onwards towards consciousness.]

And one is immediately struck by the enormous technical skill of Laforgue's own poetry.

While discussing influences, I must also mention the fashionable art theorist Hippolyte Taine, whose lectures Laforgue attended at the École des Beaux-Arts in 1880–81. He is important because Laforgue reacted so indignantly against him. Taine was a determinist who believed that art was the product of the particular social situation of a race at a particular moment in time. Hence the slogan attributed to him of '*race, milieu, moment*'. Study the man, his society and his race, Taine proposed, and you would have the complete explanation of his art. (*Philosophie de l'art*, I, 11, Paris, 1882). Such an explanation he deemed to be 'scientific'. Moral and value judgements are out of court, for works of art are causally produced by natural processes, as flowers are, and each of us has the right to prefer what best suits our own temperament.

So far, Laforgue thoroughly agreed. But no sooner has Taine uttered these tolerant principles than he begins to contradict them. As you read, it becomes clear that he is a conventional spirit, accessible to only a small range of emotions. For instance, like most of his contemporaries, he prefers classical Greek sculpture to all other traditions, yet, unaware that the ancient Greeks painted their statues, he condemns painted statuary for creating 'not pleasure but repugnance, often disgust, and sometimes horror' (I,25). He defines what is 'higher' and 'lower' in terms which had long been traditional, he condemns medieval European art for offering '*saints étiques, martyrs disloqués, vierges à la poitrine plate, aux pieds trop longs*' [emaciated saints, dislocated martyrs, flat-chested virgins with elongated feet]. To be frank, Taine dislikes both distortion and truth. His ideal is *bienfaisance* or 'wholesomeness', and a work

qui nous représente un héros vaut mieux que celle qui nous représente un pleutre (*II*, 289) [. . .] Il est déplaisant de voir de la vermine, même quand on l'écrase [. . .] (*PA*, II, 291)

[which shows us a hero is worth more than one which shows us a poltroon [. . .] The sight of vermin is unpleasant even as one crushes them [. . .]]

Laforgue was incensed by Taine's views. He protests that

Chaque homme est selon son moment dans le temps, son milieu de race et de condition sociale, son moment d'évolution individuelle, un certain clavier sur lequel le monde extérieur joue d'une certaine façon. Mon clavier est perpétuellement changeant et il n'y en a pas un autre identique au mien. Tous les claviers sont légitimes. (*MP*, 141)

[Every man is according to his moment in time, his racial milieu and his social condition, his moment of individual evolution, a certain keyboard on which the outer world plays in a certain way. My keyboard is for ever changing and there is no other identical to mine. All keyboards are valid.]

Things of universal and everlasting value – so prized by Taine – are thus no more valid than the momentary impulses of the individual; and Laforgue by contrast admires

des poésies détachées, courtes, sans sujet appréciable [. . .] mais vagues et sans raison comme un battement d'éventail, éphémères et équivoques comme un maquillage, qui font dire au bourgeois qui vient de lire 'Et après?' (*MP*, 116)

[detached brief poems without any distinguishable subject [. . .] but vague and motiveless as the wave of a fan, ephemeral and equivocal as make-up, which make the bourgeois who has just read them say 'So what?']

Laforgue's enthusiasm for the contemporary art movement Impressionism is relevant here. Truth, we may say, is not confined to eternal truths. An event which lasts a moment is just as real as one that lasts for ever. The Impressionists, and Laforgue with them, look at time from a new and different angle. They value experience, in all its instant vividness, *as* it emerges.

Moreover, to concentrate on alleged 'eternal verities', as the tradition did, had distracted attention from the actual realities of experience. Laforgue, in passages such as this, is suggesting that we may experience emotions *for which there are as yet no words*. The challenge the poet must take up is to *express* those experiences, to *find* those words! In *Derniers Vers* (where he struggles to 'say the thing which the thing really is') one finds again this awareness of the inadequacy of words. No poet can be a great poet who does not grasp the terrible gulf between experience and expression.

This is why we find him employing the most startling register of all for that master of words, a poet. Namely, the register of inarticulacy:

Oh! que les cieux sont loin, et tout! ('L'Aurore-promise')

[Oh how far off the skies are, and all that!]

Yet of course, how natural! For we are all inarticulate, faced with the immeasurable night sky. Even the greatest poet's words are mere stammerings.

Laforgue, therefore, turns against loud certainties, against eloquence, against the style of Victor Hugo which he had himself imitated (e.g. 'Hypertrophy' and the 'Autobiographical Preamble'). He writes of him:

L'ennui de ces périodiques pavés roulés du Sinaï coutumier, 350 pages de gros papier, en gros caractères [. . .] (*MP*, 130)

[The tedium of those elaborate pompositities rolled down from the customary Sinaï, 350 pages of heavy paper, in large print [. . .]]

L'envie de pousser des cris sublimes aux oreilles de mes contemporains sur les boulevards et autour de la Bourse m'est passée et je me borne à tordre mon cœur pour le faire s'égoutter en perles curieusement taillées [. . .] (*Œuvres complètes*, IV, 128)

[The desire to utter sublime cries in the ears of my contemporaries on the boulevards and around the Stock Exchange has left me, and I confine myself to torturing my heart to make it drip forth curiously cut pearls [. . .]]

In this he is entirely up to date, following the advice of Verlaine: '*Prends l'éloquence et tords-lui son cou!*' ('Art poétique') [Take eloquence and wring its neck.]

There was need to find room in art for precisely some of those feelings which Taine dislikes so much, yes, even for 'repugnance, disgust and horror'. Laforgue accepts with enthusiasm the accusation of 'decadence'. Baudelaire, who had died in 1867, had admitted into his poetry many hitherto inadmissible emotions, and for some time the young Laforgue conscientiously imitated him. Indeed one may say of some of his early poems that Baudelaire himself would have been proud to write them (e.g. 'The First Night').

It is impossible to exaggerate the importance of this move. 'Beauty' had been seen throughout the centuries as the purpose of art. It was attained by using only a part of the total range of experience and emotion open to human beings. Certain chords, certain keys, certain harmonies created beauty, and those that did not were decried. But human experience is not limited to this narrow range. The ideal of 'Beauty' was progressively abandoned by the authors of the modernist revolution. It was progressively replaced by that of emotion – of the whole expressive gamut of human experience – and this equally well in music and painting as in literature. It is a question of *claviers* (keyboards – to use one of Laforgue's own favourite metaphors) – the modern is the acceptance of modes and harmonies that had hitherto been shunned.

Art elevates? By all means, but more importantly it must disturb. It must shake you to your core! This is not to say that Laforgue does not create beauty. Clearly he does – but it is only *one* among the many effects that he achieves.

Baudelaire had famously said, '*Combien nous sommes grands et poétiques dans nos cravates et nos bottes vernies.*' [How great and poetic we are in our cravats and our patent leather boots.][4] This was an implicit rejection of the limiting of poetry to a dignified, time-hallowed vocabulary. But Laforgue goes much further than Baudelaire – he injects into his poems a great deal of slang and colloquialism. In the view of post-Baudelairean modernism, poetry is the communication of living experience – which must not be distorted even under the pretext of transforming it into 'the eternal'. That would be to take something real and replace it by a category. For Laforgue and his contemporaries, the essential is not the object but its flavour – not the eternal idea but the living instance of it. What appears

marginal and inessential to traditionalists (because 'not eternally true')
is precisely the essential – the flavour of time itself.

Littérairement, [. . .] nous pouvons être amoureux sincèrement d'un type
de femme du passé, Diane chasseresse, l'Antiope, la Joconde [. . .] ou
Poppée, femme de Néron; – mais telle grisette de Paris, telle jeune fille de
salon [. . .] nous fera seule sangloter, nous remuera jusqu'au tréfond de
nos entrailles, parce qu'elles sont les soeurs immédiates de notre éphémère,
et cela avec son allure d'aujourd'hui, sa coiffure, sa toilette, son regard
moderne. (*MP*, 161)

[In a literary way, we can be sincerely in love with a certain type of woman
from the past, Diana the huntress, Antiope, the Mona Lisa [. . .] or Nero's
wife Poppaea – but some Parisian working girl, some young lady from a
salon [. . .] will be the only one to draw tears from us, to move us to the
depths of our entrails, because they are the immediate sisters of our own
ephemeral lives, with all their up-to-date mannerisms, hair-do, outfit, and
modern-day gaze.]

Thus Laforgue gives Eiderdown and Ambulance capital letters as if
they were mythological deities (*Notre-Dame*, 'Litanies'). But of
course, such items *are* among the most important things in our
world. They deserve mythical status for they are more frightening
than the over-literary image of Diana. Not that he fails to mention
Diana or Poppaea; but he mixes them with and clashes them against
the creatures of his own time.
   It is not just the use of the 'familiar', but the way it is *combined*
with other registers that makes the great originality of Laforgue. In
one of his most famous lines, the positive is abruptly *transformed* into
the negative – the cosy winter hearth-fires, inside, away from the
drizzle, suddenly turn into factory chimneys, outside, amid the
drizzle:

Oh, dans les bruines, toutes mes cheminées! . . .
D'usines . . . (*Derniers Vers* I)

[Oh, in the drizzle, all my hearthfires! All my factory chimneys!]

It is safe to say that never had a poet assembled such a disparate set of things together:

'lainages, caoutchoucs, pharmacie, rêves' (*D V* I)

[woollens, waterproofs, chemist's shop, dreams]

Strange emotions emerge, strange tangles of emotion:

O géraniums diaphanes, guerroyeurs sortilèges, / Sacrilèges monomanes! Emballages, dévergondages, douches! [. . .] (*D V* X)

[O diaphanous geraniums, warring enchantments, obsessive blasphemies! Wrapping-paper (Cycle-sprints), spurts of shamelessness, cold showers!]

Emballages, *douches*, *caoutchoucs* were simply unmentionable in earlier poetry. As for *monomanes* or *pharmacie*, these would not have been admitted for a different reason. Namely, that they belong to a technical or scientific context – which was thought 'unpoetic'. But the point is that Laforgue is conveying a roller-coaster of moods – a whole tangle of emotions – he is not fastidiously picking out the one or two that are 'poetic', and holding his nose to the others: he is giving us something more like the complete experience.

  Nor are these bitter-sweet effects emotionless. Laforgue is not coldly, but *tormentedly* ironic. Often, the most moving poems are those where irony somehow intensifies the feeling, and gives it shade and depth, such as the 'Lament of the Organist of Notre-Dame de Nice'. Here there are very uncomfortable emotions. In one way, nothing could be more compassionate and moving – the lonely dying woman, the protestations of eternal love. On the other hand, isn't it all a bit self-conscious – overdone and self-dramatizing? On the other hand again, surely the grief and pity are genuine? And who is to feel cosmic despair if not ourselves? The tragedy in this poem is just faintly ridiculous and overdone. But that it might be ridiculous makes it more appalling still! Thus, irony deepens the sense of tragedy.

  Or take the famous 'Song of the Hypertrophic Child'. At first sight this might seem a facetious experiment in execrable taste. The elements of folksong refrain ('*tir-lan-lair*, *la-i-tou* . . .') are incongruous, and the references to death and disease lack the slightest dignity.

This, however, is simply a first reaction. Is the poem in bad taste? But then so are death and disease themselves. We are *meant* to feel uncomfortable reading it. We are meant to question our standards of what is sentimental or absurd. This poem goes beyond sentimentality and mockery into quite inadmissible emotions. We are not allowed to feel contempt. For the *persona* allegedly 'penning' it (the child) has no dignity. Critical standards interlock with our relationship to human compassion, and our sense of the grotesque renders our sense of pity more agonizing. This poem is heart-rending, and the test of its being so is that if I now go on to write (as I had intended to) that it is 'a daring experiment, which comes off amazingly well', I have a terrible sense of being cold and condescending. In other words, the poem is too close to real human experience for comfort.

Or we should look at 'Dimanches' (*FB V* 16) where the momentary comment:

. . . le petit port / Allume ses feux (Ah! connu l'décor!)

[The little port / lights its fires. (Yes, we all know the stage-setting!)]

would, you might think, undermine the tragic feeling of the poem. Oddly, it makes it more intense, because the banalities of conventional description contrast so strongly with the tragedy we have just witnessed. This is surely one of his most moving poems.

A step further into irony, and hysterical laughter becomes desperate gloom. In 'Pierrots IV' the pierrots utter a '*rire aux déchirantes gammes*'. We know this is too hysterical to be true, and is a pretence, covering up the absolutely *opposite* emotion.

As for pomposity (too often the manner of 'the sublime genius' such as Victor Hugo), Laforgue was sweating out this fever himself, in his early verse. He knows all about it, and sends it up mercilessly. Sometimes it is very broad pastiche that he employs – in this example by a set of unpoetically learned, elephantinely inelegant, heavily polysyllabic adverbs:

Chut, ultime vibration de la Débâcle, / et que Jamais soit Tout, bien
   intrinsèquement, / Très hermétiquement, primordialement!
   (*Complaintes*, 'Préludes autobiographiques')

[Hush, last vibration of the Downfall, and let Never be Everything, quite intrinsically, very hermetically, primally!]

– in the following case by the use of that time-honoured technique, bathos:

Ils vont, se sustentant d'azur! / Et parfois aussi de légumes (*N-D*,
   'Pierrots I')

[They go sustaining themselves on azure, and sometimes also on vegetables]

Like bathos perhaps is what Kenneth Burke calls 'the tangent ending', where suddenly, at the end of the tale, you move away from it at a tangent, as if some new door had opened. Laforgue is fond of this, e.g. 'Pierrots (Scène courte mais typique.)', or 'Complainte des débats mélancoliques et littéraires' (last line).

Often these moves are part of the self-irony with which he persistently views himself. An obvious case is his ironic capitalizing of *Je*. (In English, of course, the word I is always capitalized, but no irony is intended!) A similar gesture is his referring to his emotions as 'mon Sacré-Cœur', as if his heart were the Sacred Heart of Jesus – while at the same time 'sacré' is one of the French language's favourite oaths. I have therefore translated it 'my damned Sacred Heart'.

Ruchon says of him: '*son ironie vient d'un conflit entre sa sentimentalité et son intelligence*' (p. 143) – of which he is well aware, of course. He is continually sending up the most solemn things, such as love, the universe, the French language, and even himself. His overstatement, his facetiousness, serve as a defence against his own emotions. Thus, his defence against self-pity is sometimes to render it in too cheerful a tone, and thus guy it. The 'Complainte de Lord Pierrot', for instance, ends with: 'Sure of living, my whole life, / As unhappy as the stones.' To these words the poet adds the stage direction '(*Twice.*)', as if the 'Complainte' were being sung. Not only is the poet's self-pity already half debunked by the chirpy folk-song-like rhythm, but treating it as a refrain in this way further undermines it.

A more subtle case perhaps is to be found in 'Pierrots III' (*N-D*):

Jurent «je t'aime!» l'air là-bas,
D'une voix sans timbre, en extase,
Et concluent aux plus folles phrases
Par des: «Mon Dieu, n'insistons pas!»

[They swear 'I love you!' as if their minds were on something else, in a toneless, ecstatic voice, and finish off the wildest sentences with words like 'Good Lord, don't let's overdo it!']

Laforgue is laughing at the pretentiousness of eternal vows of love. But on the other hand, is he so attracted by professing such vows, that he has to use self-irony so as to defend himself against them? Except that he is only *pretending* to laugh at himself. Laforgue's irony is in fact 'unstable' and open-ended, for in *Notre-Dame la Lune* it is hard to decide what his 'real' stance is, and whether he ever quite offers his own feelings, or rather merely a set of alternative masks.

The bourgeois and aristocratic society where, in the Germany of the 1880s, Laforgue found himself, was a world of masks and pretences, of postures and impostures. But then, what social world is not? Besides, there is always a problem about the relationship of the outer personality to the inner self. It is interesting that the word '*personne*' (person) comes from the Latin 'Per-sona', which means 'through-sound', i.e. it was originally the technical word for the mask which, in classical times, was worn by play-actors when speaking their lines on stage. In *Notre-Dame la Lune* Laforgue dons a particularly impenetrable mask, that of the Pierrot who was, in late nineteenth-century France, the most popular form of the clown.

The clown is a device to create laughter. But he has a more

serious purpose in Laforgue. To defend yourself against criticism, you act yourself, and thereby overact. You turn yourself into a mask, and when challenged, you doff it, saying, 'Look, that wasn't the real me!' This resembles a conjuror's device: it is intended to deceive, in the way that stage magicians do, by getting us to look in the wrong direction.

Let's try to look in the right direction, therefore. A mask is, of course, a lie. But it also tells a part of the truth. For, what is the function of a mask? A mask conceals, because it disguises the user's real and recognizable face. A mask, however, is also chosen, and therefore reveals its wearer's deep intentions. The more the wearer is *unaware* of those intentions when he chooses the mask, the more it is likely to reveal them. (Laforgue would have said he was both aware and, partly, unaware of the Unconscious's intentions, when using the mask of the Pierrot.) The Pierrot is, therefore, not a denial of Laforgue's inner self – he is an exaggeration of it, and hence an expression of the Unconscious. This exaggeration is absurd, so allowing the poet to deny its verity. But he who chooses an exaggeration reveals what there is in himself to exaggerate.

He poses as a Pierrot, whom he claims to be a worshipper of the Moon. The title *L'Imitation de Notre-Dame la Lune* is an echo of *The Imitation of Christ*, one of Laforgue's favourite readings. Here, apparently, he is replacing God by a goddess – the virgin Diana who demands chastity and self-denial, like Jesus or the Buddha. Yet this is a hollow pretext – his worship of the Moon is less than whole-hearted: he addresses her in 'Guitare' as '*Astre sans cœur et sans reproche*'. '*Astre*' is a dignified, 'poetic' word for a heavenly body. So far so good. But the next phrase is the traditional description of the great Bayard, the legendary model of chivalry, 'the knight without fear and without reproach' – only the words '*sans peur*' (fearless) have been adjusted to '*sans cœur*' (heartless).

Now it is not the pomposity of the Moon that is being sent up. For the Moon is not pompous, she is neither this nor that. No, it is – first – Laforgue himself, in his persona as the moon-worshipping Pierrot. But is his own absurdity the ultimate target? I think not. The Moon is the goddess of virginity; she is Diana the chilly, sterile huntress; she is associated with images of death, and he even appeals to her to cause his own death ('Petits mystères'). However, she presides too over dreams of free love ('Pierrots II', verse 6), and she is also the female *ovum*: ('Jeux', verse 8). This is why the Pierrots celebrate in such a phallic way the death of a virgin ('Pierrots II', verses 2 and 8).

Behind the icy, sterile Moon, there evidently lurks the virgin-worshipping ethic of nineteenth-century bourgeois society – but at the same time this bourgeois ethic is the mask adopted by Maya so as to trick the young into continuing the race. Thus the Moon is a mask worn both by the bourgeoisie and by the Eternal Sky. As for Laforgue, he is wearing a mask to attack a mask, and in this 'dialogue' between Pierrot and Moon, neither side can be trusted, for each is concealing something from the other.

A couple more touches must be added to our picture of the clown. The Pierrot belongs to a tradition which sees clowns as comic *because* pathetic, and pathetic *because* comic. Charlie Chaplin was one of the most self-conscious exemplars of this tradition, and played this vicious circle to its comic hilt. Nor must we forget Laforgue's fondness for Shakespeare, in whose plays the King's Fool is the purveyor of wisdom – and how this fits with the Théâtre des Funambules in the Paris of Laforgue's time, where the Pierrot was allowed to utter unpalatable truths.

But of course the whole Hartmannian world-view involves Cosmic Irony. Since all is Maya, both happiness and woe are mere illusions, and the superior view is to observe all human experience with a proper detached contempt. Hartmann himself recommends

a Mephistophelian gallows-humour, that with half-suppressed pity and half-unrestrained mockery looks down with alike sovereign irony both on those caught in the illusion of happiness and on those dissolved in tearful woe [. . .] (*PU*, III, 117–18).

One can see that Laforgue follows his recommendation. This allows us to identify a major problem – one that the critics have not seen quite clearly. For Laforgue's philosophy tells him that he himself is an illusion, like the young woman he so longs for. Only, he knows he's an illusion, whereas she does not. No wonder he can't believe in himself, and he can't get on with her. No wonder he is prone to grief and despair. His self-disbelief goes right down to metaphysical depths.

On the other hand, he is not against sending up the very doctrine which tells him that everything should be sent up. Irony is so all-pervasive in Laforgue that we should even be wary of statements that seem to accord entirely with Hartmann, as for instance in the final verse of 'La Lune est stérile': 'I too get very upset! but the Unconscious guides me; / it knows what it's about, it's nothing to do with me.' The treble denial here is too much to take seriously. The poet is cocking a snook at Hartmann himself. And we should note the disrespect with which he treats the great principles of Hartmann's philosophy. 'Infini, d'où sors-tu?' he cries, for instance: 'Infinity, where did you suddenly pop out from?' ('Nobles et touchantes divagations') For why be respectful to a Universe which refuses to tell you anything, and whose purposes cannot even be guessed from its silence?

If Hartmann had founded a religion, this might almost have counted as blasphemy. But blasphemy too is an expression of irony. One does not blaspheme against one's God unless one believes in Him, and thus blasphemy holds in its very heart the most ironic of contradictions.

Most religions recoil in horror at those who reject their favourite idol. It is not generally realized that there is a great exception. In Buddhism, blasphemy can be welcomed (1) because it expresses one's frustrations at the suffering of the world, (2) because gods, goddesses, idols of all kinds and indeed ultimately the world itself are delusory, and (3) because all religions, including Buddhism itself, are absurdly inadequate to express ultimate truth. Blasphemy needs to be deeply *felt*, as a horrified and horrifying rebellion – people need to hide their heads when they hear it – otherwise the true agonized force of its protest is lacking. But in the final analysis, it is a justified outcry against the world – a protest of the sort which led Buddha himself to enlightenment.

Laforgue's attack on the sacred figures of Christianity is relatively mild. For these are powerless. The Madonna in the 'Lament of the Vigil at Polar Midnights' has a bleeding heart, is genuinely grieving – though her grief does no one any good. What Laforgue reviles are substitutes for the divine, such as those fundamental male and female principles, the Sun and Moon. The Sun stands for life – and some might say the ultimate blasphemy is that against life. But then, these impressive celestial objects, the Moon and Sun – indeed, Nature Herself – are merely phenomena, delusory creations of the Unconscious. Blasphemy is appropriate for all such objects, for it reveals their factitiousness.

Can blasphemy be mild? I think at least it is so in 'Pierrots III', where the woman is overcome by a 'need of Moon'. What this might signify is mysterious, but one should note that 'moon', in colloquial French, may mean 'backside' – and also that it means 'vagary or whim', and that there is an expression '*con comme la lune*', meaning stupid.

This reminds us that Laforgue can be savagely funny, as, famously, in 'Pierrots (Scène courte, mais typique.)' – because of its liveliness, its exact and witty observation, its sense of his *own* absurdity. Or the savage but beautifully vivid description of the girl's mouth in 'Complainte des Consolations':

'Sa bouche! à moi, ce pli pudiquement martyr / Où s'aigrissent des nostalgies des nostalgies!'

[Her mouth! . . . Be mine, you prudishly martyr-like furrow where longings grow sour on longings!]

It will already have been seen that Laforgue is a great technical innovator. His restless verbal energy leads him to coin the most pungent neologisms, mostly of an ironic sort. Some of the more famous ones are *éléphantaisiste* (elephantastical), *éternullité* (eternull-ity), *sexciproques* (sexiprocal), *voluptés* (formed from *viol* = rape + *volupté* = extreme, usually sexual, pleasure), *anomaliflore*, (based on *animaliflore/forme* – a pseudo-scientific invention). More daringly, he will take a noun and twist it by main force into verbal shape. Thus, *feu-d'artificeront* (they will firework), and *s'in-Pan-filtrer* (on the basis of 'infiltrate', I would suggest 'inPantrate') – inventions which are felt (to Laforgue's delight) to be a sacrilege against the elegances of the French language. Some of these go fluently enough into English, but two which have created problems in the past (among his finest inspirations!) are: (1) *sangsuelles*, a combination of *sangsue* (leech, literally 'blood-sucker') and *sensuel* (sensual); I propose the translation 'leecherous'. (2) *ennuiversel* (*ennui* + *universel*); I suggest 'yawniversal'.

Laforgue promised to remove some of these neologisms from his *Complaintes* – but in the event, he left them in the MS, and they were duly published. Really, I do not think this was an accident. It is possible that – reacting to someone's horror at these *trouvailles* – 'Oh yes, I'll cut them out,' he obligingly said. But, thoroughly Laforguian, he had no intention of doing so.

He plays games with sounds too, of course. The pun is in evidence, for instance in 'La vie qu'elles me font mener' we have the lines

Voir un égal d'amour en l'homme / Et non une bête de somme / Là
  pour lui remuer des sommes!

[To see man as an equal in love and not a beast of burden who's there to play the Stock Exchange!]

The second '*somme*' contains a pun which is impossible to translate – putting one's money (*sommes*) to work/disturbing (with love-making) her afternoon naps (*sommes*). Five lines later he touches the same note again, using the word *sommités* (the summits, or leading lights, of the human race).

His puns may sometimes achieve a strange beauty. One of the most surprising and beautiful of them occurs in *Derniers Vers* IX. The poem has been devoted to his imagining a young woman falling madly in love with him, and acting with all the extravagance of those romantic clichés that she expects of a young man. Suddenly, in the midst of his savage guying of these sentimental expectations, the woman cries:

Je t'attendrai / dans l'attendrissement de ma vie . . .

[I shall wait in the tender passion of my life . . .]

Something charming and beautiful has emerged from merciless irony.

    Some of his metaphors are deliberately over-contrived, as when he piles Pelion on Ossa, but it must be admitted that many of them are powerfully effective:

Amour absolu, carrefour sans fontaine $(DV$ V)]

[True love, a crossroads without a fountain]

Oh, qu'ils sont pittoresques les trains manqués! . . . $(DV$ XI)

[Missed trains! Oh, how picturesque they are! . . .]

The word 'picturesque' is beautifully chosen. 'Picturesque' stands for a reality one is gazing at, while at the same time judging how it will look once you turn it into a picture. There's a whole psychological message here, showing the poet's capacity to observe himself observing himself. If we ask whether this sort of detachment from oneself has got anything to do with the Buddhistic detachment recommended by Schopenhauer, we must say no, for it is too full of emotion. Detaching oneself in this way is to feel torn into pieces. Whatever reasons Laforgue may have for adopting Hartmannism, comfort is not one of them. His philosophy is a source of agony to him.

    As for rhymes, these too he startlingly refreshes. One might think there was less need to do so in French. For rhyming is easier in French than in English, in part because of the grammatical system of the former, which creates large numbers of identical final syllables. Even in French, however, nineteenth-century poets began to tire of the limited number of rhymes that the conventional system allowed. Naturally so, for the infinite re-use of the same rhymes ends up producing clichés. And there are certain words, of course, for which it is impossible to find a new rhyme. The traditional rules of French verse demanded rhymes for the eye as well as the ear, and rejected patterns such as *divorce* and *forcent* – where the two words are in blatantly different grammatical categories. Laforgue discards this restriction. Thus, in the 'Complainte de Lord Pierrot', he rhymes *draps* with *Léda* – a splendidly disrespectful rhyme; and in 'La Complainte du pauvre Chevalier-Errant' *s'en fichent* ('don't give a damn') is answered by *sandwiche* (sandwich). He loves to set up ironic clashes between rhymes, e.g. in 'La Lune est stérile', *Pape* (Pope) with *soupape* (valve), *lotus* with *fœtus*; *citernes* (cisterns) with *sempiternes* (the dignified 'sempiternal') – or in *Derniers Vers* IV – *violette* (violet) with *tettent* (suckle).

His rhymes are a continual delight, and contemporary critics were duly outraged. (You can see them grumbling at his experiments in Debauve, 193–215.)

His technical virtuosity is amazing. Grojnowski points to 'Complainte d'un autre Dimanche', where the first stanza contains a striking number of internal rhymes – '*vent* – *aujourd'hui* – *jalousie* – *quand* – *tachant* – *blancs* – *arbres* – *marbrent*, etc. He also engaged in many original experiments – for instance there is a feat rather prophetic of Wilfred Owen in 'Air de biniou' (*FBV*), where the final vowels all fail to rhyme, though every one ends with *-se* – a skilful exercise in expectation and teasing avoidance.

If we glance at his development, we see that he blossomed very quickly into an absolute master of form, rhyme, rhythm and metre. *Sanglot* and the early poems are, like those of any young poet, derivative – the influences of Hugo, Vigny, Gautier, Cros, Paul Bourget, Verlaine and Heine are visible – but above all of Baudelaire. After all this bookishness, Laforgue needed a breath of fresh air, and sought it in the traditional *Complainte* – a form of folk verse which I have translated as 'Street-Ballad'. He uses its rhythms, refrains and colloquial directness to open himself to a greater range of experience. The *Complaintes* perfectly fitted his message too, for, as Warren Ramsey says, 'we suspect that our lives are no more meaningful than a popular song'.

This assisted him in releasing his personal voice, or rather many voices – some of them ventriloquial – in *L'Imitation de Notre-Dame la Lune*. But I have already touched on the secrets hidden behind these masks.

Des Fleurs de Bonne Volonté was the next phase, and it marks a more controlled tone. He no longer holds up the Pierrot's mask to dazzle us, and these are among his finest poems. But Laforgue almost immediately started to use them as a quarry for his *Derniers Vers*. (This is why I have chosen only thirty-two out of the total of fifty-six for this edition.)

Finally comes the great masterpiece of the *Derniers Vers*, the first volume of French poetry to be published entirely in free verse. In France, before Laforgue's time, the poetic alternative to rhymed verse was always prose poetry. Rimbaud's *Illuminations* is largely of this form, except for two short free-verse poems, 'Marine' and 'Mouvement'. But *Illuminations* was not published until 1886. Free verse, however, was 'in the air' in the early 1880s, and some experiments in it had been published by Marie Krysinska and by Laforgue's close friend Gustave Kahn. The latter's first published essay in this line, 'Intermède IV', is not so much a piece of 'real' free verse as a normal rhymed poem, slightly 'irregularized', if I may put it thus. On the other hand, Kahn's openness to formal experiment certainly encouraged Laforgue in his own free verse. But one is really most inclined to think that it was the example of Walt Whitman which was crucial. Moreover, Laforgue studied Whitman closely, for he published some translations of the American poet in *La Vogue* in 1886.

Rémy de Gourmont has it right when he says:

Le vrai vers libre est conçu comme tel, c'est-à-dire comme fragment dessiné sur le modèle de son idée émotive, et non plus déterminé par la loi fixe du nombre. (*Esthétique de la langue française*, 1894, p. 229)

[True free verse is conceived as such, i.e. as a fragment designed on the model of its emotive idea, and no longer determined by the fixed law of number.]

That is, each idea has its own best shape, its most appropriate verbal rhythm. The claim is that free verse represents more accurately the rhythms of our shifting inner selves, with all their pauses, emphases, repetitions, departures from regularity. It is his mastery of these oscillating moods and rhythms which makes these poems such a triumph. *Derniers Vers* is a sincere record of the search for sincerity, and contains the very rhythms of that search.

THE PRESENT TRANSLATION

The stated aim of this series is to assist the reader to respond to the foreign original by producing a plain prose translation. In the case of Laforgue, no real aid can be totally 'plain'. At least two aspects of his language complicate the translator's task. In the first place, he uses a large number of colloquial idioms, and the proper translation is of course the corresponding English idiom, which is sometimes not so very 'literal'. An obvious example is 'Mettons le doigt sur la plaie' (*FBV*) which means 'This is where the shoe pinches' or 'Let's get down to the nitty-gritty'.

Secondly, a great deal of his verse is packed with polysyllables in dense proximity, lined up in battle order. The 'Autobiographical Preamble' to the *Complaintes* is particularly prone to these problems, for it is a turning-out-of-drawers of his earlier verse (when he had been at his most declamatory). Lines 40–43 run:

Draguant les chantiers d'étoiles, qu'un Cri se rue, / Mort! emballant en ses linceuls aux clapotis'/Irrévocables ces sols d'impôts abrutis!

A literal translation might give: 'Cruising the shipyards of the stars, let a Cry burst out – "Death!" wrapping in its winding cloths with irrevocable lappings these ground-floors stupefied with taxes.' This produces clogged prose – which is also hard to understand. I have inserted a note explaining '*draguant*' and those mysterious 'taxes on ground-floors', and I ended up writing:

Cruising the shipyards of the stars, let the Cry 'Death' burst out! Let it

wrap its death-shrouds, inexorably flapping, about these ground-levels
taxed to stupefaction!

I hope this is an improvement. But in any case the problem must
not be alleviated too much. For one must give a flavour of the
obstinately aggressive style that Laforgue adopts when denouncing
the Whole Universe – the volleying and thundering of adjectives,
the piling of noun upon angry noun. Nor could I move too far
from the syntax of the original, for then clarity would have been
completely lost.

By the way, these four lines are an excellent example of mixed
metaphor, of which Laforgue is either a master or else horribly
guilty, depending on your view of the matter. It is often one of his
weapons in a self-ironic attack on Hugolian verse. But as we have
seen, he has many other moods, often of extreme delicacy.

A small point: the reader should be warned also that my punctu-
ation does not always correspond to Laforgue's. To tell the truth
his is often careless or eccentric.

What is the point, however, of a translator explaining or excusing
himself? Let me simply wish the reader every enjoyment. Laforgue's
verbal play is as remarkable as anything in poetry. His irony is
startling. He does have his favourite *idées fixes*, but there is great
variety within them. His flashes of emotion are all the more powerful
for being inspected by so sharp an intelligence, he pretends to be
selfish but is really tender, he is a poet who thinks as well as feels,
and the final commitment to life and love at the end of *Derniers Vers*
(the 'ironic equilibrium' as Warren Ramsey called it) is as considered
and as deeply felt as anything in poetry.

Along with some other small masterpieces, *Derniers Vers* has always
been, and still remains, the main reason for reading Laforgue. It
consists of a number of themes, linked or in contrast. These are
explored with great variation, and to great depths of emotion – to
the accompaniment also of ironic and sarcastic cries, reminiscent of
the music of, say, Prokofiev. All the keyboards of language are used,
and the range of experience is doubtless smaller than in Mahler's
symphonies – but, as with him, there is a genuine attempt to contain

a wholeness of experience. There is great rhythmic skill, great rhythmic variety, but also an onward drive of immense power. A satisfying and, moreover, moving resolution is reached at the end, as in a symphony.

'Symphonic', when used of poetry, is usually a hollow metaphor. But here I think we may genuinely claim its aptness. Surely *Derniers Vers* is one of the *musical* masterpieces of literature.

NOTES

1. Jacques Rivière et Alain-Fournier, *Correspondance*, I, (Gallimard, 1926), p. 231–2.
2. Preface to Alain-Fournier, *Le Grand Meaulnes/Miracles*, (Garnier, Paris 1986), pp. 9–10.
3. English translation, (Kegan Paul/Trubner, London, 1931).
4. Salon de 1845', *OC*, 866.

NOTE ON THE TEXT

Complaintes and *L'Imitation* were published by Vanier in 1885, *Le Concile Féerique* by *La Vogue* in 1886, and most of *Derniers Vers* was published in either *La Vogue* or *La Revue indépendante* in the second half of 1886. The rest of Laforgue's work was not published till after his death — one should note especially the appearance of *Moralités légendaires* (Laforgue's facetious short stories) in 1887, and of *Derniers Vers* in 1890. This last edition was established with particular care by Dujardin and Fénéon, Laforgue's devoted friends, and even Pascal Pia considers it excellent.

The poems printed here are selected from the Mercure de France text (1901–3) of Laforgue's *Œuvres complètes*, with the addition of three early poems published in the 1922 edition. I have included these three here with a small selection from Laforgue's first projected collection, which he was going to entitle *Le Sanglot de la Terre*.

There are a handful of obvious errors in the Mercure de France edition, and I have corrected them. (The word *étonnante*, for instance, is missing from line 19 of *Derniers Vers* XI, though it is present in the 1890 edition of Dujardin and Fénéon.)

Pascal Pia's more recent edition is excellent, and is above all notable for printing a very large quantity of recently discovered early work (and also large numbers of variants from various manuscripts).

Finally, I want to thank most warmly Peter and France Sharratt for their invaluable help with certain obscure references, and with Laforgue's sometimes impenetrable and always quirky French.

FURTHER READING

WRITINGS BY LAFORGUE

Poésies complètes, edited by Pascal Pia (Paris, Gallimard, Livre de Poche, 1970)

Moralités légendaires, edited by Pascal Pia (Paris, Gallimard, Folio, 1977)

Œuvres complètes, Volume III: Mélanges posthumes (Paris, Mercure de France, 1901–3)

Lettres à un ami 1880–6, edited by G. Jean-Aubry (Mercure de France, 1941)

Poésies complètes, Volume I, 1860–83, edited by Jean-Louis Debauve et al., (Lausanne, 1986), (contains the poetry up to and including *Les Complaintes*)

Laforgue en son temps, edited by J.-L. Debauve (La Baconnière, Neuchâtel, 1972) (letters and critical notices).

EDITIONS

Derniers Vers, edited by Michael Collie and J.-M. L'Heureux (University of Toronto Press, 1965)

Les Complaintes, edited by Michael Collie (Athlone Press, London, 1977)

Jules Laforgue: Poems, edited by J. A. Hiddleston (Blackwell, Oxford, 1975). This selection has the most helpful notes of any edition

TRANSLATIONS

Betts, M., *Last Poems of J.L.* (Stockwell, Ilfracombe, 1973)

Dale, P., *Poems of J.L.* (Anvil Press, London, 1986)

Smith, W. J., *Selected Writings of J.L.* (Grove Press, NY, 1956)

Terry, P., *Poems of J.L.* (University of California Press, Berkeley and Los Angeles, 1958)

CRITICAL STUDIES

Betts, M., *L'Univers de J.L. à travers les mots* (Pensée Universelle, Paris, 1978)

Collie, M., *J.L.* (Athlone Press, London, 1977)

Durry, M.-J., *J.L.* (Seghers, Paris, 1952)

Grojonowski, D., *J.L. et l'originalité* (Neuchâtel, 1988)

Guichard, L., *J.L.* (PUF, Paris, 1950)

Hannoosh, M., *Parody and Decadence: Laforgue's 'Moralités légendaires'*: (Columbus, Ohio, 1989)

Hiddleston, J.A. (ed), *Laforgue aujourd'hui* (Paris, 1988)

Holmes, A., *J.L. and Poetic Innovation* (Oxford, 1993)

Ramsey, W., *J.L. and the Ironic Inheritance* (New York, 1953)

Reboul, P., *J.L.* (Hatier, 1960)

Watson, L., *Laforgue, Poet of his Age* (Mahwah, New Jersey, 1980)

BIOGRAPHIES

Arkell, D., *Looking for Laforgue: An Informal Biography* (Carcanet, Manchester, 1979)

Ruchon, F., *J.L., sa vie, son œuvre* (Ciana, Geneva, 1924)

DOCUMENTATION AND REFERENCE

Hartmann, E. von, *The Philosophy of the Unconscious* (in one volume), (Kegan Paul/Trubner, London, 1931)

Taine, H., *Philosophie de l'Art* (Paris, 1882)

BACKGROUND AND GENERAL CRITICISM

Aspey, K., and France, P. (eds.), *Poetry in France, Metamorphoses of a Muse* (Edinburgh University Press, Edinburgh, 1992)

Broome, P., and Chesters, G., *The Appreciation of Modern French Poetry* (Cambridge University Press, Cambridge, 1976)

Gibson, R., *Modern French Poets on Poetry: An Anthology* (Cambridge University Press, Cambridge, 1961, 1979)

Lewis, R., *On Reading French Verse* (Clarendon Press, Oxford, 1982)

Scott, C., *French Verse-Art, A Study* (Cambridge University Press, Cambridge, 1980)

—, *A Question of Syllables: Essays in Nineteenth-Century French Verse* (Cambridge University Press, Cambridge, 1986)

LE SANGLOT DE LA TERRE

The Grief of the Earth

AND OTHER EARLY POEMS

Ballade de retour

Le Temps met Septembre en sa hotte,
Adieu, les clairs matins d'été!
Là-bas, l'Hiver tousse et grelotte
En son ulster de neige ouaté,
Quand les casinos ont jeté
Leurs dernières ritournelles,[1]
La plage est triste en vérité!
Revenez-nous, Parisiennes!

Toujours l'océan qui sanglotte
Contre les brisants irrités,
Le vent d'automne qui marmotte
Sa complainte à satiété,
Un ciel gris à perpétuité,
Des averses diluviennes,
Cela doit manquer de gaieté!
Revenez-nous, Parisiennes!

Ballade of Home-coming

Time stuffs September in his knapsack, farewell the bright mornings of summer!
Close by, Winter coughs and shivers in his ulster of quilted snow. When the
casinos have uttered their last ritornellos, the beach is truly sad! Come home to us,
Parisiennes!

Always the ocean sobbing against the irritable breakers, the autumn wind mutter-
ing its complaint till you sicken of it, a permanent grey sky, downpours like floods,
it can't be very gay! Come home to us, Parisiennes!

Hop! le train siffle et vous cahote!
Là-bas, c'est Paris enchanté,
Où tout l'hiver on se dorlotte:
C'est l'Opéra, les fleurs, le thé,
O folles de mondanité
Allons! Rouvrez les persiennes
De l'Hôtel morne et déserté!
Revenez-nous, Parisiennes!

ENVOI

Reines de Grâce et de beauté,
Venez, frêles magiciennes,
Reprendre votre Royauté:
Revenez-nous, Parisiennes!

Up! the train whistles and jolts you! At the end of the line it's Paris the magical, where one pampers oneself all winter: it's the Opera, flowers, tea, O you devotees of high society, let's be off! Open up the shutters of the gloomy, empty Town House! Come home to us, Parisiennes!

ENVOI

Queens of grace and beauty, come, slender witches, to resume your Royal Status: Come home to us, Parisiennes!

Nuage

Eh! laisse-moi tranquille, dans mon destin,
Avec tes comparaisons illégitimes!
Un examen plus serré ferait estime
Du moindre Agent! . . .[1] Toi, tu y perds ton latin.

Preuves s'entendant comme larrons en foire,
Clins d'yeux bleus pas plus sûrs que l'afflux de sang
Qui les envoya voir: me voilà passant
Pour un beau masque d'une inconstance noire.

Ah! que nous sommes deux pauvres Bourreaux[2]
Exploités! Et sens-tu pas que ce manège
Mènera ses exploits tant que le . . . Que sais-je
N'aura pas rentré l'Infini au fourreau?

Là! faisons la paix, ô sourcils! prends ta mante:
Sans regrets apprêtés, ni scenarios vieux,
Allons baiser la brise, essuyant nos yeux
La brise . . . elle sent ce soir un peu la menthe.

Cloud

Oh! leave me in peace, in my destiny, with your unjust comparisons! A closer examination would make one suspect the presence of a teeny-weeny Agent . . . But you'll not make head nor tail of it.

Pieces of evidence in league with each other like thieves on the spree. Winks of blue eyes no more trustworthy than the rush of blood which started them seeing – and here I am, mistaken for a handsome mask of black inconstancy.

Ah! we are merely two poor exploited Executioners! And don't you feel that this double-dealing / frame-up will continue its exploits until the What-you-may-call-it slots the Infinite back into its sheath?

There! Let's make peace, O frowning eyebrows! Take your mantle. Without affected regrets or outworn scenarios, let's kiss the breeze, and dry our eyes. The breeze . . . it has a whiff of mint this evening.

Complainte du libre-arbitre

Rencontrant un jour le Christ,
Pierrot de loin lui a fait: Psitt!
Venez-ça: êtes-vous fataliste?

Pourriez-vous m'concilier un peu
Comment l'homme est libre et responsableu,[1]
Si tout c'qui s'fait est prévu d'Dieu?

Et voici que not' Seigneur Jésus,
Tout pâle, il lui a répondu:
«Ça ne serait pas de refus,

Mais . . . votre conduite accuse
Un cœur que le malheur amuse,
Et puis vous êtes sans excuse,

Pire que le méchant soldat
Romain qui m'molesta
Quand j'étais su'l' Golgotha.[2]

Dieu, qui voit tout, apprécie
Vot' conduite envers le Messie,
Que vous lui montez une scie.

Lament of Free Will

Meeting Christ one day, Pierrot from far off went: 'Hist! Come here: are you a fatalist?

Could you reconcile for me how man is free and responsible, if everything he does is foreseen by God?'

And see how our Lord Jesus, all pale, replied: 'I wouldn't refuse to answer,

but . . . your conduct reveals a heart that unhappiness amuses, and besides you are without any excuse,

worse than the wicked Roman soldier who maltreated me when I was on Golgotha.

God, who sees all, judges your conduct towards the Messiah, judges that you're poking fun at him.

En Enfer et sans façon,
Vous irez, triste polisson,
Et ce s'ra un' bonne leçon.»

Et il lui tourna les talons,
Mais Pierrot dit: «T'en sais pas long,
Car t'as déplacé la question.»

Complainte de l'Organiste de Notre-Dame de Nice

Voici que les corbeaux hivernaux
Ont psalmodié parmi nos cloches,
Les averses d'automne sont proches,
Adieu les bosquets des casinos.

Hier, elle était encor plus blême,
Et son corps frissonnait tout transi,
Cette église est glaciale aussi!
Ah! nul ici-bas que moi ne l'aime.

To Hell you'll go at once, miserable scoundrel, and let that be a lesson to you!'
And he turned his back on him. But Pierrot said: 'You don't know much about it, for you've sidestepped the issue.'

Lament of the Organist of Notre-Dame de Nice

Now the winter crows have chanted psalms among our church-bells, the autumn showers are imminent, farewell to the groves of the casino.

Yesterday she was paler still, and her body was shivering, chilled to the bone. This church is freezing too! Ah! no one in this world loves her but me.

Moi! Je m'entaillerai bien le cœur,
Pour un sourire si triste d'elle!
Et je lui en resterai fidèle
A jamais, dans ce monde vainqueur.

Le jour qu'elle quittera ce monde,
Je vais jouer un *Miserere*[1]
Si cosmiquement désespéré
Qu'il faudra bien que Dieu me réponde!

Non, je resterai seul, ici–bas,
Tout à la chère morte phtisique,
Berçant mon cœur trop hypertrophique
Aux éternelles fugues de Bach.

Et tous les ans, à l'anniversaire,
Pour nous, sans qu'on se doute de rien,
Je déchaînerai ce *Requiem*
Que j'ai fait pour la mort de la Terre!

Me! I'll make a notch in my heart for one of her sad smiles! And I'll stay faithful to her for ever, in this defeating world.

The day she departs this life I'll play a *Miserere* so cosmically despairing that God will be forced to answer me!

No, I'll stay alone, in this world, devoted to my darling, dead of TB, and I shall lullaby my over-enlarged heart with the everlasting fugues of Bach.

And every year at the anniversary, just for us, without anyone suspecting anything, I'll let loose this *Requiem* that I've composed for the death of the Earth!

La Chanson du Petit hypertrophique[1]

C'est d'un' maladie d' cœur
Qu'est mort', m'a dit l' docteur,
    Tir-lan-laire![2]
    Ma pauv' mère;
Et que j'irai là-bas,
Fair' dodo z'avec elle.
J'entends mon cœur qui bat,
C'est maman qui m'appelle!

On rit d' moi dans les rues,
De mes min's incongrues
    La-i-tou!
    D'enfant saoul;
Ah! Dieu! C'est qu'à chaqu' pas
J'étouff', moi, je chancelle!
J'entends mon cœur qui bat,
C'est maman qui m'appelle!

The Song of the Hypertrophic Child

It's from a heart disease, the doctor told me, (Tra-la-la!) that my poor mummy died; and [he says] I'm off there too, to go sleepy-byes with her. I can hear my heart beating, it's Mummy calling me!

    They laugh at me in the streets, 'cos I look grotesque (Ee-i-o!) like a drunken child. O God!, it's because at every step I'm breathless, I stagger! I can hear my heart, *etc.*

Aussi j' vais par les champs
Sangloter aux couchants,
    La-ri-rette!
    C'est bien bête.
Mais le soleil, j' sais pas,
M' semble un cœur qui ruisselle!
J'entends mon cœur qui bat,
C'est maman qui m'appelle!

Ah! si la p'tite Gen'viève
Voulait d' mon cœur qui s' crève.
    Pi-lou-i!
    Ah, oui!
J' suis jaune et triste, hélas!
Elle est ros', gaie et belle!
J'entends mon cœur qui bat.
C'est maman qui m'appelle!

Non, tout le monde est méchant.
Hors le cœur des couchants,
    Tir-lan-laire!
    Et ma mère,
Et j' veux aller là-bas
Fair' dodo z'avec elle . . .
Mon cœur bat, bat, bat . . .
Dis, Maman, tu m'appelles?

I go through the fields too, sobbing at the sunsets (Fal-lal-la!), it's very silly. But the sun, I don't know, it looks like a bleeding heart. I can hear, *etc.*

Ah! if only little Jenny wanted my breaking heart! (Heigh-ho!) Ah yes, I'm yellow and sad, alas! She's pink, happy and beautiful! I can hear, *etc.*

No, everyone's spiteful, except the hearts of the sunsets (Tra-la-la!) and my mother. And I want to be off there to go sleepy-byes with her. I can hear my heart beating, beating, beating . . . Tell me, Mummy, is that you calling me?

Hypertrophie

Astres lointains des soirs, musiques infinies,
Ce Cœur universel ruisselant de douceur
Est le cœur de la Terre et de ses insomnies.
En un pantoum[1] sans fin, magique et guérisseur
      Bercez la Terre, votre sœur.

Le doux sang de l'Hostie a filtré dans mes moelles,
J'asperge les couchants de tragiques rougeurs,
Je palpite d'exil dans le cœur des étoiles,
Mon spleen fouette les grands nuages voyageurs.
      Je beugle dans les vents rageurs.

Hypertrophy

Far-off stars of the evenings, infinite musics, this universal Heart streaming with sweetness, is the heart of Earth and its insomnias. With an endless *pantoum*, magical and healing, rock to sleep the Earth, your sister.

    The sweet blood of the Communion Host has seeped into my marrow, I splash the sunsets with tragic redness, I throb with exile in the hearts of the stars, my despair whips onwards the great voyaging clouds, I bellow in the raging winds.

Aimez-moi. Bercez-moi. Le cœur de l'œuvre immense
Vers qui l'Océan noir pleurait, c'est moi qui l'ai.
Je suis le cœur de tout, et je saigne en démence
Et déborde d'amour par l'azur constellé,
          Enfin! que tout soit consolé.

La Première nuit

(Sonnet)

Voici venir le Soir, doux au vieillard lubrique.
Mon chat Mürr accroupi comme un sphinx héraldique
Contemple, inquiet, de sa prunelle fantastique
Marcher à l'horizon la lune chlorotique.[1]

C'est l'heure où l'enfant prie, où Paris-lupanar
Jette sur le pavé de chaque boulevard
Ses filles aux seins froids qui, sous le gaz blafard
Voguent, flairant de l'œil un mâle de hasard.

Love me. Lull me to sleep. The heart of immense creation towards which the black Ocean wept – it's my heart. I'm the heart of everything, and I bleed in madness, and brim over with love starry with blue sky, that all – At last! – should be comforted.

The First Night
(Sonnet)

Here comes Evening, sweet to the old lecher. My cat Mürr crouching like a heraldic sphinx contemplates, uneasy, with his fancy-haunted eyes the chlorotic moon walking the horizon.

It's the hour when children pray, when brothel-Paris ejects onto every boulevard pavement its cold-breasted girls who, under the ashen gas-light, sail along, sniffing out with their eyes a random male.

Mais, près de mon chat Mürr, je rêve à ma fenêtre.
Je songe aux enfants qui partout viennent de naître.
Je songe à tous les morts enterrés d'aujourd'hui.

Et je me figure être au fond du cimetière,
Et me mets à la place, en entrant dans leur bière,
De ceux qui vont passer là leur première nuit.

La Cigarette

(*Sonnet*)

Oui, ce monde est bien plat: quant à l'autre, sornettes.
Moi, je vais résigné, sans espoir à mon sort,
Et pour tuer le temps, en attendant la mort,
Je fume au nez des dieux de fines cigarettes.

Allez, vivants, luttez, pauvres futurs squelettes.
Moi, le méandre bleu qui vers le ciel se tord
Me plonge en une extase infinie et m'endort
Comme aux parfums mourants de mille cassolettes.

But, my cat Mürr beside me, I dream at my window. I think of the children who, everywhere, have just been born. I think of all the corpses buried today.

I imagine myself in the heart of the graveyard, and I put myself in their place, and I enter the coffins of those who are about to spend their first night here.

The Cigarette
(*Sonnet*)

Yes, this world is pretty flat. As for the next one, it's claptrap. For my part, I go without hope, resigned to my lot, and to kill time, as I wait for death, I smoke fine cigarettes under the noses of the gods.

Carry on, you living folk, strive, you poor future skeletons. As for me, this blue meander twirling off towards the sky plunges me into infinite ecstasy and lulls me to sleep as if in the dying perfumes of a thousand incense-burners.

Et j'entre au paradis, fleuri de rêves clairs
Où l'on voit se mêler en valses fantastiques
Des éléphants en rut à des chœurs de moustiques.

Et puis, quand je m'éveille en songeant à mes vers,
Je contemple, le cœur plein d'une douce joie,
Mon cher pouce rôti comme une cuisse d'oie.

And I enter paradise, beflowered with bright dreams in which elephants in heat are seen mingling in fantastic waltzes with choirs of mosquitoes.

And then, when I wake thinking of my poems, I contemplate, my heart filled with gentle joy, my dear thumb roasted as brown as a goose's thigh.

LES COMPLAINTES

Street-ballads

Au petit bonheur de la fatalité.
Much ado about Nothing, Shakespeare

Trusting to the vagaries of the inevitable

À Paul Bourget

En deuil d'un Moi-le-Magnifique
Lançant de front les cent pur-sang[1]
De ses vingt ans tout hennissants,
Je vague, à jamais Innocent,
Par les blancs parcs ésotériques
De l'Armide[2] Métaphysique.

Un brave bouddhiste en sa châsse,
Albe, oxydé, sans but, pervers,
Qui, du chalumeau[3] de ses nerfs,
Se souffle gravement des vers,
En astres riches, dont la trace
Ne trouble le Temps ni l'Espace.

C'est tout. A mon temple d'ascète
Votre Nom de Lac[4] est piqué:
Puissent mes feuilleteurs du quai,[5]
En rentrant, se r'intoxiquer
De vos AVEUX,[6] ô pur poète!
C'est la grâce que j' me souhaite.

To Paul Bourget

In mourning for a Me-the-Magnificent, launching abreast the hundred neighing thoroughbreds of his twenty years, I wander for ever Innocent, through the esoteric white parks of the Metaphysical Armida.

A good Buddhist in his reliquary, white, oxidized, purposeless, perverse, who with the lower register of his nerves, gravely whispers verses to himself, in rich stars, whose trace troubles neither Time nor Space.

That's all. On my ascetic's temple your Lake-Name is incised: may my quayside book-browsers re-inspire themselves, on coming home, with your Confessions, O pure poet! It's the favour I wish were mine.

Préludes autobiographiques

Soif d'infini martyre? Extase en théorèmes?
Que la création est belle, tout de même!

En voulant mettre un peu d'ordre dans ce tiroir,
Je me suis perdu par mes grands vingt ans, ce soir
De Noël gras.[1]
                    Ah! dérisoire créature!
Fleuve à reflets, où les deuils d'Unique ne durent
Pas plus que d'autres! L'ai-je rêvé, ce Noël
Où je brûlais de pleurs noirs un mouchoir réel,[2]
Parce que, débordant des chagrins de la Terre
Et des frères Soleils, et ne pouvant me faire
Aux monstruosités sans but et sans témoin
Du cher Tout, et bien las de me meurtrir les poings

Autobiographical Preamble

A thirst for infinite martyrdom? An ecstasy in theorems?
How beautiful creation is, nevertheless!

Wanting to put some order in this drawer, I lost myself in my grown-up twenty years, this evening of carnival Christmas.

                    Ah! ridiculous creature! River full of reflections, where mourning for the Unique lasts no longer than for others! Did I dream it, that Christmas when I burnt a real handkerchief with my black tears, because, brimming over with the griefs of the World and of its brother Suns, and unable to bear our dear Everything's monstrous behaviour (which has no point and nobody to witness it), and weary of bruising my fists on the

Aux steppes du cobalt sourd,[3] ivre-mort de doute,
Je vivotais, altéré de *Nihil* de toutes
Les citernes de mon Amour?
                              Seul, pur, songeur,
Me croyant hypertrophique![4] comme un plongeur
Aux mouvants bosquets des savanes sous-marines,
J'avais roulé par les livres, bon misogyne.

Cathédrale anonyme! en ce Paris, jardin
Obtus et chic, avec son bourgeois de Jourdain[5]
A rêveurs, ses vitraux fardés, ses vieux dimanches
Dans les quartiers tannés où regardent des branches
Par-dessus les murs des pensionnats, et ses
Ciels trop poignants à qui l'Angélus fait: assez!

Paris qui, du plus bon bébé[6] de la Nature,
Instaure un lexicon mal cousu de ratures.

Bon Breton né sous les Tropiques, chaque soir
J'allais le long d'un quai bien nommé *mon rêvoir*,
Et buvant les étoiles à même: «ô Mystère!
«Quel calme chez les astres! ce train-train sur terre!
«Est-il Quelqu'un, vers quand,[7] à travers l'infini,

---

steppes of deaf cobalt, dead-drunk with doubt, I got along somehow, thirsting for
Nothing with all the cisterns of my Love?
                              Alone, pure, pensive, thinking myself
hypertrophic! like a diver among moving groves of under-sea savannahs, I had
roamed among books, a trusty misogynist.
    Anonymous cathedral! in this Paris, an obtuse and stylish garden, with its bourgeois
River Jordan for dreamers, its dolled-up windows, its old Sundays in the bored
districts where branches peep over the walls of the boarding schools, and its too
poignant skies to which the Angelus retorts: Enough!
    Paris, turning Nature's most easy-going baby into a disconnected dictionary of
omissions.
    A good Breton born in the Tropics, every evening I walked along a quay
well-named *My Dreamery*, drinking straight from the stars: 'O Mystery! What calm
among the heavenly host! This daily round on earth! Is there Someone, till when,
across the infinite,

«Clamer l'universel *lamasabaktani*?[8]
«Voyons; les cercles du Cercle,[9] en effets et causes,
«Dans leurs incessants vortex de métamorphoses,
«Sentent pourtant, abstrait, ou, ma foi, quelque part,
«Battre un cœur! un cœur simple; ou veiller un Regard!
«Oh! qu'il n'y ait personne et que Tout continue!
«Alors géhenne[10] à fous, sans raison, sans issue!
«Et depuis les Toujours, et vers l'Éternité!
«Comment donc quelque chose a-t-il jamais été?
«Que Tout se sache seul au moins, pour qu'il se tue!
«Draguant les chantiers d'étoiles, qu'un Cri se rue,
«Mort! emballant en ses linceuls aux clapotis
«Irrévocables ces sols d'impôts abrutis![11]
«Que l'Espace ait un bon haut-le-cœur et vomisse
«Le Temps nul, et ce Vin aux geysers de justice!
«Lyres des nerfs, filles des Harpes d'Idéal
«Qui vibriez, aux soirs d'exil,[12] sans songer à mal,
«Redevenez plasma! Ni Témoin, ni spectacle!
«Chut, ultime vibration de la Débâcle,
«Et que Jamais soit Tout, bien intrinsèquement,
«Très hermétiquement, primordialement!»

to address the universal *lama sabachthani*? Let us consider; the circles of the Circle in effects and causes, in their unceasing vortices of metamorphoses, nonetheless feel a heart beating – either apart, or by my faith somewhere! – a simple heart: or a Gaze watching! Oh! if there is nobody and yet All continues, then it's a fools' Gehenna, with no reason, no way out! since Time first began, and till Eternity! How then has anything ever managed to be? Let the All at least know itself to be alone, so it can kill itself! Cruising the shipyards of the stars, let the Cry 'Death!' burst out! Let it wrap its death-shrouds, inexorably flapping, about these ground-levels taxed to stupefaction! Let Space have a good retch, and vomit out worthless Time, and the Wine of the geysers of justice! Lyres of the nerves, daughters of the Ideal Harps which vibrated, during evenings of exile, without intending any harm, turn back into plasma! Let's have neither Witness to see nor drama to be seen! Hush, last vibration of the Downfall, and let Never be Everything, quite intrinsically, very hermetically, primally!

Ah! – Le long des calvaires de la Conscience,
La Passion des mondes studieux t'encense,
Aux Orgues des Résignations, Idéal,
O Galathée[13] aux pommiers de l'Eden-Natal!

Martyres, croix de l'Art, formules, fugues-douces,[14]
Babels d'or où le vent soigne de bonnes mousses;
Mondes vivotant, vaguement étiquetés
De livres, sous la céleste Éternullité:
Vanité, vanité, vous dis-je! – Oh! moi, j'existe,
Mais où sont, maintenant, les nerfs de ce Psalmiste?[15]
Minuit un quart; quels bords te voient passer, aux nuits
Anonymes, ô Nébuleuse-Mère? Et puis,
Qu'il doit agoniser d'étoiles éprouvées,
A cette heure où Christ naît, sans feu pour leurs couvées,
Mais clamant: ô mon Dieu! tant que, vers leur ciel mort,
Une flèche de cathédrale pointe encor
Des polaires surplis! – Ces Terres se sont tues,
Et la création fonctionne têtue!
Sans issue, elle est Tout; et nulle autre, elle est Tout.
X en soi? Soif à trucs![16] Songe d'une nuit d'août?[17]

Ah! – All through the calvaries of Consciousness, the Passion of the studious worlds burns incense to you, in tune with the Organs of Resignations, Ideal, O Galatea in the apple-trees of Birthplace-Eden!

Martyrs, crosses of Art, formulae, fine-etched fugues, golden Babels where the wind cultivates fine growths of moss, worlds struggling on, vaguely labelled with books, under Heaven's Eternullity: Vanity, vanity, I tell you! – Oh! I exist, but where now are the heart-strings of that Psalmist?

A quarter past Midnight; what shores watch you pass in the anonymous nights, O Mother-Nebula? And then, how many grief-hardened stars must be dying at this hour when Christ is born, without fire for their broods, but crying 'O my God!' as long as, towards their dead sky, a cathedral spire still pricks up out of polar surplices! – Those Earths have fallen silent, yet creation grinds stubbornly on! Purposeless, it is Everything; nothing but itself, it is Everything. X in itself? A thirst for thingummyjigs! An August night's dream?

Sans le mot, nous serons revannés, ô ma Terre!
Puis tes sœurs.[18] *Et nunc et semper, Amen.*[19] Se taire.

Je veux parler au Temps! criais-je. Oh! quelque engrais
Anonyme! Moi! mon Sacré-Cœur![20] – J'espérais
Qu'à ma mort, tout frémirait, du cèdre à l'hysope;[21]
Que ce Temps, déraillant, tomberait en syncope,
Que, pour venir jeter sur mes lèvres des fleurs,
Les Soleils très navrés détraqueraient leurs chœurs;
Qu'un soir, du moins, mon Cri me jaillissant des moelles,
On verrait, mon Dieu, des signaux dans les étoiles?

Puis, fou devant ce ciel qui toujours nous bouda,
Je rêvais de prêcher la fin, nom d'un Bouddha!
Oh! pâle mutilé, d'un: qui m'aime me suive![22]
Faisant de leurs cités une unique Ninive,[23]
Mener ces chers bourgeois, fouettés d'alléluias,
Au Saint-Sépulcre maternel du Nirvâna![24]

Maintenant, je m'en lave les mains (concurrence
Vitale, l'argent, l'art, puis les lois de la France . . .)

Without the password, we'll be winnowed again, O my Earth! And then your sisters. Now and for evermore, Amen. Silence.

'I want to speak to Time!' I cried. Oh! some anonymous compost! Myself! My damned Sacred-Heart! – I hoped that at my death, everything would tremble, from the cedar to the hyssop; that Time, raving, would fall in a faint, that, to come and cast flowers on my lips, the heartbroken Suns would wreck their choirs; that at least one evening, as my Cry burst from my marrow, we'd see, by God, distress signals in the stars?

Then, mad beneath this sky which has always cut us dead, I dreamed of preaching the end, by the name of Buddha! Oh! pale amputee! – with a cry of 'Let who loves me, follow me!' making of all their cities a single Nineveh, to lead these dear bourgeois, lashed with hallelujahs, to the motherly Holy Sepulchre of Nirvana!

Now I wash my hands of them (survival of the fittest, money, art, not to mention the laws of France . . .)

Vermis sum, pulvis es![25] où sont mes nerfs d'hier?
Mes muscles de demain? Et le terreau si fier
De Mon âme, où donc était-il, il y a mille
Siècles! et comme, incessamment, il file, file! . . .
Anonyme! et pour Quoi? – Pardon, Quelconque Loi!
L'être est forme, Brahma seul est Tout-Un en soi.[26]

O Robe aux cannelures à jamais doriques[27]
Où grimpent les Passions des grappes cosmiques;
O Robe de Maïa,[28] ô Jupe de Maman,
Je baise vos ourlets tombals éperdument!
Je sais! la vie outrecuidante est une trêve
D'un jour au Bon Repos qui pas plus ne s'achève
Qu'il n'a commencé. Moi, ma trêve, confiant,
Je la veux cuver au sein de l'INCONSCIENT.

Dernière crise. Deux semaines errabundes,
En tout, sans que mon Ange Gardien me réponde.
Dilemme à deux sentiers vers l'Eden des Élus:
Me laisser éponger mon Moi par l'Absolu?

I am a worm, thou art dust! Where are my sinews of yesterday? my muscles of tomorrow? And the proud vegetable mould of My soul, where was it, a thousand centuries ago! and how, unendingly, it rushes on, rushes past! . . . nameless! and for What? – Oh, I beg your pardon, 'for some Law or Other'! Being is form, Brahma alone is All-One in himself.

Robe with fluting that is for ever Doric, where the Passions of the cosmic clusters climb; O Robe of Maya, O Skirt of Mummy, I frantically kiss your mortuary hems! I know! impertinent life is a single day's respite at the Happy Repose which finishes no more than it's begun. As for me, I'm confidently going to brew up this respite in the bosom of the UNCONSCIOUS.

A last crisis. Two weeks of wanderings, and all without my Guardian Angel writing back to me. A dilemma offering two paths to the Eden of the Chosen: allow my Self to be rubbed out by the Absolute?

Ou bien, élixirer l'Absolu en moi-même?
C'est passé. J'aime tout, aimant mieux que Tout m'aime.
Donc Je m'en vais flottant aux orgues sous-marins,
Par les coraux, les œufs, les bras verts, les écrins,
Dans la tourbillonnante éternelle agonie
D'un Nirvâna des Danaïdes[29] du génie!
Lacs de syncopes esthétiques! Tunnels d'or!
Pastel défunt! fondant sur une langue! Mort
Mourante ivre-morte! Et la conscience unique
Que c'est dans la Sainte Piscine[30] ésotérique
D'un *lucus* à huis-clos, sans pape et sans laquais,
Que J'ouvre ainsi mes riches veines à Jamais.

En attendant la mort mortelle, sans mystère,
Lors quoi l'usage veut qu'on nous cache sous terre.

Maintenant, tu n'as pas cru devoir rester coi;
Eh bien, un cri humain! s'il en reste un pour toi.[31]

or else elixirize the Absolute in myself? That's in the past. I love everything, preferring Everything to love me. So I travel on floating to the undersea pipe-organs, past corals, eggs, green tentacles, seed-caskets, in the eternal whirling death-throes of a Nirvana of the Danaïds of genius! Lakes of aesthetic swooning! Tunnels of gold! Dead pastel drawing, toffee on a tongue! Death which dies, dead-drunk! And the unique awareness that it's in the esoteric Holy Piscina of a sacred grove behind closed doors, without pope or lackeys, that I open my rich veins to Nevermore.

Awaiting mortal death, which is unmysterious, despite the fact that custom insists on hiding us under the ground.

Now, you didn't believe you should keep silent; well, let there be a human cry! if one's still left for you.

Complainte propitiatoire à l'Inconscient[1]

Aditi.[2]

O Loi, qui êtes parce que vous Êtes,
Que votre Nom soit la Retraite!

– Elles! ramper vers elles d'adoration?
Ou que sur leur misère humaine je me vautre?
Elle m'aime, *infiniment!* Non, d'occasion!
Si non *moi*, ce serait *infiniment* un autre!

Que votre inconsciente Volonté
Soit faite dans l'Éternité![3]

– Dans l'orgue qui par déchirements se châtie.
Croupir, des étés, sous les vitraux, en langueur;
Mourir d'un attouchement de l'Eucharistie,
S'entrer un crucifix maigre et nu dans le cœur?

Que de votre communion nous vienne
Notre sagesse quotidienne!

Propitiatory Complaint to the Unconscious

Aditi

O Law, who art because thou Art, may thy Name be the Refuge!

Those women? Crawl towards them in worship? Or wallow in their human misery? She loves me, *infinitely*. No, at second hand! If not *me*, it would be *infinitely* someone else!

Let thine unconscious Will be done in Eternity!

In the church-organ which tortures itself with heart-rendings. To crouch listlessly summer after summer under the stained glass; to die from a touch of the Eucharist, to drive a thin bare cross into one's heart?

From your communion may there come our daily wisdom!

– O croisés de mon sang! transporter les cités!
Bénir la Pâque universelle, sans salaires![4]
Mourir sur la Montagne,[5] et que l'Humanité,
Aux âges d'or sans fin, me porte en scapulaires![6]

    Pardonnez-nous nos offenses, nos cris,
    Comme étant d'à jamais écrits!

– Crucifier l'infini dans des toiles comme
Un mouchoir, et qu'on dise: «Oh! l'Idéal s'est tu!»
Formuler Tout! En fugues sans fin dire l'Homme!
Être l'âme des arts à zones que-veux-tu![7]

    Non, rien; délivrez-nous de la Pensée,
    Lèpre originelle, ivresse insensée,

      Radeau du Mal[8] et de l'Exil;
      Ainsi soit-il.

O crusaders, marked by the cross of my blood! to uplift the cities! to bless the universal Passover without the wages of sin! To die on the Hill, and let Mankind through endless golden ages wear me as scapulars!

Forgive us our transgressions, our protests, as being for ever preordained!

To crucify the infinite in paintings no bigger than a handkerchief, and then say: Oh dear! the Ideal has fallen silent! To reduce everything to formulas! In endless fugues to express the meaning of Humanity! To be the soul of the arts in what-more-can-you-expect shanty towns!

No, nothing: deliver us from Thought, original leprosy, insane rapture, Raft of Evil and Exile. So be it.

Complainte-Placet de Faust Fils

Si tu savais, maman Nature,
Comme Je[1] m'aime en tes ennuis,
Tu m'enverrais une enfant pure,
   Chaste aux *«et puis?»*

Si tu savais quelles boulettes,
Tes soleils de Panurge![2] dis,
Tu mettrais le nôtre en miettes,
   En plein midi.

Si tu savais, comme la *Table*
De tes Matières est mon fort!
Tu me prendrais comme comptable,
   Comptable à mort!

Si tu savais! les fantaisies!
Dont Je puis être le ferment!
Tu ferais de moi ton Sosie,
   Tout simplement.

Plea-Complaint of Faust the Younger

If you only knew, Mummy Nature, how I love myself in the troubles you give me, you'd send me a pure young girl, chaste in face of all those 'What next?'s.

 If you knew what clangers your follow-my-leader suns make, you'd tear our sun to pieces at full noon.

 If you knew how the *Table of Your Contents* is my *forte*, you'd take me on as your accountant, accountable to death!

 If you knew the fantasies I can brew up! you'd appoint me your Double, quite simply.

Complainte à Notre-Dame des Soirs

L'Extase du soleil, peuh! La Nature, fade
Usine de sève aux lymphatiques parfums.
Mais les lacs éperdus des longs couchants défunts
Dorlotent mon voilier dans leurs plus riches rades,
      Comme un ange malade . . .
      O Notre-Dame des Soirs,
      Que Je vous aime sans espoir!

Lampes des mers! blancs bizarrants![1] mots à vertiges!
Axiomes *in articulo mortis*[2] déduits!
Ciels vrais! Lune aux échos dont communient les puits![3]
Yeux des portraits! Soleil qui, saignant son quadrige,
      Cabré, s'y crucifige!
      O Notre-Dame des Soirs,
      Certes, ils vont haut vos encensoirs!

Eux sucent des plis dont le frou-frou les suffoque;
Pour un regard, ils battraient du front les pavés;
Puis s'affligent sur maint sein creux, mal abreuvés;
Puis retournent à ces vendanges sexciproques.

Complaint to Our Lady of the Evenings

The sun's Ecstasy, faugh! Nature, insipid sap-factory with lymphatic scents. But the distraught lakes of dead, long-drawn-out sunsets cuddle my sailing-boat in their richest roadsteads, like a sick angel . . . O Our Lady of the Evenings, how hopelessly I love you!

Lamps of the seas! bizarring whites! words which make you dizzy! Axioms deduced *in articulo mortis*! True skies! Moon of echoes from which the wells receive communion! Eyes of portraits! Sun which, bleeding its four-horse chariot, rearing, crucifixes itself! O Our Lady of the Evenings, they certainly fly high, your censers!

Those other men suck at pleats whose rustling chokes them; for a glance, they'd beat their heads on the paving-stones; then, their thirst ill-slaked, they afflict themselves on many a flat chest; then return to those sexiprocal wine-harvests.

Et moi, moi, Je m'en moque!
Oui, Notre-Dame des Soirs,
J'en fais, paraît-il, peine à voir.

En voyage, sur les fugitives prairies,
Vous me fuyez; ou du ciel des eaux m'invitez;
Ou m'agacez au tournant d'une vérité;
Or vous ai-je encor dit votre fait, je vous prie?
    Ah! coquette Marie,
    Ah! Notre-Dame des Soirs,
    C'est trop pour vos seuls Reposoirs![4]

Vos Rites, jalonnés de sales bibliothèques,
Ont voûté mes vingt ans, m'ont tari de chers goûts.
Verrai-je l'oasis fondant au rendez-vous,[5]
Où . . . vos lèvres (dit-on!) à jamais nous dissèquent?
    O Lune sur la Mecque![6]
    Notre-Dame, Notre-Dame des Soirs,
    De *vrais* yeux m'ont dit: au revoir!

And *I, I* don't give a damn! Yes, Our Lady of the Evenings, it seems I'm pitiful to see.

Travelling over escaping meadows, you flee from me; or, reflected in the sky of the waters, you invite me; or madden me at the street corner of a truth; now have I yet told you to your face? Ah! coquettish Mary, Ah! Our Lady of the Evenings, you ask too much for your mere Wayside Altars!

Your Rites, waymarked by dusty libraries, have bowed my twenty-year-old back, have dried up my dearest pleasures. Shall I see the oasis melting away at the meeting-place, where . . . your lips (they say!) for ever dissect us? O Moon above Mecca, Our Lady, Our Lady of the Evenings, *true* eyes have bade me farewell!

Complainte de cette bonne Lune

On entend les Etoiles:

> Dans l'giron
> Du Patron,
> On y danse, on y danse,
> Dans l'giron
> Du Patron,
> On y danse tous en rond.[1]

– Là, voyons, mam'zelle la Lune,
Ne gardons pas ainsi rancune;
Entrez en danse, et vous aurez
Un collier de soleils dorés.

– Mon Dieu, c'est à vous bien honnête,
Pour une pauvre Cendrillon;
Mais, me suffit le médaillon[2]
Que m'a donné ma sœur planète.

– Fi! votre Terre est un suppôt
De la Pensée! Entrez en fête;
Pour sûr vous tournerez la tête
Aux astres les plus comme il faut.

Ballad of the Dear Old Moon

We hear the Stars:

In the Boss's lap, we dance, we dance; in the Boss's lap we dance, all in a ring.

'Come now, Miss Moon, don't cherish a grudge like that; join the dance, you'll have a necklace of gilded suns.'

'Goodness, you're being very kind to a poor Cinderella; but I'll content myself with the medallion my sister planet has given me.'

'Bah! your Earth is a slave of Thought! Join the party; you'll certainly turn the heads of the most respectable stars.'

– Merci, merci, je n'ai que ma mie,
Juste que je l'entends gémir!
– Vous vous trompez, c'est le soupir
Des universelles chimies!

– Mauvaises langues, taisez-vous!
Je dois veiller. Tas de traînées,
Allez courir vos guilledous!

– Va donc, rosière enfarinée![3]
Hé! Notre-Dame des gens saouls,
Des filous et des loups-garous!
Metteuse en rut des vieux matous!
            Coucou!

        Exeunt les étoiles. Silence et Lune. On entend:

            Sous l'plafond
              Sans fond,
        On y danse, on y danse,
            Sous l'plafond
              Sans fond,
        On y danse tous en rond.

'No thanks, I've no one but my darling, and I can just hear her moaning!'
  'You're wrong, it's the sighing of the universe's chemistry!'
  'Spiteful tongues, be quiet! I must keep vigil. Band of tarts, run off to your nights on the tiles!'
  'Be off with you, floury-faced prize-prude! Hey! Our Lady of drunks, rogues and werewolves! Putter-on-heat of old tomcats! Peek-a-boo!'

                        Exeunt the Stars. Silence and Moonlight. We hear:
Under the limitless ceiling, we dance, we dance, under the limitless ceiling we dance, all in a ring.

Complainte des pianos qu'on entend dans les quartiers aisés

Menez l'âme que les Lettres ont bien nourrie,
Les pianos, les pianos, dans les quartiers aisés.
Premiers soirs, sans pardessus, chaste flânerie,
Aux complaintes des nerfs incompris ou brisés.

> Ces enfants, à quoi rêvent-elles,
> Dans les ennuis des ritournelles?

> > – «Préaux des soirs,
> > Christs des dortoirs!

> «Tu t'en vas et tu nous laisses,
> Tu nous laiss's et tu t'en vas,[1]
> Défaire et refaire ses tresses,
> Broder d'éternels canevas.»

Jolie ou vague? triste ou sage? encore pure?
O jours, tout m'est égal? ou, monde, moi je veux?
Et si vierge, du moins, de la bonne blessure,[2]
Sachant quels gras couchants ont les plus blancs aveux?

Complaint of the Pianos Overheard in Prosperous Districts

Guide the soul that Literature has nurtured, pianos, pianos, in the prosperous districts!
First evenings without an overcoat, chaste strolling, in tune to the laments of nerves
misunderstood or frayed.

These young girls, what do they dream of, tediously strumming?

'School-yards at evening, Christs on the dormitory wall!

'You go away and leave us, you leave us and you go, letting down and doing up
our hair, embroidering endless samplers.'

Pretty or vague? sad or docile? still pure? O days, nothing matters? or, World, I
want it now? And so virgin at least of the good wound, for they know the reddest
sunsets make the whitest avowals?

Mon Dieu, à quoi donc rêvent-elles?
A des Roland,[3] à des dentelles?

       – «Cœurs en prison,
       Lentes saisons!

«Tu t'en vas et tu nous quittes,
Tu nous quitt's et tu t'en vas!
Couvents gris, chœurs de Sulamites,[4]
Sur nos seins nuls croisons nos bras.»

Fatales clés de l'être un beau jour apparues;[5]
Psitt! aux hérédités en ponctuels ferments,
Dans le bal incessant de nos étranges rues;
Ah! pensionnats, théâtres, journaux, romans!

       Allez, stériles ritournelles,
       La vie est vraie et criminelle.

       – «Rideaux tirés,
       Peut-on entrer?

«Tu t'en vas et tu nous laisses,
Tu nous laiss's et tu t'en vas,
La source des frais rosiers baisse,
Vraiment! Et lui qui ne vient pas . . .»

Goodness, what do they dream about? Do they dream of Rolands, or of lace-work?

'Hearts in prison, slow seasons!

'You go away and leave us, you leave us and you go! Grey nunneries, choirs of Shulamites, over our non-existent breasts let us cross our arms.'

Fateful keys to being, which appeared one fine day; hush to heredities brewing as regularly as the clock, in the unceasing dancing of our strange streets: Ah! boarding schools, theatres, newspapers, novels!

Be off with you, sterile strumming, life is real and sinful.

'Curtains drawn, may one come in?

'You go away and leave us, you leave us and you go, the spring of fresh rosebushes is drying up, it's true! And he who doesn't come . . .'

Il viendra! Vous serez les pauvres cœurs en faute,
Fiancés au remords comme aux essais sans fond,[6]
Et les suffisants cœurs cossus, n'ayant d'autre hôte
Qu'un train-train pavoisé d'estime et de chiffons.[7]

>Mourir? peut-être brodent-elles,
>Pour un oncle à dot, des bretelles?

>>– «Jamais! Jamais!
>>Si tu savais!

>«Tu t'en vas et tu nous quittes,
>Tu nous quitt's et tu t'en vas,
>Mais tu nous reviendras bien vite
>Guérir mon beau mal, n'est-ce pas?»

Et c'est vrai! l'Idéal les fait divaguer toutes,
Vigne bohême,[8] même en ces quartiers aisés.
La vie est là; le pur flacon des vives gouttes
Sera, *comme il convient*, d'eau propre baptisé.

>Aussi, bientôt, se joueront-elles
>De plus exactes ritournelles.[9]

>>«– Seul oreiller!
>>Mur familier!

He'll come! You'll be poor hearts to blame, affianced to remorse and to experiments you've had no training for. And the self-satisfied well-to-do hearts, having no host except a daily round decked out in high esteem and fashionable clothes.

Dying? Perhaps they're embroidering braces for an uncle with a dowry?

'Never! Never! If you only knew!

'You go away and leave us, you leave us and you go, but you'll come back quite quickly to heal my sweet suffering, won't you?'

And it's true! The Ideal, that Bohemian vine, sends them all raving mad, even in these prosperous districts. Life is there: the pure flask of living drops will be, *as is only decent*, baptized in clean water.

So, soon, they'll make easy play of a more precise kind of strumming.

'Single pillow! Familiar wall!

«Tu t'en vas et tu nous laisses,
Tu nous laiss's et tu t'en vas.
Que ne suis-je morte à la messe!
O mois, ô linges, ô repas!»

Complainte de l'orgue de Barbarie

Orgue, orgue de Barbarie,
Don Quichotte, Souffre-Douleur,
Vidasse, vidasse ton cœur,
Ma pauvre rosse endolorie.

Hein, étés idiots,
Octobres malades,
Printemps, purges fades,
Hivers tout vieillots?

– «Quel silence, dans la forêt d'automne,
Quand le soleil en son sang s'abandonne!»

Gaz, haillons d'affiches,
Feu les casinos,

'You go away and leave us, you leave us and you go. I wish I'd died during Mass!
O months, O underwear, O meal-times!'

Lament of the Barrel Organ

Organ, barrel organ, Don Quixote, Scapegoat, pour out, pour out your heart, my
poor tormented cur.

Hey, idiot summers, sick Octobers, springs which are insipid purges, winters all
old-fashioned?

'What stillness in the autumn forest, when the sun gives up the struggle, in its
own blood!'

Gas-lights, tatters of billboards, the late deceased casinos,

Cercueils des pianos,
Ah! mortels postiches.[1]

– «Déjà la nuit, qu'on surveille à peine
Le frou-frou de sa titubante traîne.»

Romans pour les quais,
Photos élégiaques,
Escarpins, vieux claques,
D'un coup de balai!

– «Oh! j'ai peur, nous avons perdu la route;
Paul, ce bois est mal famé! chut, écoute . . .»

Végétal fidèle,
Ève aime toujours
LUI! jamais pour
Nous, jamais pour elle.

– «O ballets corrosifs! réel, le crime?
La lune me pardonnait dans les cimes.»

pianos like coffins, Ah! mortal hairpieces!
  It's already night, we can barely hear the rustling of her drunken brood.
  Novels for the quaysides, elegiac photos, dancing shoes, old galoshes – away with
the sweep of a broom!
    'Oh, I'm afraid! We've lost the way; Paul, this wood is notorious! Hush, listen . . .'
  A faithful form of plant-life, Eve always loves HIM! never for our sake, never
for her own sake,
    'O corrosive ballets! Was it really a sin? The moon from high above forgave me.'

Vêpres, Ostensoirs,
Couchants! Sulamites[2]
De province aux rites
Exilants des soirs!

− «Ils m'ont brûlée;[3] et depuis, vagabonde
Au fond des bois frais, j'implore le monde.»

Et les vents s'engueulent,
Tout le long des nuits!
Qu'est-c'que moi j'y puis,
Qu'est-ce donc qu'ils veulent?

− «Je vais guérir, voyez la cicatrice,
Oh! je ne veux pas aller à l'hospice![4]»

Des berceaux fienteux
Aux bières de même,
Bons couples sans gêne,
Tournez deux à deux.

Orgue, Orgue de Barbarie!
Scie autant que Souffre-Douleur,
Vidasse, vidasse ton cœur,
Ma pauvre rosse endolorie.

Vespers, Monstrances, Sunsets! Provincial Shulamites at the exiling rites of evening!

'They've ruined me; and ever since, a vagabond deep in the cool woods, I implore the world.'

And the winds have a slanging match every night long! What can I do about it, what do they want?

'I'm going to heal, see the scar, Oh! I don't want to go to the workhouse!'

From cradles full of excrement to coffins in the same state − unembarrassed couples pair off and dance.

Organ, barrel organ! Old bore as much as Scapegoat, pour out, pour out your heart, my poor tormented cur.

Complainte d'un certain Dimanche

Elle ne concevait pas qu'aimer fût l'ennemi d'aimer.
SAINTE-BEUVE, *Volupté.*

L'homme n'est pas méchant, ni la femme éphémère.
Ah! fous dont au casino battent les talons,
Tout homme pleure un jour et toute femme est mère,
          Nous sommes tous filials, allons!
Mais quoi! les Destins ont des partis pris si tristes,
Qui font que, les uns loin des autres, l'on s'exile,
Qu'on se traite à tort et à travers d'égoïstes,
Et qu'on s'use à trouver quelque unique Evangile.
Ah! jusqu'à ce que la nature soit bien bonne,
          Moi je veux vivre monotone.

Dans ce village en falaises, loin, vers les cloches.
Je redescends dévisagé par les enfants
Qui s'en vont faire bénir de tièdes brioches;
          Et rentré, mon sacré-cœur se fend!

Lament for a Particular Sunday

It had not occurred to her that loving was the enemy of loving.

Man is not wicked, nor is woman transitory. Ah! mad folk whose heels beat time
at the casino, every man weeps some day and every woman is a mother, we are all
our parents' children, alas! But so what? our Destinies are so stick-in-the-mud, they
make us exile ourselves far from each other, accuse each other of selfishness without
rhyme or reason, and wear ourselves out seeking some unique Gospel. Ah! until
nature turns kind, I want a dreary life.

   In this cliffside village, far off, past the church-bells, I go back down stared at by
the children who are off to get a blessing on their newly baked buns. And on
coming home, my damned sacred-heart breaks!

Les moineaux des vieux toits pépient à ma fenêtre.
Ils me regardent dîner, sans faim, à la carte;
Des âmes d'amis morts les habitent peut-être?
Je leur jette du pain: comme blessés, ils partent!
Ah! jusqu'à ce que la nature soit bien bonne,
        Moi je veux vivre monotone.

Elle est partie hier. Suis-je pas triste d'elle?
Mais c'est vrai! Voilà donc le fond de mon chagrin!
Oh! ma vie est aux plis de ta jupe fidèle!
        Son mouchoir me flottait sur le Rhin . . .
Seul. – Le Couchant retient un moment son Quadrige[1]
En rayons où le ballet des moucherons danse,
Puis, vers les toits fumants de la soupe, il s'afflige . . .
Et c'est le Soir, l'insaisissable confidence . . .[2]
Ah! jusqu'à ce que la nature soit bien bonne,
        Faudra-t-il vivre monotone?

Que d'yeux, en éventail, en ogive,[3] ou d'inceste,
Depuis que l'Être espère, ont réclamé leurs droits!
O ciels, les yeux pourrissent-ils comme le reste?
        Oh! qu'il fait seul! oh! fait-il froid!

The sparrows on the old roofs twitter at my window. They watch me dining, without hunger, *à la carte*. Perhaps the souls of dead friends inhabit them? I throw them bread: as if offended, they fly off! Ah! until nature turns kind, I want a dreary life.

    She left yesterday. A'n't I sad about her? Yes, I am! That's the source of my grief! Oh! my life is faithful to the pleats of your dress! Her handkerchief waved to me on the Rhine . . . alone. – The Sunset restrains for a moment its four-horse chariot in rays where the ballet of midges dances, then grieves over the steaming roofs of supper . . . and it's Evening, when we are let into the elusive secret . . . Ah! until nature turns kind, must we lead a dreary life?

    Since our Species first invented hope, how many eyes, from behind a fan, from under an ogive, or in incest, have claimed their rights! O skies, do eyes rot like the rest of us? Oh! how lonely it is! how cold!

Oh! que d'après-midi d'automne à vivre encore!
Le Spleen, eunuque à froid, sur nos rêves se vautre.
Or, ne pouvant redevenir des madrépores,[4]
O mes humains, consolons-nous les uns les autres.
Et jusqu'à ce que la nature soit bien bonne,
        Tâchons de vivre monotone.

Complainte d'un autre Dimanche

C'était un très-au vent d'octobre paysage,
Que découpe, aujourd'hui dimanche, la fenêtre,
Avec sa jalousie en travers, hors d'usage,
Où sèche, depuis quand! une paire de guêtres
Tachant de deux mals blancs ce glabre[1] paysage.

Un couchant mal bâti suppurant du livide;
Le coin d'une buanderie aux tuiles sales;
En plein, le Val-de-Grâce, comme un qui préside;
Cinq arbres en proie à de mesquines rafales
Qui marbrent ce ciel crû de bandages livides.

Oh! how many autumn evenings still to be lived! World-weariness, that aloof eunuch, wallows upon our dreams. So, since we can't turn back into madrepores, O fellow-humans, let's console each other. And until nature turns kind, let's try to lead a dreary life.

Lament for Another Sunday

It was a very October-windy landscape, framed, today Sunday, by the window, with its blind at a tilt, disused, where there hang – since when! – a pair of gaiters, forming two white spots of suffering on this clean-shaven landscape.

An ill-constructed sunset, suppurating livid colours; the corner of a laundry with dirty tiles. Bang in the centre, the Val-de-Grâce, like somebody chairing a meeting. Five trees tormented by spiteful gusts which mottle this raw sky with livid bandages.

Puis les squelettes de glycines aux ficelles,
En proie à des rafales encor plus mesquines!
O lendemains de noce! ô brides de dentelles!
Montrent-elles assez la corde, ces glycines
Recroquevillant leur agonie aux ficelles!

Ah! qu'est-ce que je fais, ici, dans cette chambre!
Des vers. Et puis, après! ô sordide limace!
Quoi! la vie est unique, et toi, sous ce scaphandre,[2]
Tu te racontes sans fin, et tu te ressasses!
Seras-tu donc toujours un qui garde la chambre?

Ce fut un bien au vent d'octobre paysage . . .

Complainte de la fin des Journées

Vous qui passez, oyez donc un pauvre être,
Chassé des *Simples* qu'on peut reconnaître
Soignant, las, quelque œillet à leur fenêtre!
                Passants, hâtifs passants,
Oh! qui veut visiter les palais de mes sens?

Then the skeletons of the wisteria [like puppets] on strings, the prey of still more spiteful gusts! O morning after the wedding! O bridles of lace! Could they be more threadbare, those wisteria shrivelling up their agony on strings!

Ah! what am I doing here, in this room! Verses. And then what next! O sordid slug! What! life is unique, and you, shut in your diving suit, keep endlessly going over and over your own story and harking back to yourself! Will you be always a bedroom stay-at-home?

It was a very October-windy landscape . . .

Ballad for the End of Time

O passer-by, hear a poor creature cast out from among the *Simple Ones* whom you recognize listlessly tending some carnation at their window! Passers-by, hasty passers-by, Oh! who wants a tour round the palace of my senses?

Maints ciboires[1]
De déboires
Un encor!

Ah! l'enfant qui vit de ce nom, poète!
Il se rêvait, seul, pansant Philoctète
Aux nuits de Lemnos;[2] ou, loin, grêle ascète.
            Et des vers aux moineaux,
Par le lycée en vacances, sous les préaux!

            Offertoire,
            En mémoire
            D'un consort.

Mon Dieu, que tout fait signe de se taire!
Mon Dieu, qu'on est follement solitaire!
Où sont tes yeux, premier dieu de la Terre
            Qui ravala ce cri:
«Têtue Éternité! je m'en vais incompris . . . ?»

            Pauvre histoire!
            Transitoire
            Passeport?[3]

Many ciboria of setbacks – here's yet another!

Ah! the child who lived by the name 'poet'! He dreamt he was alone, tending Philoctetes' wound in the Lemnos nights; or, far away, a skinny ascetic. And verses to the sparrows, with the grammar school on holiday, in the school-yard.

Offertory in memory of a consort.

My God, how everything commands one to be silent! My God, how madly alone we are! Where are your eyes, first god of the Earth who choked back this cry: 'Stubborn Eternity! I quit life misunderstood . . .'?

Pathetic story! Temporary passport?

J'ai dit: mon Dieu. La terre est orpheline[4]
Aux ciels, parmi les séminaires des Routines.
Va, suis quelque robe de mousseline . . .
            – Inconsciente Loi,
Faites que ce crachoir s'éloigne un peu de moi![5]

            Vomitoire[6]
            De la Foire,
            C'est la mort.

Complainte de la Vigie aux minuits polaires

Le Globe, vers l'aimant,
Chemine exactement,
Teinté de mers si bleues
De cités tout en toits,
De réseaux de convois
Qui grignotent des lieues.

I said: My God. The earth is an orphan of Heaven, among the seminaries of Routines. Go, follow some muslin dress . . . Unconscious Law, let this spittoon pass from me!
It's the Fairground Vomitory – death.

Lament of the Vigil at Polar Midnights

The Globe steers to the magnet exactly, tinted with seas so blue, with cities full of roofs, with networks of freight-trains eating up the miles.

O ma côte en sanglots![1]
Pas loin de Saint-Malo,
Un bourg fumeux vivote,
Qui tient sous son clocher,
Où grince un coq perché,
L'Ex-Voto[2] d'un pilote!

Aux cierges, au vitrail,
D'un autel en corail,
Une jeune Madone
Tend d'un air ébaubi
Un beau cœur de rubis
Qui se meurt et rayonne!

Un gros cœur tout en sang,
Un bon cœur ruisselant,
Qui, du soir à l'aurore,
Et de l'aurore au soir,
Se meurt, de ne pouvoir
Saigner, ah! saigner plus encore!

O my sobbing coastline! Not far from Saint-Malo a smoky township just makes ends meet, keeping under its spire (where a squeaking weathercock perches) a pilot's Ex-Voto!

By the light of the candles and the stained-glass window, a young Madonna offers with a flabbergasted air, a beautiful ruby-red heart which dies and sends out beams of light!

A heavy heart all bleeding, a kind heart pouring blood which, from evening to dawn and from dawn to evening, is dying to bleed, ah! bleed still more!

Complainte de la Lune en province

Ah! la belle pleine Lune,
Grosse comme une fortune!

La retraite sonne au loin,
Un passant, monsieur l'adjoint;

Un clavecin joue en face,
Un chat traverse la place:

La province qui s'endort!
Plaquant un dernier accord,

Le piano clôt sa fenêtre.
Quelle heure peut-il bien être?

Calme Lune, quel exil!
Faut-il dire: ainsi soit-il?

Lune, ô dilettante Lune,
A tous les climats commune,

Tu vis hier le Missouri,
Et les remparts de Paris,

Complaint of the Provincial Moon

Ah! the beautiful full Moon, fat as a fortune!
    The retreat sounds far off, there's a passer-by, the deputy mayor;
    A harpsichord is playing in the house opposite, a cat crosses the square:
    The provinces falling asleep! Striking a last chord,
    The piano closes its window. Whatever can the time be?
    Calm Moon, what exile! Must we say: 'So be it'?
    Moon, O dilettante Moon, common to all climes,
    Yesterday you saw the Missouri and the ramparts of Paris,

Les fiords bleus de la Norvège,
Les pôles, les mers, que sais-je?

Lune heureuse! ainsi tu vois,
A cette heure, le convoi

De son voyage de noce!
Ils sont partis pour l'Écosse.

Quel panneau, si, cet hiver,
Elle eût pris au mot mes vers!

Lune, vagabonde Lune,
Faisons cause et mœurs communes?

O riches nuits! je me meurs,
La province¹ dans le cœur!

Et la lune a, bonne vieille,
Du coton dans les oreilles.

The blue fjords of Norway, the poles, the seas, goodness knows what!
Happy Moon! and so you can see at this moment
Her honeymoon train! They're off to Scotland.
I'd have been really trapped if, last winter, she'd taken my poems at face value!
Moon, vagabond Moon, let's make common cause and custom?
O rich nights! I'm dying, stabbed to the heart by the provinces!
And the moon, dear old lady, has stuffed cottonwool into her ears.

Complainte des Printemps

Permettez, ô sirène,
Voici que votre haleine
Embaume la verveine;
C'est l'printemps qui s'amène!

– Ce système,[1] en effet, ramène le printemps,
Avec son impudent cortège d'excitants.

Otez donc ces mitaines;
Et n'ayez, inhumaine,
Que mes soupirs pour traîne:
Ous'qu'il y a de la gêne . . .

– Ah! yeux bleus méditant sur l'ennui de leur art!
Et vous, jeunes divins, aux soirs crus de hasard!

Du géant à la naine,[2]
Vois, tout bon sire entraîne
Quelque contemporaine,
Prendre l'air, par hygiène . . .

Complaint for the Springtimes

Allow me to say, O siren, here is your breath making the vervain fragrant; springtime is on her way!

'This system does in fact bring spring again, with her impudent retinue of stimulants.'

Take off those mittens; and, cruel one, have only my sighs for your train. Or are you embarrassed . . .

'Ah! blue eyes meditating on the tedium of their art! and you, divine young things, in the crude evenings of chance!'

From the male giant to the lady dwarf, see, every good sir brings along some female of his own age to take a constitutional in the fresh air . . .

– Mais vous saignez ainsi pour l'amour de l'exil!
Pour l'amour de l'Amour! D'ailleurs, ainsi soit-il . . .

> T'ai-je fait de la peine?
> Oh! viens vers les fontaines
> Où tournent les phalènes
> Des Nuits Elyséennes![3]

– Pimbèche aux yeux vaincus, bellâtre aux beaux jarrets,
Donnez votre fumier à la fleur du Regret.

> Voilà que son haleine
> N'embaum' plus la verveine!
> Drôle de phénomène . . .
> Hein, à l'année prochaine?

– Vierges d'hier, ce soir traîneuses de fœtus,
A genoux! voici l'heure où se plaint l'Angélus.

> Nous n'irons plus au bois,[4]
> Les pins sont éternels,
> Les cors ont des appels! . . .

> Neiges des pâles mois,
> Vous serez mon missel![5]
> – Jusqu'au jour de dégel.

'But you bleed too for the love of exile! for the love of Love! Besides, so be it . . .'

Have I hurt your feelings? Oh! come to the fountains where the moths of the Elysian Nights flutter!

'Stuck-up bitch with the vanquished eyes, smoothie with the well-turned calf, feed the flower of Regret with your manure.'

And now her breath no longer makes the vervain fragrant! A strange phenomenon . . . Well, goodbye till next year?

'Virgins of yesterday, this evening carriers of embryos – on your knees! this is the hour when the Angelus mourns.

We'll go no more to the woods, the pines are eternal, the horns utter haunting cries! . . .

Snows of the pale months, you shall be my missal! – until the day of the thaw.

Complainte de l'Automne monotone

Automne, automne, adieux de l'Adieu!
La tisane bout, noyant mon feu;
        Le vent s'époumonne
A reverdir la bûche où mon grand cœur tisonne.
        Est-il de vrais yeux?
Nulle ne songe à m'aimer un peu.

        Milieux aptères,
        Ou sans divans;
        Regards levants,[1]
        Deuils solitaires,
        Vers des Sectaires!

Le vent, la pluie, oh! le vent, la pluie!
Antigone,[2] écartez mon rideau;
        Cet ex-ciel tout suie,
Fond-il *decrescendo, statu quo, crescendo*?
        Le vent qui s'ennuie,
Retourne-t-il bien les parapluies?

Complaint of Monotonous Autumn

Autumn, autumn, when Goodbye itself says goodbye! The herb tea boils over, putting my fire out; the wind shouts itself hoarse enough to put new leaves on the log where my heavy heart fans the flames. Are there true eyes? None thinks to give me a little love.

Places without wings or divans; glances dawning, lonely mournings, the poetry of Cliques.

The wind, the rain, Oh! the wind, the rain! Antigone, draw my curtain; that soot-black ex-sky, is it melting *decrescendo, status quo,* or *crescendo*? Is the bored wind turning the umbrellas properly inside out?

Amours, gibiers!
Aux jours de givre,
Rêver sans livre,
Dans les terriers
Chauds de fumiers!

Plages, chemins de fer, ciels, bois morts,
Bateaux croupis dans les feuilles d'or,[3]
Le quart aux étoiles,
Paris grasseyant par chic aux prises de voiles;[4]
De trop poignants cors
M'ont hallalisé ces chers décors.

Meurtres, alertes,
Rêves ingrats!
En croix, les bras;
Roses ouvertes,[5]
Divines pertes!

Le soleil mort, tout nous abandonne.
Il se crut incompris. Qu'il est loin!
Vent pauvre, aiguillonne
Ces convois de martyrs se prenant à témoins!
La terre, si bonne,
S'en va, pour sûr, passer cet automne.

Loves, quarries at bay! On frosty days to dream with no book, in the warm burrows of dunghills!

Beaches, railways, skies, dead-wood, boats stagnating in gold-leaf, on lookout under the stars, Paris affectedly telling dirty jokes at takings of the veil; Horns far too poignant have death-knelled for me these dear stage-sets.

Murders, alerts, ungrateful dreams! Cross your arms; open roses bring divine ruin!

Once the sun is dead, everything abandons us. He thought himself misunderstood. How far away he is! Wretched wind, goad on those processions of martyrs calling each other to witness! The earth, so kindly, is surely going to die this autumn.

Nuits sous-marines!
Pourpres forêts,
Torrents de frais,
Bancs en gésines,
Tout s'illumine!

– Allons, fumons une pipette de tabac,
En feuilletant un de ces si vieux almanachs,

En rêvant de la petite qui unirait
Aux charmes de l'œillet ceux du chardonneret.

Complainte de l'Ange incurable

Je t'expire mes Cœurs[1] bien barbouillés de cendres;
Vent esquinté de toux des paysages tendres!

Où vont les gants d'avril, et les rames d'antan?[2]
L'âme des hérons fous sanglote sur l'étang.

Et vous, tendres
D'antan?

Underwater nights! Purple forests, torrents of expenses, shoals in childbirth, everything is luminous!
   Come, let's smoke a little pipe of tobacco and leaf through one of these old almanacs,
   Dreaming of the darling who'd unite the charm of the carnation and the goldfinch.

Complaint of the Incurable Angel

I gasp you out my Hearts well smeared with ashes; wind exhausted with coughs from the landscapes of love!
   Where do the gloves of April go, the oars of yesteryear? The souls of mad herons weep across the pond.
   And you, romances of yesteryear?

Le hoche-queue pépie aux écluses gelées;
L'amante va, fouettée aux plaintes des allées.

Sais-tu bien, folle pure, où sans châle tu vas?
– Passant oublié des yeux gais, j'aime là-bas . . .

      – En allées
        Là-bas!

Le long des marbriers (Encore un beau commerce!)
Patauge aux défoncés un convoi, sous l'averse.

Un trou, qu'asperge un prêtre âgé qui se morfond,
Bâille à ce libéré de l'être; et voici qu'on

      Le déverse
      Au fond.

Les moulins décharnés, ailes hier allègres,
Vois, s'en font les grands bras du haut des coteaux maigres!

Ci-gît n'importe qui. Seras-tu différent,
Diaphane d'amour, ô Chevalier-Errant?

The wagtail twitters on the frozen locks; the sweetheart goes her way, lashed by the avenues' laments.

Are you quite clear, pure fool, where you're off to without a shawl? 'O passer-by whom happy eyes forget, I have a lover there . . .'

That way, along the avenues!

Past the marble masons' yards (That's another fine trade!) a funeral procession squelches through the potholes, under the downpour.

A hole, sprinkled by an aged moping priest, yawns for this person released from life; and now they

tip him right down to the bottom.

The skeletal mills, whose wings were happy yesterday – see, they're waving huge arms at each other from the tops of the gaunt hillsides!

Here lies no matter who. Will you be different, transparent with love, O Knight Errant?

Claque, ô maigre
Errant!

Hurler avec les loups, aimer nos demoiselles,
Serrer ces mains sauçant dans de vagues vaisselles!

Mon pauvre vieux, il le faut pourtant! et puis, va,
Vivre est encor le meilleur parti ici-bas.

Non! vaisselles
D'ici-bas!

Au-delà plus sûr que la Vérité! des ailes
D'Hostie ivre et ravie aux cités sensuelles!

Quoi! Ni Dieu, ni l'art, ni ma Sœur Fidèle; mais
Des ailes! par le blanc suffoquant! à jamais,

Ah! des ailes
A jamais!

— Tant il est vrai que la saison dite d'automne
N'est aux cœurs mal fichus rien moins que folichonne.

Drop dead, O skinny Errant!

To howl with the wolves, to love our young ladies, to clasp these hands that mop the sauce from who knows what dishes!

My poor old friend, you've no alternative! and after all, in this world, living is still the best policy.

No! the dishes of this world!

A next world surer than Truth! wings of rapturous Communion Host snatched away from the cities of the senses!

What! Neither God, nor art, nor my Loyal Sister; but wings for ever! so white they choke you!

Ah! wings for ever!

— It's so true that the season called autumn isn't much fun for off-colour souls.

Complainte des Nostalgies préhistoriques

La nuit bruine sur les villes.
Mal repu des gains machinals,
On dîne; et, gonflé d'idéal,
Chacun sirote son idylle,
  Ou furtive, ou facile.

Échos des grands soirs primitifs!
Couchants aux flambantes usines,
Rude paix des sols en gésine,
Cri jailli là-bas d'un massif,
  Voluptés à vif!

Dégringolant une vallée,
Heurter, dans des coquelicots,
Une enfant bestiale et brûlée
Qui suce, en blaguant les échos,
  De jûteux abricots.

Complaint of Feeling Home-Sick for Primeval Times

Night drizzles down on the cities. Ill-rewarded by our industrial earnings, we dine; and, puffed up with the Ideal, each of us sips at his idyll, whether it be furtive or facile.

Echoes of the long evenings of primeval times! Sunsets like factories ablaze, rough peace of soils in childbed, shriek bursting from the shrubs over there, violuptuated to the quick.

Stumbling down a valley, running into a feral sunburnt girl among the poppies, who is sucking juicy apricots, while making fun of the echoes.

Livrer aux langueurs des soirées
Sa toison où du cristal luit,
Pourlécher ses lèvres sucrées,
Nous barbouiller le corps de fruits
    Et lutter comme essui!

Un moment, béer, sans rien dire,
Inquiets d'une étoile là-haut;
Puis, sans but, bien gentils satyres,
Nous prendre aux premiers sanglots
    Fraternels des crapauds.

Et, nous délèvrant[1] de l'extase,
Oh! devant la lune en son plein,
Là-bas, comme un bloc de topaze,
Fous, nous renverser sur les reins,
    Riant, battant des mains!

La nuit bruine sur les villes;
Se raser le masque, s'orner
D'un frac deuil, avec art dîner,
Puis, parmi des vierges débiles,
    Prendre un air imbécile.

Freeing to the languors of the evenings her mane of hair where crystal gleams, licking her sugared lips, daubing our bodies with fruit, and tussling to dry them off.

For a moment gaping, saying nothing, uneasy at a star high above, then aimlessly, gentle satyrs, to make love in time to the first brotherly sobs of the toads.

And dekissing ourselves from this ecstasy, Oh! under the full moon up there like a chunk of topaz, madly throwing ourselves on our backs, laughing, clapping our hands!

Night drizzles on the cities: shave your mask, dress up in a tailcoat of mourning-black, dine with artistry, then among feeble-minded virgins, adopt a stupid air.

Autre Complainte de l'orgue de Barbarie

Prolixe et monocorde,
Le vent dolent des nuits
Rabâche ses ennuis,
Veut se pendre à la corde
　　Des puits! et puis?
　　Miséricorde!

　– Voyons, qu'est-ce que je veux?
Rien. Je suis-t-il malhûreux!

Oui, les phares aspergent
Les côtes en sanglots,
Mais les volets sont clos
Aux veilleuses des vierges,
　　Orgue au galop,
　　Larmes des cierges!

　– Après? qu'est-ce qu'on y peut?
　– Rien. Je suis-t-il malhûreux!

Another Lament from the Barrel Organ

Prolix and monotonous, the doleful night wind harps on its troubles, tries to hang itself by the well-rope! and then? Have pity!

'Let's see, what do I want?' Nothing. Am'n't I mis'ble!

Yes, the lighthouses spray the coasts with sobs of light, but the shutters are closed on the virgins' night-lights, galloping church-organ, weeping candles!

'So? What's to be done about it?' – Nothing. Am'n't I mis'ble!

Vous, fidèle madone,
Laissez! Ai-je assisté,
Moi, votre puberté?
O jours où Dieu tâtonne,
    Passants d'été,
    Pistes d'automne!

– Eh bien! aimerais-tu mieux . . .
– Rien. Je suis-t-il malhûreux!

Cultes, Littératures,
Yeux chauds, lointains ou gais,
Infinis au rabais,
Tout train-train, rien qui dure,
    Oh! à jamais
    Des créatures![1]

– Ah! ça qu'est-ce que je veux?
– Rien. Je suis-t-il malhûreux!

Bagnes des pauvres bêtes,
Tarifs d'alléluias,
Mortes aux camélias,[2]
Oh! lendemain de fête
    Et paria,
    Vrai, des planètes!

You, faithful Madonna, leave me alone! Did I attend *your* adolescence? O days when God can hardly feel his way, passers-by of summer, tracks of autumn!

'Well, would you prefer . . . ?' – Nothing. Am'n't I mis'ble!

Cults, literatures, warm eyes, far off or joyous, Infinites at a knock-down price, everything's humdrum, nothing lasts, Oh! nothing but critters for ever!

'Ah! what do I want?' – Nothing. Am'n't I mis'ble!

Penal servitude for poor animals, price list of hallelujahs, dead women with camelias, oh! the morning after the night before, and, yes, pariah of the planets!

– Enfin! quels sont donc tes vœux?
– Nuls. Je suis-t-il malhûreux!

La nuit monte, armistice
Des cités, des labours.
Mais il n'est pas, bon sourd,
En ton digne exercice,
  De raison pour
  Que tu finisses?

– Bien sûr. C'est ce que je veux.
Ah! Je suis-t-il malhûreux!

Complainte du pauvre Chevalier-Errant

Jupes des quinze ans, aurores de femmes,
Qui veut, enfin, des palais de mon âme?
Perrons d'œillets blancs, escaliers de flamme,
  Labyrinthes alanguis,
   Edens qui
Sonneront sous vos pas reconnus, des airs reconquis.

'Okay, so what are your wishes?' – None. Am'n't I mis'ble!
Night comes up, armistice for cities and ploughed fields. But, my deaf friend, in your worthy activity, can't you see sense in stopping?
'Of course. That's what I want. Ah! Am'n't I mis'ble?'

Complaint of the Poor Knight Errant

Fifteen-year-old skirts, daysprings of women, who'll buy the palaces of my soul? Steps of white carnations, staircases of flame, languid labyrinths, Edens which, under your recognized footsteps, will ring out reconquered tunes.

Instincts-levants[1] souriant par les fentes,
Méditations un doigt à la tempe,
Souvenirs clignotant comme des lampes,
Et, battant les corridors,
Vains essors,
Les Dilettantismes chargés de colliers de remords.

Oui, sans bruit, vous écarterez mes branches,
Et verrez comme, à votre mine franche,
Viendront à vous mes biches les plus blanches,
Mes ibis sacrés, mes chats,
Et, rachats!
Ma Vipère de Lettres aux bien effaçables crachats.[2]

Puis, frêle mise au monde![3] ô Toute Fine,
O ma Tout-universelle orpheline,
Au fond de chapelles de mousseline
Pâle, ou jonquille à poids noirs,
Dans les soirs,
Feu d'artificeront envers vous mes sens encensoirs![4]

Sunrising-instincts smiling through the chinks, meditations with finger on temple, memories flashing on and off like lamps, and, scouring the corridors, vain flights, dilettantisms weighed down with necklaces of remorse.

Yes, noiselessly you'll part my branches, and see how, at your fresh face, my whitest hinds will come to you, my holy ibises, my cats, and – redemptions! – my Literary Viper whose spittle is so easily wiped off.

Then, frail delicate birth! All-Delicate, O my Omni-Universal Orphaness, behind chapels of muslin, pale, or daffodil with black dots, in the evenings, my censer senses will firework towards you!

Nous organiserons de ces parties!
Mes caresses, naïvement serties,
Mourront, de ta gorge aux vierges hosties,
Aux amandes de tes seins!
O tocsins,
Des cœurs dans le roulis⁵ des empilements de coussins.

Tu t'abandonnes au Bon, moi j'abdique;
Nous nous comblons de nos deux Esthétiques;
Tu condimentes mes piments mystiques,
J'assaisonne tes saisons;
Nous blasons,
A force d'étapes sur nos collines, l'Horizon!

Puis j'ai des tas d'éternelles histoires,
O mers, ô volières de ma Mémoire!
Sans compter les passes évocatoires!
Et quand tu t'endormiras,
Dans les draps
D'un somme, je t'éventerai de lointains opéras.

We'll hold such parties! My caresses, naïvely jewel-set, will die, from your throat
with its virgin holy wafers, to the almonds of your breasts! O alarm bells, of hearts
in the wave-swell of the piles of cushions.

You abandon yourself to the Good, I abdicate; we fulfil each other with our two
Aesthetics; you spice my mystical pimentos, I give seasoning to your seasons; upon
our hills, by dint of rapid stages climbed, we cloy the Horizon!

And then I've loads of everlasting stories, O seas, O aviaries of my Memory!
without counting my spell-casting gestures! and when you fall asleep in the sheets
of a doze, I'll fan you with far-off operas.

Orage en deux cœurs, ou jets d'eau des siestes,
Tout sera Bien, contre ou selon ton geste,
        Afin qu'à peine un prétexte te reste
            De froncer tes chers sourcils,
                Ce souci:
«Ah! suis-je née, infiniment, pour vivre par ici?»

— Mais j'ai beau parader, toutes s'en fichent!
Et je repars avec ma folle affiche,
    Boniment incompris, piteux *sandwiche*:[6]
            Au Bon Chevalier-Errant,
                Restaurant,
Hôtel meublé, Cabinets de lecture, prix courants.

Tempest in two hearts, or siestas like fountains, all will be Well, with or without your assent, so that barely a pretext will remain for you to knit your dear eyebrows, worrying: 'Ah! was I born, through all eternity, to live in a place like this?'
— But it's no good parading myself, none of them gives a damn! And I set off again with my crazy advertisement, misunderstood sales-talk, pitiable sandwich-man: 'At the Good Knight-Errant, Restaurant, Furnished Hotel, Reading Rooms, run-of-the-mill prices.'

Complainte des Consolations

Quia voluit consolari.

Ses yeux ne me voient pas, son corps serait jaloux;
Elle m'a dit: «monsieur . . .» en m'enterrant d'un geste;
Elle est Tout, l'univers moderne et le céleste.
Soit! draguons donc Paris, et ravitaillons-nous,
          Tant bien que mal, du reste.

Les Landes sans espoir de ses regards brûlés
Semblaient parfois des paons prêts à mettre à la voile . . .
Sans chercher à me consoler vers les étoiles,
Ah! Je trouverai bien deux yeux aussi sans clés,
          Au Louvre, en quelque toile![1]

Oh! qu'incultes, ses airs, rêvant dans la prison
D'un *cant*[2] sur le qui-vive au travers de nos hontes!
Mais, en m'appliquant bien, moi dont la foi démonte
Les jours, les ciels, les nuits, dans les quatre saisons
          Je trouverai mon compte.[3]

Complaint of the Consolations

For he wished to be comforted.

Her eyes don't see me, for her body would be jealous. She said to me, 'Sir . . .' burying me with a gesture. She is Everything, the universe both modern and celestial. So be it! Let's go cruising round Paris, and refuel ourselves – though rather poorly, I admit.

    The despairing Heathlands of her fire-scorched gaze resembled sometimes peacocks ready to set sail . . . Without seeking to console myself in the stars' direction, Ah! I'll easily find two equally keyless eyes in the Louvre, in some painting or other!

    Oh! how uncivilized, her airs and graces, dreaming away in the prison of a pose, on the look-out right into our shames! But, by properly applying myself, I whose faith dismantles the days, skies, nights, in the course of the four seasons I'll get what I deserve.

Sa bouche! à moi, ce pli pudiquement martyr
Où s'aigrissent des nostalgies de nostalgies!
Eh bien, j'irai parfois, très sincère vigie,
Du haut de Notre-Dame aider l'aube au sortir
    De passables orgies.

Mais, Tout va la reprendre! – Alors Tout m'en absout.
Mais, Elle est ton bonheur! – Non! je[4] suis trop immense,
Trop chose. Comment donc! mais ma seule présence
Ici-bas, vraie à s'y mirer,[5] est l'air de Tout:
    De la Femme au Silence![6]

Complainte des bons Ménages

L'Art sans poitrine m'a trop longtemps bercé dupe.
Si ses labours sont fiers, que ses blés décevants!
Tiens, laisse-moi bêler tout aux plis de ta jupe
    Qui fleure le couvent.

 Her mouth! Be mine, you prudishly martyrlike furrow where longings grow
sour on longings! Well well, on my emergence from second-rate orgies, sometimes
I'll go in very sincere vigil to the top of Notre-Dame – to help the dawn up.
 'But Everything will reproach her!' 'In that case Everything lets me off doing
so.' 'But She is your happiness!' – 'No! I am too immense, too elemental. Come
now! my mere presence In This World, so true you can see yourself in me as in a
mirror, is the way Everything looks: the Woman of the Silence!'

The Lament of Respectable Households

Flat-chested art has lulled and duped me for too long. Though its ploughed fields
are impressive, how disappointing are its wheat-harvests! Come, let me bleat at the
folds of your skirt, which smells of the convent.

Le Génie avec moi, serf, a fait des manières;
Toi, jupe, fais frou-frou, sans t'inquiéter pourquoi,
Sous l'œillet bleu de ciel de l'unique théière,
      Sois toi-même, à part moi.

Je veux être pendu, si tu n'es pas discrète
Et *comme il faut*, vraiment! Et d'ailleurs tu m'es tout.
Tiens, j'aimerai les plissés de ta collerette
      Sans en venir à bout.

Mais l'Art, c'est l'Inconnu! qu'on y dorme et s'y vautre.
On peut ne pas l'avoir constamment sur les bras!
Eh bien, ménage au vent! Soyons Lui, Elle et l'Autre.
      Et puis, n'insistons pas.

I'm a serf to my Genius, which poses and pouts. Rustle on, skirt, rustle on without worrying why, under the sky-blue carnation of the single teapot, be yourself – in my private thoughts.

I'll be hanged if you're not discreet and ladylike, really! and besides you're everything to me. Come, I shall love the pleats of your collar and never come to an end of them.

But Art is the Unknown! Whether you sleep or wallow in it, you don't have to have it under your feet all the time! So, let's throw this relationship to the winds! Let's be He, She and the Other. And then, let's give the subject a rest.

Complainte de Lord Pierrot

Au clair de la lune,
Mon ami Pierrot,
Filons, en costume,
Présider là-haut!
Ma cervelle est morte.
Que le Christ l'emporte!
Béons à la Lune,
La bouche en zéro.[1]

Inconscient, descendez en nous par réflexes:
Brouillez les cartes, les dictionnaires, les sexes.

Tournons d'abord sur nous-même, comme un fakir!
(Agiter le pauvre être, avant de s'en servir.)[2]

J'ai le cœur chaste et vrai comme une bonne lampe;
Oui, je suis en taille-douce, comme une estampe.

Lord Pierrot's Complaint

By the light of the moon, Pierrot my friend, let's go dressed up to preside up above!
My brain is dead. May Christ bear it away! Let's gape at the Moon, our mouths
shaped like zeros.

Unconscious, descend into us by reflexes, shuffle the cards, the dictionaries, the
sexes.

Let's spin round upon ourselves, like dervishes! (Shake well, before using your
wretched self.)

My heart is as chaste and true as an old lamp; yes, I'm in copper-plate, like a
print.

Vénus, énorme comme le Régent,[3]
Déjà se pâme à l'horizon des grèves;
Et c'est l'heure, ô gens nés casés, bonnes gens,
De s'étourdir en longs trilles de rêves!
Corybanthe,[4] aux quatre vents tous les draps!
Disloque tes pudeurs, à bas les lignes!
En costume blanc, je ferai le cygne,
Après nous le Déluge,[5] ô ma Léda![6]
Jusqu'à ce que tournent tes yeux vitreux,
Que tu grelottes en rires affreux,
Hop! enlevons sur les horizons fades
Les menuets de nos pantalonnades!
            Tiens! l'Univers
            Est à l'envers . . .

        – Tout cela vous honore,
        Lord Pierrot, mais encore?

    – Ah! qu'une, d'elle-même, un beau soir sût venir,
    Ne voyant que boire à mes lèvres, ou mourir!

    Je serais, savez-vous, la plus noble conquête
    Que femme, au plus ravi du Rêve, eût jamais faite!

    Venus, as huge as the Kohinoor, is already swooning on the horizon of the riversides; and it's the hour, O folk born housebound, decent folk, to dull your wits with long trills of dreams! Corybant, all sheets to the four winds! Dislocate your modesties, follow no line! In a white costume I'll play the swan, after us the Flood, O my Leda! Until your glassy eyes turn, and you shiver in frightful laughter, Up! let's joyously play on the dull horizons the minuets of our burlesques! What a surprise! the Universe is upside down . . .
    'These sentiments honour you, Lord Pierrot, but what else?'
    Ah! that someone, of her own free will, could come one fine evening, wishing only to drink at my lips, or die!
    I should be, you know, the noblest conquest that woman, in her most ravished Dream, had ever made!

D'ici-là, qu'il me soit permis
De vivre de vieux compromis.

Où commence, où finit l'humaine
Ou la divine dignité?

Jonglons avec les entités,
Pierrot s'agite et Tout le mène!⁷
Laissez faire, laissez passer;
Laissez passer, et laissez faire;
Le semblable, c'est le contraire,

Et l'univers, c'est pas assez!
Et je me sens, ayant pour cible
Adopté la vie impossible,
De moins en moins localisé!

    – Tout cela vous honore,
     Lord Pierrot, mais encore?

– Il faisait, ah! si chaud, si sec.
Voici qu'il pleut, qu'il pleut, bergères!⁸
Les pauvres Vénus bocagères
Ont la roupie à leur nez grec!

In the meantime, allow me to live old compromises.
Where does human or divine dignity begin, where does it end?
Let's juggle with entities. Pierrot bustles to and fro, and the All controls him. Let be, let by; let by and let be; the same is the opposite,
and the universe is not enough! And I, having for my target adopted the impossibility of life, I feel less and less localized!
'These sentiments honour you, Lord Pierrot, but what else?'
It was, ah! so hot, so dry. Now it's raining, raining, shepherdesses! The poor woodland Venuses have drips hanging from their Greek noses!

    – Oh! de moins en moins drôle;
    Pierrot sait mal son rôle?

– J'ai le cœur triste comme un lampion forain . . .
Bah! j'irai passer la nuit dans le premier train;

    Sûr d'aller, ma vie entière,
    Malheureux comme les pierres. (*Bis.*)[9]

Autre Complainte de Lord Pierrot

Celle qui doit me mettre au courant de la Femme!
Nous lui dirons d'abord, de mon air le moins froid:
«La somme des angles d'un triangle, chère âme,
    «Est égale à deux droits.»

Et si ce cri lui part: «Dieu de Dieu! que je t'aime!»
– «Dieu reconnaîtra les siens.»[1] Ou piquée au vif:
– «Mes claviers ont du cœur, tu seras mon seul thème.»
    Moi: «Tout est relatif.»

'Oh! less and less funny; has Pierrot forgotten his lines?'
My heart is as sad as a paper lantern at a funfair . . . Bah! I'll go spend the night in the first train that comes;
Sure of living my whole life as miserable as the stones. (*Twice.*)

Another Complaint from Lord Pierrot

She who's sure to give me the low-down on Woman! I'll say to her first, with my least cold air, 'The sum of the angles of a triangle, dear soul, is equal to two right angles.'
And if this cry issues from her: 'God of Gods! how I love you!' – 'God will recognize his own.' Or, if she's pricked to the quick: 'My keyboards have hearts, you'll be my only theme' – I: 'All is relative.'

De tous ses yeux,[2] alors! se sentant trop banale:
«Ah! tu ne m'aimes pas; tant d'autres sont jaloux!»
Et moi, d'un œil qui vers l'Inconscient s'emballe:
      «Merci, pas mal; et vous?»

– «Jouons au plus fidèle!» – «A quoi bon, ô Nature!»
«Autant à qui perd gagne!» Alors, autre couplet:
– «Ah! tu te lasseras le premier, j'en suis sûre . . .»
      – «Après vous, s'il vous plaît.»[3]

Enfin, si, par un soir, elle meurt dans mes livres,
Douce; feignant de n'en pas croire encor mes yeux,
J'aurai un: «Ah çà, mais, nous avions De Quoi vivre!
      «C'était donc sérieux?»

Complainte sur certains ennuis

Un couchant des Cosmogonies!
Ah! que la Vie est quotidienne . . .
Et, du plus vrai qu'on se souvienne,[1]
Comme on fut piètre et sans génie . . .

All her eyes on me then, feeling herself too banal: 'Ah! you don't love me; so many others are jealous!' And I, with one eye intent on the Unconscious: 'Thank you, not bad; and you?'

'Let's play at "Who's the more faithful"!' – 'What's the point, O Nature?' – 'It's as good as playing "Loser takes all"!' – Next, another little set phrase: 'Ah, you'll tire of me first, I'm sure . . .' – 'No, after you, please.'

At last, if one evening she dies among my books, quietly; pretending not to believe my eyes, I'll react with a: 'Drat it, we had the Wherewithal to live on! Was it serious after all?'

Complaint about Certain Annoyances

A sunset of Cosmogonies! Ah! how day-to-day Life is . . . And as true as one can remember, how paltry and lacking in genius we were . . .

On voudrait s'avouer des choses,
Dont on s'étonnerait en route,
Qui feraient, une fois pour toutes!
Qu'on s'entendrait à travers poses.

On voudrait saigner le Silence,
Secouer l'exil des causeries;
Et non! ces dames sont aigries
Par des questions de préséance.

Elles boudent là, l'air capable.
Et, sous le ciel, plus d'un s'explique,
Par quels gâchis suresthétiques
Ces êtres-là sont adorables.

Justement, une nous appelle,
Pour l'aider à chercher sa bague,
Perdue (où dans ce terrain vague?)
Un souvenir D'AMOUR, dit-elle!

Ces êtres-là sont adorables!

We'd wish to confess to one another, things which would keep us amazed, so that – once and for all! – we'd understand each other through our poses.

We'd like to bleed the Silence, shake off the exile of conversations. But ah no! These ladies are embittered by questions of precedence.

They pout there, looking competent, and under heaven more than one man tries to explain to himself by what overdone bungling these creatures are supposed to be adorable.

This very moment, here's one calling us to help her find her ring, lost (where, in this no man's land?) a souvenir of LOVE, she says!

These creatures are adorable!

Complainte des noces de Pierrot

Où te flatter pour boire dieu,
Ma provisoire corybante?[1]
Je sauce mon âme en tes yeux,
Je ceins ta beauté pénitente,
Où donc vis-tu? Moi si pieux,
    Que tu m'es lente, lente!

Tes cils m'insinuent: c'en est trop;
Et leurs calices[2] vont se clore,
Sans me jeter leur dernier mot,
Et refouler mes métaphores,
De leur petit air comme il faut?
    Isis,[3] levez le store!

Car cette fois, c'est pour de bon;
Trop d'avrils, quittant la partie
Devant des charmes moribonds,
J'ai bâclé notre eucharistie
Sous les trépieds où ne répond
    Qu'une aveugle Pythie![4]

The Ballad of Pierrot's Wedding

Where can I caress you, my temporary corybant, so as to drink of god? I dip my soul in the flavour of your eyes, I besiege your penitent beauty, where is your life hidden? Though I am so devoted, how unresponsive you are to me, how unresponsive!

Your eyelashes hint to me: 'You're going too far'; And are their calyxes about to close, without telling me their last word, and to repress my metaphors with their delicate genteel look? Isis, raise the shutters!

For this time, I've really gone and done it! Too many Aprils, abandoning the contest before dying attractions, I've botched our communion under tripods where only a blind Pythia responds!

Ton tabernacle est dévasté?
Sois sage, distraite égoïste!
D'ailleurs, suppôt d'éternité,
Le spleen de tout ce qui n'existe[5]
Veut qu'en ce blanc matin d'été,
     Je sois ton exorciste!

Ainsi, fustigeons ces airs plats
Et ces dolentes pantomimes
Couvrant d'avance du vieux glas
Mes tocsins à l'hostie ultime!
Ah! tu me comprends, n'est-ce pas,
     Toi, ma moins pauvre rime?

Introïbo,[6] voici l'Époux!
Hallali! songe au pôle, aspire;
Je t'achèterai des bijoux,
Garde-moi ton *ut*[7] de martyre . . .
Quoi! bébé bercé, c'est donc tout?
     Tu n'as plus rien à dire?

Your altar is desecrated? Behave yourself, you inattentive, selfish thing! Besides, you minion of eternity, the resentment of everything which (doesn't) exist insists (this white summer morning) on my being your exorcist!

Thus, let us castigate these dreary tunes and doleful pantomimes – forewarned, the old death-knell shouting down my alarm bells in honour of the ultimate communion host! Ah! you understand me, don't you, [my love,] you who are my least dreadful rhyme!

Introibo, Here comes the Husband! View Halloo! Think of the North Pole, breathe in; I'll buy you jewels, keep for me your keynote of martyrdom! Hey, rockabyed baby, is that everything? You've nothing more to say?

– Mon dieu, mon dieu! je n'ai rien eu,
J'en suis encore aux poncifs thèmes!
Son teint me redevient connu,
Et, sur son front tout au baptême,[8]
Aube déjà l'air ingénu!
L'air vrai! l'air non mortel quand même!

      Ce qui fait que je l'aime,

   Et qu'elle est même, vraiment,
      La chapelle rose
      Où parfois j'expose
      Le Saint-Sacrement
   De mon humeur du moment.

Complainte du Vent qui s'ennuie la nuit

Ta fleur se fane, ô fiancée?
Oh! gardes-en encore un peu
La corolle qu'a compulsée
Un soir d'ennui trop studieux!

'My God, my God, I've had nothing, I'm still stuck among banalities! I begin to recognize her complexion again and, on her forehead (submitted to baptism) there dawns already the look of innocence! the look of truth! well, at least the look of not being mortal!

Which is why I love her,

And why she's even, truly, the rose chapel where sometimes I exhibit the Holy Sacrament of my transient mood.

Complaint of the Wind which gets bored at night

Is your flower fading, my betrothed? Oh! for a while preserve from that fate the corolla that was examined on an evening of too studious boredom!

Le vent des toits qui pleure et rage,
Dans ses assauts et ses remords,
Sied au nostalgique naufrage
Où m'a jeté ta Toison-d'Or.[1]

    Le vent assiège,
       Dans sa tour,
    Le sortilège
       De l'Amour;
    Et, pris au piège,
    Le sacrilège
    Geint sans retour.[2]

Ainsi, mon idéal sans bride
T'ubiquitait de ses sanglots,
O calice loyal mais vide
Qui jouais à me rester clos?
Ainsi dans la nuit investie,
Sur tes pétales décevants,
L'Ange fileur d'eucharisties
S'afflige tout le long du vent.

The wind weeping and raging on the roofs, suits well, in its assaults and its remorses, the nostalgic shipwreck where your Golden Fleece has driven me.

The wind besieges, in its tower, the spell of Love; and caught in its own trap, the sacrilege complains unrequitedly.

Thus, the sobs of my uncontrolled ideal made me see you everywhere, O calyx, faithful but empty, who made a game of remaining closed to me. Thus, in the besieged night, over your disappointing petals, the Angel who spins communions mourns in the wind's every note.

Le vent assiège,
  Dans sa tour,
Le sortilège
  De l'Amour,
Et, pris au piège,
  Le sacrilège
Geint sans retour.

O toi qu'un remords fait si morte,
Qu'il m'est incurable, en tes yeux,
D'écouter se morfondre aux portes
Le vent aux étendards de cieux!
Rideaux verts de notre hypogée,[3]
Marbre banal du lavabo,
Votre hébétude ravagée
Est le miroir de mon tombeau.

O vent, allège
  Ton discours
Des vains cortèges
  De l'humour;
Je rentre au piège,
Peut-être y vais-je
Tuer l'Amour!

The wind besieges in its tower the spell of Love, and caught in its own trap, the sacrilege complains irrevocably.

O you whom a remorse turns icy cold, how unforgivable in your eyes that I hear the wind with heaven's banners moping around our doors! Green curtains of our hypogeum, banal marble of the washbasin, your ravaged numbness is the mirror of my tomb.

O wind, lighten your speech with empty processions of humour; I am drawn back into the trap, there perhaps I shall kill Love!

Complainte du pauvre corps humain

L'homme et sa compagne sont serfs
De corps, tourbillonnants cloaques
Aux mailles de harpes de nerfs
Serves de tout et que détraque
Un fier répertoire d'attaques.

> Voyez l'homme, voyez!
> Si ça n'fait pas pitié!

Propre et correct en ses ressorts,[1]
S'assaisonnant de modes vaines,
Il s'admire, ce brave corps,
Et s'endimanche pour sa peine,
Quand il a bien sué la semaine.

> Et sa compagne! allons,
> Ma bell', nous nous valons.

Ballad of the Wretched Human Body

Man and his mate are slaves of their bodies, swirling sewers, with meshes of nerve-harps in serfdom to everything, and knocked out of kilter by a proud repertoire of fits.

Look at man, look at him! Dunnit myke you weep!

Fit and accurate in its suspension, dolled up with empty fashions, this handsome body admires itself, and decks itself in its Sunday best, to repay its trouble for having sweated all week long.

And his mate! Come, my charmer, we're no better than each other.

Faudrait le voir, touchant et nu
Dans un décor d'oiseaux, de roses;
Ses tics réflexes d'ingénu,
Ses plis pris de mondaines poses;
Bref, sur beau fond vert, sa chlorose.[2]

    Voyez l'homme, voyez!
    Si ça n'fait pas pitié!

Les Vertus et les Voluptés
Détraquant d'un rien sa machine,
Il ne vit que pour disputer
Ce domaine à rentes divines
Aux lois de mort qui le taquinent.

    Et sa compagne! allons,
    Ma bell', nous nous valons.

Il se soutient de mets pleins d'art,
Se drogue, se tond, se parfume,
Se truffe tant, qu'il meurt trop tard;
Et la cuisine se résume
En mille infections posthumes.

You ought to see it, touching and bare in a décor of birds and roses; its reflex tics of affected innocence, its habits picked up from social posturing; in short, on a fine green background, its chlorosis.

Look at man, look at him! Dunnit myke you weep!

Since the Virtues and the Pleasures knock its machine out of gear for a trifle, it lives only to defend this domain, with its divine annuities, against the laws of death which pester it.

And his mate! Come, my charmer, we're no better than each other.

It sustains itself on refined dishes, drugs itself, takes the clippers to itself, perfumes itself, stuffs itself so full of delicacies that it dies too late; and high-class cookery sums itself up in a thousand posthumous infections.

Oh! ce couple, voyez!
Non, ça fait trop pitié.

Mais ce microbe subversif
Ne compte pas pour la Substance,
Dont les déluges corrosifs
Renoient vite pour l'Innocence
Ces fols germes de conscience.[3]

Nature est sans pitié
Pour son petit dernier.

Complainte du Roi de Thulé

Il était un roi de Thulé,[1]
    Immaculé,
Qui loin des jupes et des choses,
Pleurait sur la métempsychose
        Des lys en roses,
        Et quel palais![2]

Oh! this couple, take a look! No, it's too pathetic.

But this subversive microbe counts for nothing in the eyes of Substance, whose corrosive floods quickly drown back into Innocence these foolish seeds of consciousness.

Nature has no pity on her youngest baby.

Ballad of the King of Thulé

There was a king of Thulé, immaculate, who far from skirts and realities, wept over the reincarnation of lilies as roses – and what a palace!

Ses fleurs dormant, il s'en allait,
        Traînant des clés,
Broder aux seuls yeux des étoiles,
Sur une tour, un certain Voile.
        De vive toile,
        Aux nuits de lait!

Quand le voile fut bien ourlé,
        Loin de Thulé,
Il rama fort sur les mers grises,
Vers le soleil qui s'agonise,
        Féerique Église!
        Il ululait:

«Soleil-crevant,[3] encore un jour,
Vous avez tendu votre phare
Aux holocaustes vivipares,[4]
Du culte qu'ils nomment l'Amour.

«Et comme, devant la nuit fauve,
Vous vous sentez défaillir,
D'un dernier flot d'un sang martyr
Vous lavez le seuil de l'Alcôve![5]

When his flowers slept, he would go off, dragging his keys, to embroider, under the eyes of the stars alone, on a tower, a certain Veil of living linen in the milky nights!

When the veil was well stitched, far from Thulé, he rowed strongly on the grey seas towards the self-agonizing sun, fey Church! He howled:

'O clapped-out sun, for yet another day you held out your beacon to the viviparous holocausts of the cult they call Love.

And as, before the tawny night, you feel yourself fainting, with a last flood of martyr's blood you wash the threshold of the Alcove!

«Soleil! Soleil! moi je descends
Vers vos navrants palais polaires,
Dorloter dans ce Saint-Suaire
        Votre cœur bien en sang,
        En le berçant!»

Il dit, et, le Voile étendu,
        Tout éperdu,
Vers les coraux et les naufrages,
Le roi raillé des doux corsages,
        Beau comme un Mage
        Est descendu!

Braves amants! aux nuits de lait,
        Tournez vos clés!
Une ombre, d'amour pur transie,
Viendrait vous gémir cette scie:
«Il était un roi de Thulé
        Immaculé . . .»

Sun, Sun!, I descend towards your heartbreaking polar palaces, to cuddle in this
Holy Shroud your very bleeding heart, and lullaby it!'

He spoke! and stretching out the Veil, all frantic, towards corals and shipwrecks,
the king mocked by soft bodices descended, handsome as a Magus!

Fine lovers! on milky nights, turn your keys! A shade, transfixed by pure love,
would come to wail to you this old catch-phrase: 'There was a king of Thulé,
immaculate . . .'

Complainte des Cloches

Dimanche, à Liége.

Bin bam, bin bam,
Les cloches, les cloches,
Chansons[1] en l'air, pauvres reproches!
Bin bam, bin bam,
Les cloches en Brabant!

Petits et gros, clochers en fête,
De l'hôpital à l'Évêché,
Dans ce bon ciel endimanché,
Se carillonnent, et s'entêtent,
A tue-tête! à tue-tête!

Bons vitraux, saignez impuissants
Aux allégresses hosannahlles
Des orgues lâchant leurs pédales,
Les tuyaux bouchés par l'encens!
Car il descend! il descend!

Ballad of the Bells

Sunday, Liège

Ding dong, ding dong, the bells, the bells, songs of nonsense in the air, feeble reproaches! Ding dong, ding dong, the bells in Brabant!

Little and big, bell-towers in celebration from the hospital to the Bishop's Palace, in this fine sky in its Sunday best, carilloning and carrying on, ear-splittingly!

Good stained-glass windows, bleed helplessly in the hosannalian joys of organs letting their pedals rip, their pipes plugged with incense! for he's coming to Earth! he's coming to Earth!

Voici les lentes oriflammes
Où flottent la Vierge et les Saints!
Les cloches, leur battant des mains,
S'étourdissent en jeunes gammes
   Hymniclames! hymniclames!

Va, Globe aux studieux pourchas,[2]
Où Dieu à peine encor s'épèle!
Bondis, Jérusalem nouvelle,
Vers les nuits grosses de rachats,
   Où les lys ne filent pas![3]

Edens mûrs. Unique Bohême![4]
Nous, les beaux anges effrénés;
Elles, les Regards incarnés,
Pouvant nous chanter, sans blasphème:
   Que je t'aime! pour moi-même!

Here are the slow banners where Virgin and Saints hover! the bells, clapping their hands, deafen themselves in young hymn-clamouring scales!

Come, Globe of the studious quest, where God can still barely spell his name! Leap up, new Jerusalem, towards nights pregnant with redemptions, where the lilies do not spin!

Ripe Edens, Unique Bohemia! We, the beautiful frantic angels; the women, incarnate Gazes, able to sing to us, without blasphemy, 'How I love you! for myself!'

Oui, les cloches viennent de loin!
Oui, oui, l'Idéal les fit fondre
Pour rendre les gens hypocondres,
Vêtus de noir, tendant le poing
    Vers un Témoin! Un Témoin![5]

Ah! cœur-battant, cogne à tue-tête
Vers ce ciel niais endimanché!
Clame, à jaillir de ton clocher,
Et nous retombe à jamais BÊTE.
    Quelle fête! quelle fête!

    Bin bam, bin bam,
    Les cloches! les cloches!
Chansons en l'air, pauvres reproches!
    Bin bam, bin bam,
Les cloches en Brabant (1)!

(1) Et ailleurs.[6]

Yes, the bells are an old story! Yes, yes, the Ideal had them cast to turn us all into hypochondriacs, dressed in black, stretching out our hands towards a Witness! a Witness!

Ah! beating heart, knock deafeningly at the silly sky in its Sunday best! – shout so you spurt from your spire – and fall to earth for ever WITLESS. What a feast! What fun!

Ding dong, ding dong, the bells! the bells! songs of nonsense in the air, feeble reproaches! Ding dong, ding dong, the bells in Brabant! (1)

(1) And elsewhere.

Complainte des grands Pins dans une villa abandonnée

A Bade.

Tout hier, le soleil a boudé dans ses brumes,
Le vent jusqu'au matin n'a pas décoléré,
Mais, nous point des coteaux là-bas, un œil sacré[1]
Qui va vous bousculer ces paquets de bitume![2]

> – Ah! vous m'avez trop, trop vanné,
> Bals de diamants, hanches roses;
> Et, bien sûr, je n'étais pas né
>> Pour ces choses.

– Le vent jusqu'au matin n'a pas décoléré.
Oh! ces quintes de toux d'un chaos bien posthume,[3]

> – Prés et bois vendus! Que de gens,
> Qui me tenaient mes gants, serviles,
> A cette heure, de mes argents,
>> Font des piles!

Complaint of the Tall Pines in an Abandoned Villa

Baden

All yesterday, the sun sulked in its mists, the wind till morning stayed bad-tempered. But now there peeps over the hills a sacred eye which will hustle away those asphalt-coloured parcels.

'Ah! you've winnowed me too much, dances full of diamonds, rosy hips. And of course I wasn't born for those things.'

The wind till morning stayed bad-tempered. Oh! those coughing fits of a truly posthumous chaos.

'Meadows and woods sold! How many people who held my gloves, servile, now make piles out of my money!'

– Délayant en ciels bas ces paquets de bitume
Qui grimpaient talonnés de noirs Misérérés![4]

    – Elles, coudes nus dans les fruits,
    Riant, changeant de doigts leurs bagues;
    Comme nos plages et nos nuits
        Leur sont vagues!

– Oh! ces quintes de toux d'un chaos bien posthume,
Chantons comme Memnon,[5] le soleil a filtré,

    – Et moi, je suis dans ce lit cru
    De chambre d'hôtel, fade chambre,
    Seul, battu dans les vents bourrus
        De novembre.

– Qui, consolant des vents les noirs Misérérés,[6]
Des nuages en fuite éponge au loin l'écume.

    – Berthe aux sages yeux de lilas,
    Qui priais Dieu que je revinsse,
    Que fais-tu, mariée là-bas,
        En province?

Watering down into low skies those asphalt parcels which climbed, hounded on by black Misereres!

Those girls, bare elbows in the fruit, laughing, switching their rings from finger to finger; how vague our beaches and nights are to them!

Oh! those coughing fits of truly posthumous chaos, let's sing like Memnon, the sun has filtered through,

And I'm in this crude bed in a dreary hotel bedroom, alone, battered by the surly November winds.'

Which far away, consoling the black Misereres of the winds, soaks up the wetness of the fleeing clouds.

Bertha with your docile lilac eyes, who prayed God for my return, what are you doing, married in the provinces far away?

– Memnons, ventriloquons! le cher astre a filtré
Et le voilà qui tout authentique s'exhume!

> – Oh! quel vent! adieu tout sommeil;
> Mon Dieu, que je suis bien malade!
> Oh! notre croisée au soleil
> Bon, à Bade.

– Il rompt ses digues! vers les grands labours qui fument!
Saint Sacrement! et *Labarum*[7] des *Nox irae*![8]

> – Et bientôt, seul, je m'en irai,
> A Montmartre, en cinquième classe,[9]
> Loin de père et mère, enterrés
> En Alsace.[10]

Complainte de l'oubli des Morts

Mesdames et Messieurs,
Vous dont la mère est morte.
C'est le bon fossoyeux
Qui gratte à votre porte.

Let's Memnonize, let's ventriloquize! the darling sun has filtered through and here he is, truly authentic, disinterring himself!

Oh what a wind! farewell all sleep. My God, how sick I am! Oh for our window at Baden, warm in the sunshine!

He breaks his dykes! towards the big fields, which start to steam! Holy Sacrament! and Labarum of the Nox Irae!

And soon I'll be on my way alone to Montmartre, in fifth class, far from father and mother, buried in Alsace.

Complaint for the Forgetting of the Dead

Ladies and Gents, you whose mother's dead. It's the good old gravedigger scratching at your door.

Les morts
C'est sous terre;
Ça n'en sort
Guère.

Vous fumez dans vos bocks,
Vous soldez quelque idylle,
Là-bas chante le coq,
Pauvres morts hors des villes![1]

Grand-papa se penchait,
Là, le doigt sur la tempe,
Sœur faisait du crochet,
Mère montait la lampe.

Les morts
C'est discret,
Ça dort
Trop au frais.

Vous avez bien dîné,
Comment va cette affaire?
Ah! les petits mort-nés
Ne se dorlotent guère!

Them corpses is underground, they don't come out hardly at all.

You smoke over your beer glasses, you settle up for some treat. Far off crows the cock, poor dead ones outside town!

Grandaddy used to lean, just there, one finger on his temple, Sister was crocheting, Mother was turning up the lamp.

Them corpses is tactful, they sleep too much out of doors.

You've had a good nosh-up, how's business? Ah! the little stillborn ones don't hardly coddle theirselves!

Notez, d'un trait égal,
Au livre de la caisse,
Entre deux frais de bal:
Entretien tombe et messe.

> C'est gai,
> Cette vie;
> Hein, ma mie,
> O gué?[2]

Mesdames et Messieurs,
Vous dont la sœur est morte,
Ouvrez au fossoyeux
Qui claque à votre porte;

Si vous n'avez pitié,
Il viendra (sans rancune)
Vous tirer par les pieds,
Une nuit de grand'lune!

> Importun
> Vent qui rage!
> Les défunts?
> Ça voyage.

Mark, with a steady hand, on the cash-book between two dance tickets: 'upkeep of grave, and Mass.'

This life's cheery, ain't it, dearie?

Ladies and Gents, you whose sister has died, open to the gravedigger rapping at your door.

If you've no pity, he'll come (nothing personal!) and haul you out by the feet, one night of full moon!

Pestering, raging wind! The dead? They're of no fixed abode.

Complainte de l'Époux outragé

Sur l'air populaire: «Qu'allais-tu faire à la fontaine?»

– Qu'alliez-vous faire à la Mad'leine,
    Corbleu, ma moitié,
– Qu'alliez-vous faire à la Mad'leine?

– J'allais prier pour qu'un fils nous vienne,
    Mon Dieu, mon ami;
J'allais prier pour qu'un fils nous vienne.

– Vous vous teniez dans un coin, debout,
    Corbleu, ma moitié!
Vous vous teniez dans un coin debout.

– Pas d'chaise économis' trois sous,[1]
    Mon Dieu, mon ami;
Pas d'chaise économis' trois sous.

– D'un officier, j'ai vu la tournure,
    Corbleu, ma moitié!
D'un officier, j'ai vu la tournure.

– C'était ce Christ grandeur nature,
    Mon Dieu, mon ami;
C'était ce Christ grandeur nature.

Ballad of the Outraged Husband

To the popular tune 'What were you doing at the fountain?'

What were you doing at the Madeleine, Corblimey, my other half . . . ?
    I went to pray for us to have a son, by God, my dear . . .
    You were in a corner, standing.
    If you don't take a chair you save three ha'pence . . .
    I saw an officer, to judge by his bearing . . .
    It was that life-size Christ . . .

– Les Christs n'ont pas la croix d'honneur,
      Corbleu, ma moitié!
Les Christs n'ont pas la croix d'honneur.

– C'était la plaie du Calvaire, au cœur,
      Mon Dieu, mon ami;
C'était la plaie du Calvaire au cœur.

– Les Christs n'ont qu'au flanc seul la plaie,
      Corbleu, ma moitié!
Les Christs n'ont qu'au flanc seul la plaie!

– C'était une goutte envolée,
      Mon Dieu, mon ami;
C'était une goutte envolée.

– Aux Crucifix on n'parl' jamais,
      Corbleu, ma moitié!
Aux Crucifix on n' parl' jamais!

– C'était du trop d'amour qu' j'avais,
      Mon Dieu, mon ami,
C'était du trop d'amour qu' j'avais!

Et moi j' te brûl'rai la cervelle,
      Corbleu, ma moitié,
Et moi j' te brûl'rai la cervelle!

Christs don't wear the Military Cross . . .
It was the wound of Calvary . . .
Christs have that wound only on one side . . .
It was a splash of blood gone astray . . .
To Crucifixes you never talk . . .
It was all because I felt too much love . . .
And I'll blow your brains out . . .

– Lui, il aura mon âme immortelle,
    Mon Dieu, mon ami,
Lui, il aura mon âme immortelle!

Complainte du Temps et de sa Commère l'Espace

Je tends mes poignets universels dont aucun
N'est le droit ou le gauche, et l'Espace, dans un
Va-et-vient giratoire, y détrame les toiles
D'azur pleines de cocons à fœtus d'Étoiles.
Et nous nous blasons tant, je ne sais où, les deux
Indissolubles nuits aux orgues vaniteux
De nos pores à Soleils, où toute cellule
Chante: Moi! Moi! puis s'éparpille, ridicule!

Elle est l'infini sans fin, je deviens le temps
Infaillible. C'est pourquoi nous nous perdons tant.
Où sommes-nous? Pourquoi? Pour que Dieu s'accomplisse?
Mais l'Éternité n'y a pas suffi! Calice

He'll have my immortal soul,
my God, my lover,
he'll have my immortal soul!

Ballad of Time and of his Old Crony, Space

I offer my universal wrists of which none is either right or left, and Space, spiralling to and fro, unweaves the azure cloths full of the Stars' foetus-cocoons. And we care so little, I don't know where, we two indissoluble nights with conceited organs, for our Sun-pores where every cell chants: 'Me! me!' then scatters, absurd!

    She is the endless infinite, I become infallible time. That's why we get so lost. Where are we? Why? So God can accomplish himself? But Eternity has not been long enough for that!

Inconscient, où tout cœur crevé se résout,
Extrais-nous donc alors de ce néant trop tout!
Que tu fisses de nous seulement une flamme,
Un vrai sanglot mortel, la moindre goutte d'âme!

Mais nous bâillons de toute la force de nos
Touts, sûrs de la surdité des humains échos.
Que ne suis-je indivisible! Et toi, douce Espace,
Où sont les steppes de tes seins, que j'y rêvasse?
Quand t'ai-je fécondée à jamais? Oh! ce dut
Être un spasme intéressant! Mais quel fut mon but?
Je t'ai, tu m'as. Mais où? Partout, toujours. Extase
Sur laquelle, quand on est le Temps, on se blase.

Or, voilà des spleens infinis que je suis en
Voyage vers ta bouche, et pas plus à présent
Que toujours, je ne sens la fleur triomphatrice
Qui flotte, m'as-tu dit, au seuil de ta matrice.

Unconscious calyx where every broken heart is solved, extract us from this nothing which is too everything! If you'd only made of us a flame, a real mortal sob, the tiniest drop of a soul!

But we yawn with all the strength of our Everythings, sure of the deafness of human echoes. Why a'n't I indivisible! And you, sweet Space, where are the steppes of your breasts, that I may daydream on them? When did I impregnate you for ever? Oh! It must have been an interesting spasm! But what was my purpose? I have you, you have me. But where? Everywhere, always. An ecstasy about which, when one is Time, one can be blasé.

Now during infinite tediums I've been travelling towards your mouth. But I can't feel – any more than I ever could – the triumphal flower which floats, you told me, on the threshold of your womb.

Abstraites amours! quel infini mitoyen
Tourne entre nos deux Touts? Sommes-nous deux? ou bien
(Tais-toi si tu ne peux me prouver à outrance,
Illico, le fondement de la connaissance,

Et, par ce chant: Pensée, Objet, Identité!
Souffler le Doute, songe d'un siècle d'été)[1]
Suis-je à jamais un solitaire Hermaphrodite,
Comme le Ver solitaire,[2] ô ma Sulamite?[3]
Ma complainte n'a pas eu de commencement,
Que je sache, et n'aura nulle fin; autrement,
Je serais l'anachronisme absolu. Pullule
Donc, azur possédé du mètre et du pendule![4]

O Source du possible, alimente à jamais
Des pollens des soleils d'exil, et de l'engrais
Des chaotiques hécatombes, l'automate[5]
Universel où pas une loi ne se hâte.
Nuls à tout, sauf aux rares mystiques éclairs
Des élus, nous restons les deux miroirs d'éther[6]
Réfléchissant, jusqu'à la mort de ces Mystères,
Leurs Nuits que l'Amour jonche de fleurs éphémères.

Abstract love-affair! What halfway-house infinity revolves between our two Every-things? Are we two? or else — (Keep silent if you can't prove to me, to the bitter end, forthwith, the foundation of knowledge,

and by this chant: 'Thought, Object, Identity!' blow away Doubt, like a mid-summer century's dream) — am I for ever a lonely Hermaphrodite, like the solitary Worm, O my Shulamite? My lament has had no beginning, as far as I know, and will have no end; otherwise I would be the absolute anachronism. So pullulate, azure possessed of the metre and the pendulum!

O Source of the possible, for ever feed with the pollens of the suns of exile, and with the composts of chaotic hecatombs, the Universal Robot in which not a single law hurries itself. Null for everyone, except for the rare mystical illuminations of the elect, we remain the two mirrors of Ether, reflecting — until the death of these Mysteries — their Nights which Love strews with perishable flowers.

Complainte-Litanies de mon Sacré-Cœur[1]

Prométhée et Vautour,[2] châtiment et blasphème,
Mon Cœur, cancer sans cœur, se grignote lui-même.

Mon Cœur est une urne où j'ai mis certains défunts,
Oh! chut, refrains de leurs berceaux! et vous, parfums . . .

Mon Cœur est un lexique où cent littératures
Se lardent sans répit de divines ratures.

Mon Cœur est un désert altéré, bien que soûl
De ce vin revomi, l'universel dégoût.

Mon Cœur est un Néron, enfant gâté d'Asie,
Qui d'empires de rêve en vain se rassasie.

Mon Cœur est un noyé vidé d'âme et d'essors,
Qu'étreint la pieuvre Spleen en ses ventouses d'or.

Complaint-Litanies of my Damned Sacred Heart

Prometheus and Vulture, punishment and blasphemy, my Heart, a heartless cancer, gnaws at itself.

My Heart is an urn where I have put certain dead people, Oh! hush, lullabies of their cradles! and you, perfumes . . .

My Heart is a lexicon where a hundred literatures are peppered without respite by divine erasures.

My Heart is a thirsty desert, though drunk with the revomited wine of universal disgust.

My Heart is a Nero, spoiled child of Asia, who vainly sates himself with dream empires.

My Heart is a drowned man emptied of soul and impulses, which the octopus Spleen grips in its golden suckers.

C'est un feu d'artifice hélas! qu'avant la fête,
A noyé sans retour l'averse qui s'embête.

Mon Cœur est le terrestre Histoire-Corbillard,[3]
Que traînent au néant l'instinct et le hasard.

Mon Cœur est une horloge oubliée à demeure,
Qui, me sachant défunt, s'obstine à sonner l'heure!

Mon aimée était là, toute à me consoler;
Je l'ai trop fait souffrir, ça ne peut plus aller.

Mon Cœur, plongé au Styx[4] dè nos arts danaïdes,[5]
Présente à tout baiser une armure de vide.

Et toujours, mon Cœur, ayant ainsi déclamé,
En revient à sa complainte: Aimer, être aimé!

It's a firework, alas! which before the festivity, has been irrevocably drowned by the bored downpour.

My Heart is the earthly Hearse-History, which instinct and chance drag towards nothingness.

My Heart is a clock left forgotten at home, which, knowing me dead, persists in striking the hour!

My beloved was there, devoted to consoling me; I've hurt her feelings too much, it won't work any more.

My Heart, plunged in the Styx of our Danaïd arts, presents to every kiss an armour of emptiness.

And always my Heart, having declaimed thus, returns to its complaint: 'To love, to be loved!'

Complainte des Débats mélancoliques et littéraires

On peut encore aimer, mais confier toute son âme est
   un bonheur qu'on ne retrouvera plus.

Corinne ou l'Italie.[1]

Le long d'un ciel crépusculâtre,[2]
Une cloche angéluse en paix
L'air exilescent et marâtre
Qui ne pardonnera jamais.

Paissant des débris de vaisselle,
Là-bas, au talus des remparts,
Se profile une haridelle
Convalescente; il se fait tard.

Qui m'aima jamais? Je m'entête
Sur ce refrain bien impuissant,
Sans songer que je suis bien bête
De me faire du mauvais sang.

Complaint of Mournful Literary Debates

One can still love, but to commit one's entire soul is
a bliss one will never feel again.

Corinne ou l'Italie

All round a twilightish sky, a bell peacefully angeluses the exilescent and step-
motherish air which never will forgive.

   Grazing on broken crockery, over on the slope of the ramparts, is the silhouette
of a convalescent old nag; it's getting late.

   Who ever loved me? I stubbornly persist with this powerless refrain, without
dreaming that I'm silly to fret and fume.

Je possède un propre physique,
Un cœur d'enfant bien élevé,
Et pour un cerveau magnifique
Le mien n'est pas mal, vous savez.

Eh bien, ayant pleuré l'Histoire,
J'ai voulu vivre un brin heureux;
C'était trop demander, faut croire;
J'avais l'air de parler hébreux.

Ah! tiens, mon cœur, de grâce, laisse!
Lorsque j'y songe, en vérité,
J'en ai des sueurs de faiblesse,
A choir dans la malpropreté.

Le cœur me piaffe de génie
Eperdument pourtant, mon Dieu!
Et si quelqu'une veut ma vie,
Moi je ne demande pas mieux!

Eh va, pauvre âme véhémente!
Plonge, être, en leurs Jourdains blasés,[3]
Deux frictions de vie courante
T'auront bien vite exorcisé.

I have a sound physique, the heart of a well-bred child, and as for a splendid brain, mine isn't bad, you know.

Well, having wept for History, I wanted to live just a wee bit happy; this was too much to ask, believe me; I seemed to be talking double Dutch.

Ah! look here, my heart, for pity's sake shut up! When I think about it, truly I'm in sweats of weakness for fear of falling into dishonour.

Yet, my God, my heart prances with genius, frantically! And if anyone wants to share my life, I couldn't ask for better!

Be off with you, poor vehement soul! Drench yourself, creature, in their jaded Jordans, two rub-downs of present-day life will quickly exorcize you.

Hélas, qui peut m'en répondre!
Tenez, peut-être savez-vous
Ce que c'est qu'une âme hypocondre?
J'en suis une dans les prix doux.

O Hélène, j'erre en ma chambre;
Et tandis que tu prends le thé,
Là-bas dans l'or d'un fier septembre,
Je frissonne de tous mes membres,
En m'inquiétant de ta santé.

Tandis que, d'un autre côté . . .

Complainte d'une Convalescence en Mai

Nous n'avons su toutes ces choses qu'après sa mort.
        Vie de Pascal, par Mme Périer.

Convalescent au lit, ancré de courbatures,
Je me plains aux dessins bleus de ma couverture,

Las de reconstituer dans l'art du jour baissant
Cette dame d'en face auscultant[1] les passants:

Alas! who can promise me that! Look here, perhaps you know what a hypochon-
driac soul is like? I'm one at a knock-down price.

O Helen, I pace up and down my room; and while you are taking tea, over there
in the gold of a proud September, I'm shivering in every limb, as I fret about your
health.

Whilst, seen from another point of view . . .

Complaint of a Convalescence in May

We knew all this only after his death
        Life of Pascal, Mme Périer

Convalescent in bed, pinned down by aches and pains, I complain to the blue
pattern of my blanket,
    Tired of reconstructing in the art of fading day that lady in the house opposite
stethoscoping the passers-by;

Si la Mort, de son van, avait chosé[2] mon être,
En serait-elle moins, ce soir, à sa fenêtre? . . .

Oh! mort, tout mort! au plus jamais, au vrai néant
Des nuits où piaule en longs regrets un chat-huant!

Et voilà que mon Ame est tout hallucinée!
Mais s'abat, sans avoir fixé sa destinée.

Ah! que de soirs de mai pareils à celui-ci;
Que la vie est égale; et le cœur endurci!

Je me sens fou d'un tas de petites misères.
Mais maintenant, je sais ce qu'il me reste à faire.

Qui m'a jamais rêvé? Je voudrais le savoir!
Elles vous sourient avec âme, et puis bonsoir,

Ni vu ni connu. Et les voilà qui rebrodent
Le canevas ingrat de leur âme à la mode;

if Death with his winnowing fan had reduced me to thing-hood, she'd be there this evening at her window just the same.

Oh! dead, quite dead! in the nevermore, the true nothingness of the nights where a screech-owl moans its long sorrows!

And here's my soul quite hallucinated! but it flops back again without having resolved its destiny.

Ah! how many May evenings just like this one; life is so flat; and how hardened is the heart!

I'm driven mad by a heap of little miseries, but now I know what remains for me to do.

Who has ever dreamed of me? I'd like to know! They smile at you soulfully, and then bye-bye,

you're cut dead and ignored. And there they are re-embroidering the thankless tapestry of their souls in the latest fashion;

Fraîches à tous, et puis reprenant leur air sec
Pour les christs déclassés et autres gens suspects

Et pourtant, le béni grand bol de lait de ferme
Que me serait un baiser sur sa bouche ferme!

Je ne veux accuser personne, bien qu'on eût
Pu, ce me semble, mon bon cœur étant connu . . .

N'est-ce pas; nous savons ce qu'il nous reste à faire,
O Cœur d'or pétri d'aromates littéraires,

Et toi, cerveau confit dans l'alcool de l'Orgueil!
Et qu'il faut procéder d'abord par demi-deuils . . .

Primo: mes grandes angoisses métaphysiques
Sont passées à l'état de chagrins domestiques;

Deux ou trois spleens locaux. – Ah! pitié, voyager
Du moins, pendant un an ou deux à l'étranger . . .

open and vivacious with everyone, and then adopting a dry manner to Christs who've gone down in the world and other dubious people,

and yet the big bowl of blessed farm-milk that a kiss on her firm mouth would be!

I don't want to accuse anyone, although one might, it seems to me, since my good heart is known . . .

isn't it? We know what remains for us to do, O Heart of gold stuffed with literary spices,

and you, brain pickled in the alcohol of Pride! And that we must first proceed by half-mournings . . .

First: my great metaphysical anguishes have decayed to the state of household vexations:

two or three local grumbles. – Ah! for pity's sake, at least to take a trip abroad for a year or two . . .

Plonger mon front dans l'eau des mers, aux matinées
Torrides, m'en aller à petites journées,

Compter les clochers, puis m'asseoir, ayant très chaud,
Aveuglé des maisons peintes au lait de chaux . . .

Dans les Indes du Rêve aux pacifiques Ganges,[3]
Que j'en ai des comptoirs, des hamacs de rechange!

– Voici l'œuf à la coque et la lampe du soir.
Convalescence bien folle, comme on peut voir.

Complainte du sage de Paris

Aimer, uniquement, ces jupes éphémères?
Autant dire aux soleils: fêtez vos centenaires.

Mais tu peux déguster, dans leurs jardins d'un jour,
Comme à cette dînette unique Tout concourt;

to plunge my brow into sea-water, on torrid mornings, to travel by short stages,
    To count the spires, then sit down, boiling hot, dazzled with whitewashed houses . . .
    in the Indies of Dream on the peaceful Ganges, how many counters to stand at, how many spare hammocks!
    – Here's the boiled egg and the evening lamp. A crazy convalescence, as you can see.

Lament of the Wise Man of Paris

To love nothing but these ephemeral skirts? As well say to the suns: celebrate your centenaries.
    But you can taste, in their gardens which last but a day, how Everything conspires towards this unique dolls' tea-party;

Déguster, en menant les rites réciproques,
Les trucs Inconscients dans leur œuf, à la coque.

Soit en pontifiant, avec toute ta foi
D'Exécuteur des hautes-œuvres[1] de la Loi;

Soit en vivisectant ces claviers anonymes,
Pour l'art, sans espérer leur *ut*[2] d'hostie ultime.

Car, crois pas que l'hostie où dort ton paradis
Sera d'une farine aux levains inédits.

Mais quoi, leurs yeux sont tout! et puis la nappe est mise.
Et l'Orgue juvénile à l'aveugle improvise.

Et, sans noce, voyage, curieux, colis,
Cancans, et fadeur d'hôpital du même lit,

Mais pour avoir des vitraux fiers à domicile,
Vivre à deux seuls est encore le moins imbécile.

Vois-la donc, comme d'ailleurs, et loyalement,
Les passants, les mots, les choses, les firmaments.

Taste, as you conduct the reciprocal rites, the devices of the Unconscious in their eggs, soft-boiled.

Whether while pontificating, with all the faith of an Executioner of the high tasks of the Law;

Or whether while vivisecting anonymous keyboards, for art's sake, without hoping for their keynote of ultimate holy wafer.

For do not believe that the wafer where your paradise sleeps will be of a flour with unprecedented leaven.

But so what, their eyes are everything! and besides the tablecloth is spread, and the childish Organ is blindly improvising.

And, without wedding, honeymoon, nosy parkers, packages, tittle-tattle, and the hospital staleness of the same bed,

But to have proud stained-glass windows at home, to live as a couple is still the least stupid.

See her, then, as you faithfully see passers-by, words, things and firmaments.

Vendange chez les arts enfantins; sois en fête
D'une fugue, d'un mot, d'un ton, d'un air de tête.[3]

La science, outre qu'elle ne peut rien savoir,
Trouve, tels les ballons,[4] l'Irrespirable Noir.

Ne force jamais tes pouvoirs de Créature,[5]
Tout est écrit et vrai, rien n'est contre-nature.

Vivre et peser selon le Beau, le Bien, le Vrai?
O parfums, ô regards, ô fois! soit, j'essaierai;

Mais, tel Brennus[6] avec son épée, et d'avance,
Suis-je pas dans l'un des plateaux de la balance?

Des casiers de bureau, le Beau, le Vrai, le Bien;
Rime et sois grand, la Loi reconnaîtra les siens.[7]

Ah! démaillote-toi, mon enfant, de ces langes
D'Occident! va faire une pleine eau dans le Gange.

La logique, la morale, c'est vite dit;
Mais! gisements d'instincts, virtuels paradis,

Wine-harvest of childish arts; take delight in a fugue, a word, a tone, a tilt of the head.

Science, apart from the fact that it can know nothing, discovers (like balloons) the Unbreathable Blackness.

Never force your powers as a Creature, everything is written and true, nothing is unnatural.

To live and base your values on the Beautiful, the Good, the True? O scents, glances, faiths! Very well, I'll try;

but, like Brennus with his sword, before I start, a'n't I in one of the pans of the scale?

They are office pigeonholes, the Beautiful, the True, the Good; rhyme and be great, the Law will recognize its own.

Ah! my child, strip off the nappies of the West! Go and swim right out into the Ganges!

It's easy to say 'Logic and morality'; but! prehistoric relics of instincts, potential paradises,

Nuit des hérédités et limbes des latences!
Actif? passif? ô pelouses des Défaillances

Tamis de pores! Et les bas-fonds sous-marins,
Infini sans foyer, forêt vierge à tous crins!

Pour voir, jetez la sonde, ou plongez sous la cloche
Oh! les velléités, les anguilles sous roche,[8]

Les polypes sournois attendant l'hameçon,
Les vœux sans état-civil, ni chair, ni poisson!

Les guanos à Geysers,[9] les astres en syncope,
Et les métaux qui font loucher nos spectroscopes!

Une capsule éclate, un monde de facteurs
En prurit, s'éparpille assiéger les hauteurs;

D'autres titubent sous les butins génitoires,[10]
Ou font un feu d'enfer dans leurs laboratoires!

Allez! laissez passer, laissez faire; l'Amour
Reconnaîtra les siens:[11] il est aveugle et sourd.

---

nights of heredities and limbos of latencies! Active? passive? O lawns of Lapses,
sieves of pores! And submarine depths, homeless Infinite, diehard virgin forest!
   To see, do a sounding, or go down in a diving bell; oh! the impulses, the fishy
things under rocks,
   the sly polyps waiting for the hook, the wishes without civic status, neither flesh
nor fish!
   the Geysering guanos, the stars in a faint, and the metals which make our
spectroscopes squint!
   A capsule bursts, an itching world of factors scatters to besiege the heights;
   others stagger under their genital booty, or make a hellfire in their laboratories!
   Come! let them pass, let them act; Love will recognize its own: it's blind and
deaf.

Car la vie innombrable va, vannant les germes
Aux concurrences des êtres sans droits, sans terme.

Vivotez et passez, à la grâce de Tout;
Et voilà la pitié, l'amour et le bon goût.

L'Inconscient, c'est l'Éden-Levant[12] que tout saigne;
Si la Terre ne veut sécher, qu'elle s'y baigne!

C'est la grande Nounou où nous nous aimerions
A la grâce des divines sélections.[13]

C'est le Tout-Vrai, l'Omniversel Ombelliforme
Mancenilier,[14] sous qui, mes bébés, faut qu'on dorme!

(Nos découvertes scientifiques étant
Ses feuilles mortes, qui tombent de temps en temps.)

Là, sur des oreillers d'étiquettes d'éthiques,
Lévite[15] félin aux égaux ronrons lyriques,

Sans songer: «Suis-je moi? Tout est si compliqué!
«Où serais-je à présent, pour tel coche manqué?»

For multitudinous life goes sifting the seeds, in the competitions of creatures without rights, without limit.

Soldier on and pass on, by the grace of Everything; and that's all that pity, love and good taste are.

The Unconscious, it's Dawning-Eden from which everything draws its blood; if Earth doesn't wish to go dry, let her bathe there!

It's our big Nanny where we're supposed to love each other, thanks to divine selections.

It's the All-True, the Omniversal Umbelliform Manchineel-Tree, under which, my babies, we gotta sleep!

(Our scientific discoveries being its dead leaves, which fall from time to time.)

There, on pillows of ethical etiquettes, a feline Levite droning away, smoothly lyrical,

without thinking, 'Am I myself? Everything's so complicated! Where can I be now, waiting for what missed bus?'

Sans colère, rire, ou pathos, d'une foi pâle,
Aux riches flirtations des pompes argutiales,

Mais sans rite emprunté, car c'est bien malséant,
Sirote chaque jour ta tasse de néant;

Lavé comme une hostie, en quelconques costumes
Blancs ou deuil, bref calice au vent qu'un rien parfume.

– «Mais, tout est rire à la Justice! et d'où vient
Mon cœur, ah! mon sacré-cœur, s'il ne rime à rien?»

– Du calme et des fleurs. Peu t'importe de connaître
Ce que tu fus, dans l'à jamais, avant de naître?

Eh bien, que l'autre éternité qui, Très-Sans-Toi,
Grouillera, te laisse aussi pieusement froid.

Quant à *ta* mort, l'éclair aveugle en est en route
Qui saura te choser,[16] va, sans que tu t'en doutes.

without anger, laughter or pathos, in pallid faith, to the rich flirtations of quibbling pumps,

but without any borrowed ritual, for that's unseemly, sip every day at your cup of nothingness;

wishy-washy as a holy wafer, in nondescript white or mourning-coloured suits, brief chalice in the wind perfumed by a trifle.

'But it's all a mockery of Justice! And where does my heart come from, ah! my damned sacred-heart, if there's no rhyme or reason in it?'

'Calm and flowers. You don't mind not knowing what you were, in the Forever, before being born?

Well, let the other eternity, which will teem Very-Much-Without-You, leave you just as piously cold.

As to *your* death, the blind thunderbolt is on its way which will know how to thing you without your suspecting it.

– «Il rit d'oiseaux, le pin dont *mon* cercueil viendra
– Mais *ton* cercueil sera *sa* mort! etc . . .

Allons, tu m'as compris. Va, que ta seule étude
Soit de vivre sans but, fou de mansuétude.

Complainte des Complaintes

Maintenant, pourquoi ces complaintes?
Gerbes d'ailleurs d'un défunt Moi
Où l'ivraie[1] art mange la foi?
Sot tabernacle où je m'éreinte
A cultiver des roses peintes?
Pourtant ménage et sainte-table!
Ah! ces complaintes incurables,
      Pourquoi? pourquoi?

'It's joyous with birds, the pine from which *my* coffin will come!' 'But *your* coffin will be *its* death! Etcetera . . .'

You see, you've understood me. Go, let your sole concern be to live without purpose, mad with mildness.

Complaint for these Complaints

And now, why these complaints? Sheaves, besides, of a dead Self where art (the tares) consumes faith? Daft tabernacle where I wear myself out growing painted roses? Nonetheless household and holy table! Ah, these incurable laments, why, why?

Puis, Gens à qui les fugues vraies
Que crie, au fond, ma riche voix
– N'est-ce pas, qu'on les sent parfois? –
Attoucheraient sous leurs ivraies
Les violettes d'une Foi,
Vous passerez, imperméables
A mes complaintes incurables?
      Pourquoi? pourquoi?

Chut! tout est bien, rien ne s'étonne.
Fleuris, ô Terre d'occasion,
Vers les mirages des Sions!
Et nous, sous l'Art qui nous bâtonne,
Sisyphes[2] par persuasion,
Flûtant des christs les vaines fables,
Au cabestan de l'incurable
      POURQUOI! – Pourquoi?

And then, People for whom the true fugues which despite everything my rich voice cries out (You feel them sometimes, don't you?) might touch under their tares the violets of a Faith – will you pass by, waterproofed against my incurable laments? Why, why?

Hush! All is well, nothing is puzzled. Blossom, O Second-hand World, towards the mirages of the Zions! And we, under Art which gives us the stick, we are all of us Sisyphuses by persuasion, swigging the empty fables of the Christs at the capstan of the incurable WHY – Why?

Complainte-Épitaphe

La Femme,
Mon âme:
Ah! quels
Appels!

Pastels
Mortels,
Qu'on blâme
Mes gammes!

Un fou
S'avance,
Et danse.

Silence . . .
Lui, où?
Coucou.

Complaint-Epitaph

Woman, my soul: Ah! what allurements! Mortal pastel-colours, let's blame my
spectrums! A madman steps forward, and dances. Silence . . . Where's he gone?
Peek-a-boo.

L'IMITATION DE
NOTRE–DAME LA LUNE

The Imitation of Our Lady the Moon

> Ah! quel juillet nous avons hiverné,
> *Per amica silentia lunæ*!
> ÎLE DE LA MAINAU.[1]
(Lac de Constance)

> Ah! what a July we wintered
> By the friendly silence of the moon!

Un mot au Soleil pour commencer

Soleil! soudard[1] plaqué d'ordres et de crachats,
Planteur mal élevé, sache que les Vestales[2]
A qui la Lune, en son équivoque œil-de-chat,[3]
Est la rosace[4] de l'Unique Cathédrale,

Sache que les Pierrots, phalènes des dolmens
Et des nymphéas blancs des lacs où dort Gomorrhe,[5]
Et tous les bienheureux qui pâturent l'Éden
Toujours printanier des renoncements, – t'abhorrent.

Et qu'ils gardent pour toi des mépris spéciaux,
Bellâtre, Maquignon, Ruffian, Rastaqouère
A breloques d'œufs d'or qui le prends de si haut
Avec la terre et son Orpheline lunaire.

An Opening Word to the Sun

Sun! swashbuckler splattered with medals and spit-and-polish, ill-bred planter, know that the Vestals for whom the Moon, in her ambiguous cat's-eye, is the rose-window of the One Cathedral –

Know that the Pierrots, moths of the megaliths and the white water-lilies of the lakes where Gomorrha sleeps, and all the blessed folk who graze upon the always springlike Eden of renunciations – abhor you.

And that they retain a special contempt for you, fop, huckster, pander, mountebank with trinkets of golden eggs, who take such a lofty attitude to Earth and its lunar Orphaness.

Continue à fournir de couchants avinés
Les lendemains vomis des fêtes nationales,
A styler tes saisons, à nous bien déchaîner
Les drames de l'Apothéose Ombilicale![6]

Va, Phœbus![7] mais, Déva,[8] dieu des Réveils cabrés,
Regarde un peu parfois ce Port-Royal[9] d'esthètes
Qui, dans leurs décamérons lunaires au frais,[10]
Ne parlent de rien moins que mettre à prix ta tête.

Certes, tu as encor devant toi de beaux jours;
Mais la tribu s'accroît, de ces vieilles pratiques
De l'A QUOI BON? qui vont rêvant l'art et l'amour
Au seuil lointain de l'Agrégat inorganique.[11]

Pour aujourd'hui, vieux beau, nous nous contenterons
De mettre sous le nez de Ta Badauderie
Le mot dont l'Homme t'a déjà marqué au front;
Tu ne t'en étais jamais douté, je parie?

Continue providing vinous sunsets on those 'mornings-after' vomited up by our national holidays, giving polish to your seasons, unloosing upon us the dramas of the Umbilical Apotheosis!

Onward, Phoebus! but, Deva, god of the rearing Reveilles, take a look sometimes at this Port-Royal of aesthetes who, in their lunar Decamerons in the cooler, talk of nothing less than putting a price on your head.

Yes, you've still got fine sunlit days before you; but the tribe is growing of those old practices of WHAT'S THE POINT who go dreaming of art and love on the far-off threshold of the Inorganic Aggregate.

Just for today, old dandy, we'll content ourselves with sticking under Your Nosy Parkership's nose, the Word which Man has already cut upon your forehead. You'd never suspected it, I bet?

– Sache qu'on va disant d'une belle phrase, os
Sonore, mais très nul comme suc médullaire,
De tout boniment creux enfin: c'est du pathos,
C'est du PHŒBUS! —[12] Ah! pas besoin de commentaires . . .

O Vision du temps où l'être trop puni,
D'un: «Eh! va donc, Phœbus!» te rentrera ton prêche
De vieux *Crescite et multiplicamini*,[13]
Pour s'inoculer à jamais la Lune fraîche!

Litanies des premiers quartiers de la Lune

Lune bénie
Des insomnies,

Blanc médaillon
Des Endymions,[1]

Astre fossile
Que tout exile,

Jaloux tombeau
De Salammbô,[2]

Know that we say of a fine phrase, a bone that flutes out a good note but is
lacking in marrow, i.e. empty sales-talk: 'It's pathetic, it's a Phoebus!' – Enough
said . . .

O Vision of the time when mankind will have taken enough punishment and,
with a 'Get along, Phoebus!', will slap back at you your sermon on the old *Increase
and Multiply*, and inoculate itself for ever with cool Moon!

Litanies of the First Two Quarters of the Moon

Blessed moon of insomnias,
    White medallion of Endymions,
    Fossil star which everything banishes,
    Jealous tomb of Salammbô

Embarcadère
Des grands Mystères,

Madone et miss
Diane-Artémis,³

Sainte Vigie⁴
De nos orgies,

Jettatura
Des baccarats,⁵

Dame très lasse
De nos terrasses,

Philtre attisant
Les vers-luisants,

Rosace et dôme
Des derniers psaumes,

Bel œil-de-chat⁶
De nos rachats,

Sois l'Ambulance
De nos croyances!

Sois l'édredon
Du Grand-Pardon!

Embarcation-Point for the Great Mysteries,
Madonna and Miss Diana-Artemis,
Sainted Vigil of our orgies,
Evil eye of the baccarats
Most weary lady of our terraces,
Love potion setting the glow-worms on fire,
Rose-window and dome of the last psalms,
Lovely cat's-eye of our redemptions,
Be the Ambulance of our Beliefs!
Be the Eiderdown of the Grand Forgiveness!

Au Large

Comme la nuit est lointainement pleine
De silencieuse infinité claire!
Pas le moindre écho des gens de la terre,
Sous la Lune méditerranéenne!

Voilà le Néant dans sa pâle gangue,
Voilà notre Hostie et sa Sainte-Table,
Le seul bras d'ami par l'Inconnaissable,
Le seul mot solvable en nos folles langues!

Au delà des cris choisis des époques,
Au delà des sens, des larmes, des vierges,
Voilà quel astre indiscutable émerge,
Voilà l'immortel et seul soliloque!

On the Deep Ocean

How the night is distantly full of silent clear infinity! Not the least echo of earthly
people under the Mediterranean Moon!

Here is Nothingness in its pale matrix, here is our Holy Wafer and its Holy Altar,
the only friendly arm throughout the Unknowable, the only word solvable in our
crazy languages!

Far beyond the most distinguished outcries of the ages, beyond meanings, tears
and virgins, see what indisputable star emerges, admire the one immortal soliloquy!

Et toi, là-bas, pot-au-feu, pauvre Terre!
Avec tes essais de mettre en rubriques
Tes reflets perdus du Grand Dynamique![1]
Tu fais un métier, ah! bien sédentaire!

Clair de lune

Penser qu'on vivra jamais dans cet astre,
Parfois me flanque un coup dans l'épigastre.

Ah! tout pour toi, Lune, quand tu t'avances
Aux soirs d'août par les féeries du silence!

Et quand tu roules, démâtée, au large
A travers les brisants noirs des nuages!

Oh! monter, perdu, m'étancher à même
Ta vasque de béatifiants baptêmes!

And you, down there below, stewpot, poor Earth! With your attempts to put in headlines your random reflections of the Great Dynamic! Your job is Ugh! so sedentary!

Music by Moonlight

To think we'll ever live upon that star, sometimes winds me in the solar plexus.

Ah! All for you, Moon, when you progress on August evenings through fairylands of silence!

And when you roll, dismasted, on the deep, through the black breakers of the clouds!

Oh! to mount, lost, to slake myself straight from your basin of beatifying baptisms!

Astre atteint de cécité, fatal phare
Des vols migrateurs des plaintifs Icares![1]

Œil stérile comme le suicide,
Nous sommes le congrès des las, préside;

Crâne glacé, raille les calvities
De nos incurables bureaucraties;

O pilule des léthargies finales,
Infuse-toi dans nos durs encéphales!

O Diane à la chlamyde très dorique,[2]
L'Amour cuve, prend ton carquois et pique

Ah! d'un trait inoculant l'être aptère,
Les cœurs de bonne volonté sur terre!

Astre lavé par d'inouïs déluges,
Qu'un de tes chastes rayons fébrifuges,

Ce soir, pour inonder mes draps, dévie,
Que je m'y lave les mains de la vie!

Heavenly body struck with blindness, fatal lighthouse of migrating flights of plaintive Icaruses!

Eye as sterile as suicide, we are the congress of the weary, be our chairwoman;
Frozen skull, scoff at the baldness of our incurable bureaucracies;

O pill of the final lethargies, infuse yourself into our hard brains!

O Diana in your hyper-Doric chlamys, Love is fermenting away, take up your quiver, and prick,

Ah! with a contraceptive arrow the wingless species, the hearts of good will on earth!

Luminary washed by unheard-of floods, may one of your chaste fever-fleeing rays

change course this evening to soak my sheets, and in it let me wash my hands of life!

Guitare

Astre[1] sans coeur et sans reproche,[2]
O Maintenon[3] de vieille roche!

Très Révérende Supérieure
Du cloître où l'on ne sait plus l'heure,

D'un Port-Royal[4] port de Circée[5]
Où Pascal n'a d'autres *Pensées*

Que celles du roseau qui jase[6]
Ne sait plus quoi, ivre de vase . . .

Oh! qu'un Philippe de Champaigne,[7]
Mais né pierrot, vienne et te peigne!

Un rien, une miniature
De la largeur d'une tonsure;

Ça nous ferait un scapulaire[8]
Dont le contact anti-solaire,

Par exemple aux pieds de la femme,
Ah! nous serait tout un programme!

Piece for Guitar

Star without heart and without reproach, O Maintenon of old rock!
   Very Reverend Mother Superior of the cloister where all have lost their bearings
Of a Port-Royal port of Circe where Pascal has no other thoughts
   than those of the reed which jabbers about who knows what, drunk on slime . . .
   Oh if only a Philippe de Champaigne (but born a pierrot) could come and paint you!
   A mere nothing, a miniature of the width of a tonsure:
   It'd make us a scapular whose anti-solar contact,
   For example when we kneel at women's feet, Ah!, would be the real policy to follow!

Pierrots

I

C'est, sur un cou qui, raide, émerge
D'une fraise empesée *idem*,
Une face imberbe au cold-cream,
Un air d'hydrocéphale asperge.

Les yeux sont noyés de l'opium
De l'indulgence universelle,
La bouche clownesque ensorcèle
Comme un singulier géranium.

Bouche qui va du trou sans bonde
Glacialement désopilé,
Au transcendental en-allé[1]
Du souris vain de la Joconde.

Campant leur cône enfariné
Sur le noir serre-tête en soie,
Ils font rire leur patte d'oie
Et froncent en trèfle[2] leur nez.

Pierrots

I

On a neck which stiffly emerges from a ruff just as stiffly starched, it's a hairless cold-creamed face, with the look of a swollen-headed asparagus.

Its eyes are drowned in the opium of universal indulgence, the clownish mouth casts a spell like a singular geranium.

A mouth which varies from the bungless hole, glacially convulsed with laughter, to the transcendental gone-ness of the Mona Lisa's empty smile.

Planting a floury-white cone on their black silk skull-cap, they make their crow's-feet laugh and pucker their noses into a trefoil.

Ils ont comme chaton de bague
Le scarabée[3] égyptien,
A leur boutonnière fait bien
Le pissenlit des terrains vagues.

Ils vont, se sustentant d'azur,
Et parfois aussi de légumes,
De riz plus blanc que leur costume,
De mandarines et d'œufs durs.

Ils sont de la secte du Blême,
Ils n'ont rien à voir avec Dieu,
Et sifflent: «Tout est pour le mieux
«Dans la meilleur» des mi-carême!»[4]

II

Le cœur blanc tatoué
De sentences lunaires,
Ils ont: «Faut mourir, frères!»
Pour mot-d'ordre-Evohé.[5]

   The stone on their rings is the Egyptian scarab, the dandelion of waste grounds
is stylish in their buttonholes.
   They go sustaining themselves on azure, and sometimes also on vegetables, on
rice whiter than their costume, on mandarins and hard-boiled eggs.
   They belong to the sect of the Wan, they have nothing to do with God, and
they whistle: 'All is for the best in the best of all possible Mid-Lents!'

II
Their white hearts tattooed with lunar maxims, they take 'We must die, brothers!'
as their slogan-*cum*-Evohé.

Quand trépasse une vierge,
Ils suivent son convoi,
Tenant leur cou tout droit
Comme on porte un beau cierge.

Rôle très fatigant,
D'autant qu'ils n'ont personne
Chez eux, qui les frictionne
D'un conjugal onguent.

Ces dandys de la Lune
S'imposent, en effet,
De chanter «s'il vous plaît?»
De la blonde à la brune.

Car c'est des gens blasés;
Et s'ils vous semblent dupes,
Çà et là, de la Jupe,
Lange à cicatriser,'

Croyez qu'ils font la bête
Afin d'avoir des seins,
Pis-aller de coussins
A leurs savantes têtes.

When a virgin dies, they follow her cortège, holding their necks quite straight, like someone carrying a handsome candle.

A very wearying part to play, all the more so as they have nobody at home to massage them with a marital ointment.

These dandies of the Moon insist in fact on singing, 'Please?' to every brunette and blonde.

For they are blasé folk, and if you think they are taken in now and then by the Skirt, a nappy for healing,

know that they play the fool so as to have breasts – a stopgap for cushions – under their learned heads.

Ecarquillant le cou
Et feignant de comprendre
De travers, la voix tendre,
Mais les yeux si filous!

– D'ailleurs, de mœurs très fines,
Et toujours fort corrects,
(Ecole des cromlechs
Et des tuyaux d'usines).

III

Comme ils vont molester, la nuit,
Au profond des parcs, les statues,
Mais n'offrant qu'aux moins dévêtues
Leur bras et tout ce qui s'ensuit,

En tête à tête avec la femme
Ils ont toujours l'air d'être un tiers,
Confondent demain avec hier,
Et demandent *Rien* avec âme!

Necks goggling and pretending to misunderstand, their voices tender, but their eyes so rascally!

Besides, very punctilious morals, and always very polite (the school of stone henges and factory pipes).

III

Since they go assaulting the statues at night deep in the parks, but offering only to the most scantily clothed ones their arms and everything that ensues,

alone with a woman they always have the air of playing gooseberry, they mix up tomorrow with yesterday, and plead for *Nothing* with deep emotion!

Jurent «je t'aime!» l'air là-bas,
D'une voix sans timbre, en extase,
Et concluent aux plus folles phrases
Par des: «Mon Dieu, n'insistons pas?»

Jusqu'à ce qu'ivre, Elle s'oublie,
Prise d'on ne sait quel besoin
De lune?[7] dans leurs bras, fort loin
Des convenances établies.

IV

Maquillés d'abandon,[8] les manches
En saule, ils leur font des serments,
Pour être vrais trop véhéments!
Puis tumultuent en gigues blanches,

Beuglant: Ange! tu m'as compris,
A la vie, à la mort! – et songent:
Ah! passer là-dessus l'éponge! . . .
Et c'est pas chez eux parti pris,

They swear 'I love you!' as if their minds were on something else, in a toneless, ecstatic voice, and finish off the wildest sentences with words like 'Good Lord, don't let's overdo it!'

until in rapture, overcome by God knows what need of moon, She forgets herself in their arms, far far away from established proprieties.

IV

Painted and powdered with forlornness their sleeves drooping like a willow, they plight their troth, too vehement to be true! then tumultuate in white jigs,

bellowing: 'Angel! you have understood me, for life, for death!' – and then think: 'Ah! let's call the whole thing off!' And it isn't that they're prejudiced,

Hélas! mais l'idée de la femme
Se prenant au sérieux encor
Dans ce siècle, voilà, les tord
D'un rire aux déchirantes gammes!

Ne leur jetez pas la pierre, ô
Vous qu'affecte une jarretière!
Allez, ne jetez pas la pierre
Aux blancs parias, aux purs pierrots!

v

Blancs enfants de chœur de la Lune,
Et lunologues⁹ éminents,
Leur Eglise ouvre à tout venant,
Claire d'ailleurs comme pas une.

Ils disent, d'un œil faisandé,
Les manches très sacerdotales,
Que ce bas monde de scandale
N'est qu'un des mille coups de dé

Alas! but the idea of woman still taking herself seriously in this century, you see, doubles them up with heart-rending laughter!

Cast no stone at them, O you who are roused by a garter! Come, cast no stone at the white pariahs, the pure Pierrots!

v

White choirboys of the Moon and eminent lunologists, their church is open to all and sundry, and besides it's pretty damn bright.

They say, with a sybaritic air (their sleeves very priestly) that this low world of scandal is only one of the thousand dice-throws

Du jeu que l'Idée et l'Amour,
Afin sans doute de connaître
Aussi leur propre raison d'être,
Ont jugé bon de mettre au jour.

Que nul d'ailleurs ne vaut le nôtre,
Qu'il faut pas le traiter d'hôtel
Garni vers un plus immortel,
Car nous sommes faits l'un pour l'autre;

Qu'enfin, et rien de moins subtil,
Ces gratuites antinomies
Au fond ne nous regardant mie,
L'art de tout est l'*Ainsi soit-il*;

Et que, chers frères, le beau rôle
Est de vivre de but en blanc
Et, dût-on se battre les flancs,
De hausser à tout les épaules.

in the game that the Idea and Love – doubtless so as to understand the purpose of their own existence too – judged it right to create.

[They say too] that no world is worth as much as ours, that we mustn't treat it as a hotel furnished in view of a more immortal one, for we are made for each other,

and that finally (and nothing is less subtle) – since these gratuitous contradictions basically are no concern of ours, the art of everything is *So be it*;

and that, dear brethren, the starring role in the play is to live point-blank and – even if it's a futile waste of effort – to shrug your shoulders at everything.

Pierrots

(*On a des principes*)

Elle disait, de son air vain fondamental:
«Je t'aime pour toi seul!» – Oh! là, là, grêle histoire;
Oui, comme l'art! Du calme, ô salaire illusoire
       Du capitaliste Idéal![1]

Elle faisait: «J'attends, me voici, je sais pas . . .»
Le regard pris de ces larges candeurs des lunes;
– Oh! là, là, ce n'est pas peut-être pour des prunes,
       Qu'on a fait ses classes ici-bas?

Mais voici qu'un beau soir, infortunée à point,
Elle meurt! – Oh! là, là; bon, changement de thème!
On sait que tu dois ressusciter le troisième
       Jour, sinon en personne, du moins

Pierrots:
(*One has principles*)

She said, in her downright empty way: 'I love you for your own sake!' – (Oh dear, what a thin tale! Yes, like art for art's sake! Keep calm, O illusory reward, the capitalist's Ideal!)

  She uttered: 'I'm waiting, here I am, what am I to think?', her eyes filled with great moon-like candours. (Oh well, then it isn't perhaps for peanuts that one's gone to school in this world?)

  But now one fine evening, with perfectly timed ill-luck, she dies! – Oh goodness, let's change the subject! We know you must resurrect on the third day, if not in person, at least

Dans l'odeur, les verdures, les eaux des beaux mois!
Et tu iras, levant encore bien plus de dupes
Vers le Zaïmph[2] de la Joconde, vers la Jupe!
      Il se pourra même que j'en sois.

Pierrots

(*Scène courte, mais typique.*)

Il me faut, vos yeux! Dès que je perds leur étoile,
Le mal des calmes plats s'engouffre dans ma voile,
Le frisson du *Væ soli!*[1] gargouille en mes moelles . . .

Vous auriez dû me voir après cette querelle!
J'errais dans l'agitation la plus cruelle,
Criant aux murs: Mon Dieu! mon Dieu! Que dira-t-elle?

Mais aussi, vrai, vous me blessâtes aux antennes
De l'âme, avec les mensonges de votre traîne.
Et votre tas de complications mondaines.

in the odour, the greenery, the waters of the best months! And you'll be on your way, flushing out still more dupes towards the Veil of the Mona Lisa, towards the Skirt! I might even myself be one of those dupes.

Pierrots
(*A short, but typical, scene.*)

I must have your eyes! The moment I lose their guiding star, the seasickness of flat calms engulfs itself in my sail, the shudder of *Væ soli!* gurgles in my marrow . . .

    You should have seen me after that quarrel! I wandered about in the most cruel agitation, crying to the walls: 'My God! my God! What will she say?'

    But it's also true that you wounded the antennae of my soul, with your trawl-net of lies, and your stack of social complications.

Je voyais que vos yeux me lançaient sur des pistes,
Je songeais: Oui, divins, ces yeux! mais rien n'existe
Derrière! Son âme est affaire d'oculiste.

Moi, je suis laminé d'esthétiques loyales!
Je hais les trémolos, les phrases nationales;
Bref, le violet gros deuil est ma couleur locale.

Je ne suis point «ce gaillard-là!» ni Le Superbe!
Mais mon âme, qu'un cri un peu cru exacerbe,
Est au fond distinguée et franche comme une herbe.

J'ai des nerfs encor sensibles au son des cloches,
Et je vais en plein air sans peur et sans reproche,[2]
Sans jamais me sourire en un miroir de poche.

C'est vrai, j'ai bien roulé! j'ai râlé dans des gîtes
Peu vous; mais, n'en ai-je pas plus de mérite
A en avoir sauvé la foi en vos yeux? dites . . .

I saw that your eyes were setting me off on tracks. I thought: 'Yes, divine, those eyes! but nothing exists behind them! Her soul is a matter for the oculist.'

I, on the other hand, am laminated with trusty aesthetic principles! I hate tremolos and nationalistic overstatements; in short, deep mourning purple is my camouflage.

I am not at all 'Lord Muck'! nor 'The Swanker'! but my soul, which is set on edge by too sharp a cry, is fundamentally noble and as candid as grass.

I have nerves which are still sensitive to the sound of bells, and I walk in the open air without fear or reproach, and without ever smirking at myself in a pocket mirror.

It's true I've been about! I've groaned in dens which weren't at all your thing; but isn't my merit in your eyes all the greater for keeping my faith pure despite it? Tell me . . .

– Allons, faisons la paix, Venez, que je vous berce,
Enfant. Eh bien?
     – C'est que, votre pardon me verse
Un mélange (confus) d'impressions . . . diverses . . .

              (*Exit.*)

Locutions des Pierrots

I

Les mares de vos yeux aux joncs de cils,
   O vaillante oisive femme,
   Quand donc me renverront-ils
La Lune-levante de ma belle âme?

'Come, let's make our quarrel up. Come here, let me cradle you, poor child. Isn't that better?'
 'The problem is, your forgiveness provides me with a (confused) jumble of various . . . impressions . . . (*Exit*)

The Things that Pierrots Say

I

The duckponds of your eyes with eyelashes for rushes, O valiant futile woman, when will they give me a reflection of the Rising Moon of my high-minded soul?

Voilà tantôt[1] une heure qu'en langueur
    Mon cœur si simple s'abreuve
    De vos vilaines rigueurs,
Avec le regard bon d'un terre-neuve.

Ah! madame, ce n'est vraiment pas bien,
    Quand on n'est pas la Joconde,
    D'en adopter le maintien
Pour induire en spleens tout bleus le pauv' monde.

II

Ah! le divin attachement
Que je nourris pour Cydalise,[2]
Maintenant qu'elle échappe aux prises
De mon lunaire entendement!

Vrai, je me ronge en des détresses,
Parmi les fleurs de son terroir
A seule fin de bien savoir
Quelle est sa faculté-maîtresse![3]

Eftsoons 'twill be an hour that, listless, my so artless heart has been drinking in your nasty spitefulness, with the adoring eyes of a Newfoundland dog.

    Ah! Madam, it really isn't nice, when one is not the Mona Lisa, to adopt her manner so as to give poor old everybody the blue sulks.

II

Ah! the divine attachment that I nourish for Cydalise, now that she escapes the grasp of my lunar understanding!

    It's true, I gnaw myself away in fits of distress among the flowers of her native soil, with the sole object of deciding which is her dominant faculty!

– C'est d'être la mienne, dis-tu?
Hélas! tu sais bien que j'oppose
Un démenti formel aux poses
Qui sentent par trop l'impromptu.

III

Ah! sans Lune, quelles nuits blanches,[4]
Quels cauchemars pleins de talent!
Vois-je pas là nos cygnes blancs?
Vient-on pas de tourner la clenche?

Et c'est vers toi que j'en suis là.
Que ma conscience voit double,
Et que mon cœur pèche en eau trouble,
Ève, Joconde[5] et Dalila![6]

Ah! par l'infini circonflexe
De l'ogive[7] où j'ahanne en croix,
Vends-moi donc une bonne fois
La raison d'être de Ton Sexe!

It's 'To be mine,' you say? Alas, you know quite well that I issue an official rejection of all affectations which have too strong a whiff of being improvised.

III

Ah! without a Moon, what sleepless nights, what nightmares full of genius! Can't I see there our white swans? Hasn't someone just clicked the sneck?

And it's with you that I've got to this point, that my conscience is seeing double, and my heart fishing in troubled waters, Eve, Mona Lisa and Delilah!

Ah! by the infinite circumflex of the ogive where I gasp, crucified, sell me for good and all the *raison d'être* of Your Sex!

IV

Tu dis que mon cœur est à jeun
De quoi jouer tout seul son rôle,
Et que mon regard ne t'enjôle
Qu'avec des infinis d'emprunt!

Et tu rêvais avoir affaire
A quelque pauvre in-octavo . . .
Hélas! c'est vrai que mon cerveau
S'est vu, des soirs, trois hémisphères.[8]

Mais va, l'œillet de tes vingt ans,
Je l'arrose aux plus belles âmes
Qui soient! – Surtout, je n'en réclame
Pas, sais-tu, de ta part autant!

V

T'occupe pas, sois Ton Regard,
Et sois l'âme qui s'exécute;
Tu fournis la matière brute,
Je me charge de l'œuvre d'art.

IV

You say my heart is empty-bellied of what it needs to perform its lonely part, and
that my gaze cajoles you only with borrowed infinities!

And you dreamed of having to deal with some poor octavo volume . . . Alas! it's
true, some evenings, my brain has thought it possesses three hemispheres.

But see here, I'm watering the carnation of your twenty years with the finest
souls which ever were! – Besides, you know, I don't ask as much of *you*!

V

Don't worry, be Thy Gaze, and be the compliant soul; you provide the raw material,
I'll take care of the work of art.

Chef-d'œuvre d'art sans idée-mère
Par exemple! Oh! dis, n'est-ce pas
Faut pas nous mettre sur les bras
Un cri des Limbes[9] prolifères?

Allons, je sais que vous avez
L'égoïsme solide au poste,
Et même prêt aux holocaustes[10]
De l'ordre le plus élevé.

VI

Je te vas dire:[11] moi, quand j'aime,
C'est d'un cœur, au fond sans apprêts,
Mais dignement élaboré
Dans nos plus singuliers problèmes.

Ainsi, pour mes mœurs et mon art,
C'est la période védique[12]
Qui seule à bon droit revendique
Ce que j'en «attelle à ton char».[13]

Masterpiece of art without mother-idea, for God's sake! Oh! say . . . we mustn't burden ourselves with a wail from child-bearing Limbo!

Come, I know your self-centredness will never desert its post, and is even ready for holocausts of the most exalted order.

VI

I tell you straight: when I love, it's with a heart fundamentally without affectations, but praiseworthily convoluted by humanity's most special problems.

So, as regards my manners and my art, this is my Vedic period which alone has the right to claim what part of them I 'yoke to your chariot'.

Comme c'est notre Bible hindoue
Qui, tiens, m'amène à caresser,
Avec ces yeux de cétacé,[14]
Ainsi, et bien sans but, ta joue.

VII

Cœur de profil, petite âme douillette,
Tu veux te tremper un matin en moi,
Comme on trempe, en levant le petit doigt,
Dans son café au lait une mouillette!

Et mon amour, si blanc, si vert, si grand.
Si tournoyant! ainsi ne te suggère
Que pas-de-deux, silhouettes légères
A enlever sur ce solide écran![15]

Adieu. – Qu'est-ce encor? Allons bon, tu pleures!
Aussi pourquoi ces grands airs de vouloir,
Quand mon Étoile t'ouvre son peignoir,
D'Hélas, chercher midi flambant à d'autres heures![16]

As it is our Hindu Bible which – oh surprise! – leads me to stroke, with these
cetacean eyes – like this . . . quite aimlessly . . . your cheek.

VII

Heart in profile, downy little soul, you seek to dip yourself for a morning in me,
as one dips (with pinkie raised) a finger of bread in one's white coffee!

And so my love, so white, so green, so great, so dizzying! suggests to you merely
two-steps, light silhouettes to be picked out against this solid screen!

Farewell. – What now? Dear dear, you're weeping! So why those great appearances
of wanting, when my Star opens to you its dressing-gown, Alas, to look for flaming
noon at the wrong time of day?

VIII

Ah! tout le long du cœur
Un vieil ennui m'effleure . . .
M'est avis qu'il est l'heure
De renaître moqueur.

Eh bien? je t'ai blessée?
Ai-je eu le sanglot faux,
Que tu prends cet air sot
De *la Cruche cassée?*[17]

Tout divague d'amour;
Tout, du cèdre à l'hysope,[18]
Sirote sa syncope;
J'ai fait un joli four.

IX

        Ton geste,
        Houri,[19]
M'a l'air d'un *memento mori*[20]
Qui signifie au fond: va, reste . . .

VIII

Ah! an old anxiety prickles all round my heart . . . I think it's time to be reborn as a scoffer.

Well? Did I hurt your feelings? Did my sob ring hollow, so you took on that stupid *Broken Jug* look?

Everything raves with love; everything from cedar to hyssop, sips at the swoon of it. I've really cocked it up.

IX

Your gesture, houri, looks to me like a *memento mori* which really means, 'Come, stay.'

Mais, je te dirai ce que c'est,
Et pourquoi je pars, foi d'honnête
        Poète
        Français.

Ton cœur a la conscience nette,
Le mien n'est qu'un individu
        Perdu
        De dettes.

x

Que loin l'âme type
Qui m'a dit adieu
Parce que mes yeux
Manquaient de principes!

Elle, en ce moment,
Elle, si pain tendre,
Oh! peut-être engendre
Quelque garnement.

But I'll tell you what the problem is, and why I'm leaving, on my honour as a true French Poet.
    Your heart has a clear conscience, mine is merely a bloke crippled with debts.

x

How distant now is that soul (of standard model) who bade me farewell because my eyes lacked principles!
    She, tender as new-baked bread, at this moment perhaps, oh! she's engendering some brat.

Car on l'a unie
Avec un monsieur,
Ce qu'il y a de mieux,
Mais pauvre en génie.

XI

Et je me console avec la
        Bonne fortune
        De l'alme Lune.
O Lune, *Ave Paris stella*![21]

Tu sais si la femme est cramponne;
        Eh bien, déteins,
        Glace sans tain,
Sur mon œil! qu'il soit tout atone,

Qu'il déclare: ô folles d'essais,
        Je vous invite
        A prendre vite,
Car c'est à prendre et à laisser.

    For she's been united with a gentleman of great respectability, but short on genius.

XI

And I console myself with the good fortune of the gracious Moon. O Moon, *Ave Paris stella*!
    You know how clinging women are; so, fade, two-way mirror, on my eye! Let it be quite colourless,
    Let it declare: 'You women mad for experiments, I invite you to take quickly, for you must take it and leave it.'

XII

Encore un livre; ô nostalgies
Loin de ces très goujates gens,
Loin des saluts[22] et des argents,
Loin de nos phraséologies!

Encore un de mes pierrots mort;
Mort d'un chronique orphelinisme;
C'était un cœur plein de dandysme
Lunaire, en un drôle de corps.

Les dieux s'en vont; plus que des hures;
Ah! ça devient tous les jours pis;
J'ai fait mon temps, je déguerpis
Vers l'Inclusive Sinécure![23]

XIII

Eh bien, oui, je l'ai chagrinée,
Tout le long, le long de l'année;
Mais quoi! s'en est-elle étonnée?

XII
Yet another book; O yearning to be far away from these boorish folk, from saluting and [talk of] money, from 'our' ways of putting things!

Another of my pierrots dead. Dead of chronic orphanism; his was a heart full of lunar dandyism, in a freakish body.

The gods are departing; they're nothing now but hunting trophies on the wall. Ah! every day it gets worse; my life is done, I'm slipping away to the All-Inclusive Sinecure!

XIII
Well yes, I made her suffer, right through, right through the year; but so what? Did this surprise her?

Absolus, drapés de layettes,
Aux lunes de miel de l'Hymette,[24]
Nous avions par trop l'air vignette!

Ma vitre pleure, adieu! l'on bâille
Vers les ciels couleur de limaille
Où la Lune a ses funérailles.

Je ne veux accuser nul être,
Bien qu'au fond tout m'ait pris en traître.
Ah! paître, sans but là-bas! paître . . .

XIV

Les mains dans les poches,
Le long de la route,
        J'écoute
    Mille cloches
Chantant: «Les temps sont proches,
    Sans que tu t'en doutes!»

Absolute, draped in baby-clothes, on the honeymoons of Hymettus, we looked far too much the perfect picture!

My window's weeping, farewell! we're yawning for skies the colour of iron filings where the Moon celebrates her funeral.

I don't want to accuse anyone, although basically everything has played me false. Ah! to browse, aimlessly there! to browse . . .

XIV

Hands in pockets, right down the road, I listen to a thousand bells chanting: 'The time is near, though you don't suspect it!'

Ah! Dieu m'est égal!
Et je suis chez moi!
        Mon toit!
      Très natal
C'est Tout. Je marche droit,
    Je fais pas de mal.

Je connais l'Histoire,
Et puis la Nature,
        Ces foires
      Aux ratures;
Aussi je vous assure
    Que l'on peut me croire!

XV

J'entends battre mon Sacré-Cœur[25]
Dans le crépuscule de l'heure,
Comme il est méconnu, sans sœur,
Et sans destin, et sans demeure!

J'entends battre ma jeune chair
Equivoquant par mes artères,
Entre les Edens de mes vers
Et la province de mes pères.

Ah! God's of no interest to me! and I'm at home! My very natal roof is the All.
I tread the straight and narrow, I harm nobody.
    I know History, and Nature too, those bedlams full of second thoughts; so I tell
you straight, you can believe me!

XV

I hear my damned Sacred-Heart throbbing in the twilight of this hour, how
misunderstood it is, sisterless, without a destiny, homeless!
    I hear my young flesh throbbing, equivocating through my arteries between the
Edens of my verse and the province of my ancestors.

Et j'entends la flûte de Pan[26]
Qui chante: «Bats, bats la campagne!
«Meurs, quand tout vit à tes dépens;
«Mais entre nous, va, qui perd gagne!»

XVI

Je ne suis qu'un viveur lunaire
Qui fait des ronds[27] dans les bassins,
Et cela, sans autre dessein
Que devenir un légendaire.

Retroussant d'un air de défi
Mes manches de mandarin pâle,
J'arrondis ma bouche et – j'exhale
Des conseils doux de Crucifix.

Ah! oui, devenir légendaire,
Au seuil des siècles charlatans!
Mais où sont les Lunes d'antan?[28]
Et que Dieu n'est-il à refaire?

And I hear the pipes of Pan singing: 'Explore the terrain! Die, since everything lives at your expense; but, between you and me, so what! loser takes all!'

XVI

I'm merely a Moon-dweller making ripples in ponds, without any other purpose than to become legendary.

Rolling up, with a defiant air, my pale mandarin's sleeves, I make my mouth round and – I breathe out gentle Crucifix advice.

Ah! yes, to become legendary on the threshold of the charlatan centuries! But where are the Moons of yesteryear? And why is God not to be created anew?

Dialogue avant le Lever de la Lune

– Je veux bien vivre; mais vraiment,
L'Idéal est trop élastique!

– C'est l'Idéal, son nom l'implique,
Hors son non-sens, le verbe ment.

– Mais, tout est conteste; les livres
S'accouchent, s'entretuent sans lois!

– Certes! l'Absolu perd ses droits,
Là, où le Vrai consiste à vivre.

– Et, si j'amène pavillon
Et repasse au Néant ma charge?

– L'Infini, qui souffle du large,
Dit: «Pas de bêtises, voyons!»

– Ces chantiers du Possible ululent
A l'Inconcevable, pourtant!

– Un degré, comme il en est tant
Entre l'aube et le crépuscule.

Dialogue before the Moon's Rising

'Yes, I do want to live; but really, the Ideal is too elastic!'
    'It's the Ideal, its name implies it. Apart from its meaning nothing, the word is a lie.'
    'But everything's a struggle; books give birth, kill each other lawlessly!'
    'Certainly! When Truth consists of living, the Absolute loses its rights.'
    'And if I haul down my flag and pass my responsibility back to Nothingness?'
    'The Infinite, which blows from the deep sea, says, "Come now, don't be an idiot!"'
    'And yet, these building sites of the Possible yell at the Unimaginable!'
    'A degree, of which there are many between dawn and dusk.'

– Être actuel, est-ce, du moins,
Être adéquat à Quelque Chose?

– Conséquemment, comme la rose
Est nécessaire à ses besoins.

– Façon de dire peu commune
Que Tout est cercles vicieux?

– Vicieux, mais Tout!
              – J'aime mieux
Donc m'en aller selon la Lune.

Petits Mystères

Chut! Oh! ce soir, comme elle est près!
Vrai, je ne sais ce qu'elle pense,
Me ferait-elle des avances?
Est-ce là le rayon qui fiance
Nos cœurs humains à son cœur frais?

'Is existing at least being adequate to Something?'
'Causally, as the rose is necessary to its needs.'
'Is that an unusual way of saying that Everything is vicious circles?'
'Vicious, but still Everything!' – 'Then I prefer to depart by the Moon's path.'

Small Mysteries

Hush! Oh! this evening, how close she is! It's true I don't know what she's thinking. Might she make advances to me? Is this the ray which betrothes our human hearts to her cool heart?

Par quels ennuis kilométriques
Mener ma silhouette encor,
Avant de prendre mon essor
Pour arrimer, veuf de tout corps,
A ses dortoirs madréporiques.

Mets de la Lune dans ton vin,
M'a dit sa moue cadenassée;
Je ne bois que de l'eau glacée,
Et de sa seule panacée
Mes tissus qui stagnent ont faim.

Lune, consomme mon baptême,
Lave mes yeux de ton linceul;
Qu'aux hommes, je sois ton filleul;
Et pour nos compagnes, le seul
Qui les délivre d'elles-mêmes.

Lune, mise au ban du Progrès
Des populaces des Etoiles.
Volatilise-moi les moelles,
Que je t'arrive à pleines voiles,
Dolmen, Cyprès, Amen, au frais![1]

By what kilometre-long tediums must I still lead my silhouette before, widowed of my body, I shall dock in her coral dormitories!

'Put Moon in your wine,' her padlocked pout told me; 'I drink only frozen water, and for its sole panacea my stagnating tissues are thirsty.'

Moon, consummate my baptism, wash my eyes with your winding sheet; let men accept me as your godson; and may I be for our women companions the only one who liberates them from themselves.

O Moon who are banished from the Progress of the Star-peoples, evaporate my marrow, let me come to you at full sail, Megalith, Cypress, Amen, into the cool!

Nuitamment

O Lune, coule dans mes veines
Et que je me soutienne à peine,

Et croie t'aplatir sur mon cœur!
Mais, elle est pâle à faire peur!

Et montre par son teint, sa mise,
Combien elle en a vu de grises!

Et ramène, se sentant mal,
Son cachemire sidéral,

Errante Delos,[1] nécropole,
Je veux que tu fasses école;

Je te promets en ex-voto
Les Putiphars[2] de mes manteaux!

Et tiens, adieu; je rentre en ville
Mettre en train deux ou trois idylles,

En m'annonçant par un Péan
D'épithalame à ton Néant.

Nightly

O Moon, flow in my veins and may I hardly be able to stand,
  and believe I flatten you against my heart! But she's terrifyingly pale!
  and shows by her complexion and expression what a rough time she's gone through!
  and pulls around her, feeling ill, her cashmere of stars.
  Wandering Delos, necropolis, I want you to set the fashion;
  I promise you as ex-voto the Potiphars of my cloaks!
  Oh by the way, goodbye; I'm going into town to set two or three idylls going,
  announcing myself with a wedding-song Paean in honour of your Nothingness.

La Lune est stérile

Lune, Pape abortif à l'amiable, Pape
Des Mormons pour l'art, dans la jalouse Paphos[1]
Où l'État tient gratis les fils de la soupape
D'échappement des apoplectiques Cosmos!

C'est toi, léger manuel d'instincts, toi qui circules,
Glaçant, après les grandes averses, les œufs
Obtus de ces myriades d'animalcules
Dont les simouns mettraient nos muqueuses en feu!

Tu ne sais que la fleur des sanglantes chimies;
Et perces nos rideaux, nous offrant le lotus
Qui constipe les plus larges polygamies,
Tout net, de l'excrément logique des fœtus.[2]

Carguez-lui vos rideaux, citoyens de mœurs lâches;
C'est l'Extase qui paie comptant, donne son Ut
Des deux sexes et veut pas même que l'on sache
S'il se peut qu'elle ait, hors de l'art pour l'art, un but.[3]

The Moon is Sterile

Moon, you abortive courtesy Pope, you Mormons' Pope for art's sake, in jealous
Paphos where the State holds *gratis* every string of the exhaust-valve of the apoplectic
Cosmoses!

It is you, short practical guide to the instincts, you who circulate, freezing, after
great downpours, the obtuse eggs of those myriads of animalcules whose sandstorms
would set our mucuses on fire!

You know only the flower of the chemistries of blood; and you pierce our
curtains, offering us the lotus which constipates the most extensive polygamies –
stops them dead! – with the logical excrement of embryos . . .

Brail up your curtains, citizens of lax morals; it's Ecstasy which pays in cash, gives
the note to which the sexes tune their instruments, and doesn't even want us to
know if it's possible that there might be – apart from art for art's sake – any purpose.

On allèche de vie humaine, à pleines voiles,
Les Tantales[4] virtuels, peu intéressants
D'ailleurs, sauf leurs cordiaux, qui rêvent dans nos moelles.
Et c'est un produit net qu'encaissent nos bons sens.[5]

Et puis, l'atteindrons-nous, l'Oasis aux citernes,
Où nos cœurs toucheraient les payes qu'On leur doit?
Non, c'est la rosse aveugle aux cercles sempiternes
Qui tourne pour autrui les bons chevaux de bois.

Ne vous distrayez pas, avec vos grosses douanes;
Clefs de fa, clefs de sol, huit stades de claviers,
Laissez faire, laissez passer la caravane
Qui porte à l'Idéal ses plus riches dossiers!

L'Art est tout, du droit divin de l'Inconscience;
Après lui, le déluge![6] et son moindre regard
Est le cercle infini dont la circonférence
Est partout, et le centre immoral nulle part.[7]

Human life at full sail baits the potential Tantaluses – who are not very interesting
except for their stimulants slumbering in our marrows. And these are net earnings,
which our good senses put in the till.

Besides, shall we reach it, the Oasis with the cisterns, where our hearts will be
paid the wages that Somebody owes us? No, it's the blind beast, eternally circling,
turning for someone else the obedient horses of the merry-go-round.

Don't distract yourselves, with your huge taxes; the keys of F, of G, eight rows
of keyboards, stand aside, give way to the caravan which carries to the Ideal its
richest dossiers!

Art is all, by the divine right of Unconsciousness; after art, the deluge! and its
least glance is the infinite circle whose circumference is everywhere and its immoral
centre nowhere.

Pour moi, déboulonné du pôle de stylite[8]
Qui me sied, dès qu'un corps a trop de son secret,
J'affiche: celles qui voient tout, je les invite
A venir, à mon bras, des soirs, prendre le frais.

Or voici: nos deux Cris, abaissant leurs visières,
Passent mutuellement, après quiproquos,
Aux chers peignes du cru leurs moelles épinières
D'où lèvent débusqués tous les archets locaux.[9]

Et les ciels familiers liserés de folie
Neigeant en charpie éblouissante, faut voir
Comme le moindre appel: c'est pour nous seuls! rallie
Les louables efforts menés à l'abattoir![10]

Et la santé en deuil ronronne ses vertiges,
Et chante, pour la forme: «Hélas! ce n'est pas bien,
«Par ces pays, pays si tournoyants, vous dis-je,
«Où la faim d'Infini justifie les moyens.»[11]

  As for me, kicked off the Stylites pole which suits me – as soon as a body has
had enough of its own secret, I stick up this advertisement: 'Those ladies who see
everything, I invite them to take my arm, and walk in the evening cool.'
  Now see what happened. After the usual misunderstandings, our two Cries,
lowering their vizors, mutually pass their two spinal chords through the fine tooth
comb of the heartland . . . from which all the local violin bows rise, driven from
hiding.
  And, as the familiar skies, fringed with folly, were snowing in dazzling shreds,
it's remarkable how the slightest call: 'It's for us alone!' rallies praiseworthy efforts
intended for the abattoir!
  And health in mourning drones out its vertigos, and sings, for form's sake: 'Alas!
it isn't nice, in these countries, countries that are so dizzying, I tell you, where
hunger for the Endless justifies the means.'

Lors, qu'ils sont beaux les flancs tirant leurs révérences
Au sanglant capitaliste berné des nuits,
En s'affalant cuver ces jeux sans conséquence!
Oh! n'avoir à songer qu'à ses propres ennuis!

– Bons aïeux qui geigniez semaine sur semaine,
Vers mon Cœur, baobab[12] des védiques terroirs,
Je m'agite aussi! mais l'Inconscient me mène;
Or, il sait ce qu'il fait, je n'ai rien à y voir.

Nobles et touchantes divagations sous la Lune

Un chien perdu grelotte en abois à la Lune . . .
Oh! pourquoi ce sanglot quand nul ne l'a battu?
Et, nuits! que partout la même Ame! En est-il une
Qui n'aboie à l'exil ainsi qu'un chien perdu?

And oh, how beautiful they are, those haunches curtseying to the bloodstained capitalist whom the nights deceive, sinking down to sleep off these inconsequential games! Oh! to have only one's own troubles to think of!

Dear ancestors who used to groan week after week towards my Heart, baobab of Vedic homelands, I too am overactive! but the Unconscious guides me; it knows what it's about, it's none of my business.

Noble and Touching Divagations under the Moon

A lost dog shivers as it barks at the Moon . . . Oh! why this grief when no one has been beating him? And, O nights! everywhere the same Soul! Is there a single one who doesn't bark at exile like a lost dog?

Non, non; pas un caillou qui ne rêve un ménage,
Pas un soir qui ne pleure: encore un aujourd'hui!
Pas un Moi qui n'écume aux barreaux de sa cage
Et n'épluche ses jours en filaments d'ennui.

Et les bons végétaux! des fossiles qui gisent
En pliocènes tufs de squelettes parias,
Aux printemps aspergés par les steppes kirghyses,
Aux roses des contreforts de l'Himalaya!

Et le vent qui beugle, apocalyptique Bête
S'abattant sur des toits aux habitants pourris,
Qui secoue en vain leur huis-clos, et puis s'arrête,
Pleurant sur son cœur à Sept-Glaives d'incompris.[1]

Tout vient d'un seul impératif catégorique,[2]
Mais qu'il a le bras long, et la matrice loin!
L'Amour, l'amour qui rêve, ascétise et fornique;
Que n'aimons-nous pour nous dans notre petit coin?

No, no, there's not one pebble that doesn't dream of setting up a home, not one evening which doesn't weep: 'Yet another today!' not one Myself who doesn't foam at the bars of his cage and shred away his days in slivers of world-weariness.

And the dear old plants! fossils lying in pliocene tufas of pariah skeletons, in springtimes watered by the Kirghiz steppes, among the roses of Himalayan counterscarps!

And the bellowing wind, apocalyptic Beast pouncing on roofs full of loathsome householders, vainly shaking their bolted doors, then pausing to bewail its heart pierced by Seven Swords of misunderstanding.

Everything comes from a single categorical imperative, but isn't its arm long and its womb far away! Love, love that dreams, denies itself and fornicates; why don't we love for our own sakes in our own little inglenook?

Infini, d'où sors-tu? Pourquoi nos sens superbes
Sont-ils fous d'au delà les claviers[3] octroyés,
Croient-ils à des miroirs plus heureux que le Verbe,
Et se tuent? Infini, montre un peu tes papiers!

Motifs décoratifs, et non but de l'Histoire,
Non le bonheur pour tous, mais de coquets moyens
S'objectivant en nous, substratums sans pourboires,
Trinité de Molochs,[4] le Vrai, le Beau, le Bien.

Nuages à profils de kaïns?[5] vents d'automne
Qui, dans l'antiquité des Pans[6] soi-disant gais,
Vous lamentiez aux toits des temples heptagones,
Voyez, nous rebrodons les mêmes Anankès.[7]

Jadis les gants violets des Révérendissimes
De la Théologie en conciles cités,
Et l'évêque d'Hippone attelant ses victimes
Au char du Jaggernaut Œcuménicité,[8]

Infinity, where did you suddenly pop out from? Why are our proud senses mad
for something beyond the permitted spectrums? Do they believe in mirrors which
are more fortunate than the Word – and kill themselves? Infinite, why don't you
give us a peep at your identity cards!

Repetitive patterns, and not a Historical Purpose; not happiness for all, but
methods of seduction objectivizing themselves in us, substrata offering no rewards,
trinity of Molochs, the True, the Beautiful, the Good.

Clouds with the profiles of sarongs? winds of autumn which, in the ancient time
of the so-called joyous Pans, lamented in the roofs of seven-cornered temples, see,
we re-embroider the same Anankés.

Once upon a time it was the violet gloves of the Most Reverend Doctors of
Theology, who were quoted in synods, and the Bishop of Hippo harnessing his
victims to the chariot of the Juggernaut Ecumenicity;

Aujourd'hui; microscope de télescope!⁹ Encore,
Nous voilà relançant l'Ogive au toujours Lui,
Qu'il y tourne casaque, à neuf qu'il s'y redore
Pour venir nous bercer un printemps notre ennui.

Une place plus fraîche à l'oreiller des fièvres,
Un mirage inédit au détour du chemin,
Des rampements plus fous vers le bonheur des lèvres,
Et des opiums plus longs à rêver. Mais demain?

Recommencer encore? Ah! lâchons les écluses,¹⁰
A la fin! Oublions tout! nous faut convoyer
Vers ces ciels où, s'aimer et paître étant les Muses,¹¹
Cuver sera le dieu pénate des foyers!¹²

Oh! l'Eden immédiat des braves empirismes!
Peigner ses fiers cheveux avec l'arête des
Poissons qu'on lui offrit crus dans un paroxysme
De dévouement! s'aimer sans serments, ni rabais.

Today, from telescope to microscope! Here we are again, relaunching the Ogive
to the Always-Himself, let him be a turncoat, let him re-gild himself anew, and
come and rock our world-weariness to sleep for a springtime.

A cooler place on fevers' pillow, an unprecedented mirage at the bend of a path,
insaner clamberings towards the bliss of lips, and opiums providing longer dreams.
But tomorrow?

Start all over again? Ah! for God's sake let's open the sluicegates and weep! Let's
forget everything! Convey us to the skies where, since the Muses' message is 'Love
one another, and browse away!', the protective god of our homes will be –
wine-making!

Oh! the instant Eden of brave empiricisms! To comb your proud hair with a
fishbone, from fish you were offered raw in a fit of devotion! to love each other
without vows or price reductions.

Oui, vivre pur d'habitudes et de programmes,
Pacageant mes milieux, à travers et à tort,
Choyant comme un beau chat ma chère petite âme,
N'arriver qu'ivre-mort de Moi-même à la mort!

Oui, par delà nos arts, par delà nos époques
Et nos hérédités, tes îles de candeur,
Inconscience![13] et elle, au seuil, là, qui se moque
De mes regards en arrière, et fait: N'aie pas peur.

Que non, je n'ai plus peur; je rechois en enfance;
Mon bateau de fleurs est prêt, j'y veux rêver à
L'ombre de tes maternelles protubérances,
En t'offrant le miroir de mes *et cætera* . . .[14]

Yes, to live pure of habits and programmes, pasturing on my social circles, without rhyme or reason, cherishing like a beautiful cat my dear little soul, and arriving at death dead-drunk on Myself alone!

Yes, beyond our arts, beyond our epochs and our heredities, your isles of candour, Unconsciousness! and she, on the threshold there, mocking my backward glances and saying: 'Don't be afraid.'

Of course not, I'm not frightened any more; I'm relapsing into childhood; my float decked with flowers is ready, I want to dream there in the shade of your maternal protuberances, while I offer you the mirror of my *etcetera* . . .

Jeux

Ah! la Lune, la Lune m'obsède . . .
Croyez-vous qu'il y ait un remède?

Morte? Se peut-il pas qu'elle dorme
Grise de cosmiques chloroformes?

Rosace en tombale efflorescence
De la Basilique du Silence.

Tu persistes dans ton attitude,
Quand je suffoque de solitude!

Oui, oui, tu as la gorge bien faite;
Mais, si jamais je m'y allaite? . . .

Encore un soir, et mes berquinades
S'en iront rire à la débandade,

Traitant mon platonisme si digne
D'extase de pêcheur à la ligne![1]

Salve, Regina[2] *des Lys*! reine,
Je te veux percer de mes phalènes![3]

Pastimes

Ah! the Moon, the Moon obsesses me . . . D'you think there's a cure?
  Dead? Can't she be sleeping, drunk on cosmic chloroforms?
  Rose-window flowering like a tomb in the Basilica of Silence.
  You persist in your attitude, while I suffocate from solitude!
  Yes, yes, your bosom's shapely; but, if I never taste its milk? . . .
  One more evening, and my infantile books will go off laughing helterskelter,
  treating my so dignified Platonism as a poet's deluded rapture!
  Salve, Regina of the Lilies! Queen, I long to pierce you with my moths!

Je veux baiser ta patène[4] triste,
Plat veuf du chef de saint Jean-Baptiste!

Je veux trouver un *lied*![5] qui te touche
A te faire émigrer vers ma bouche!

– Mais, même plus de rimes à Lune . . .
Ah! quelle regrettable lacune!

Avis, je vous prie

Hélas! des Lunes, des Lunes,
Sur un petit air en bonne fortune . . .[1]
Hélas! de choses en choses
Sur la criarde corde des virtuoses! . . .

Hélas! agacer d'un lys
La violette d'Isis! . . .[2]
Hélas! m'esquinter, sans trêve, encore,
Mon encéphale anomaliflore[3]
En floraison de chair par guirlandes d'ennuis!
O Mort, et puis?

I want to kiss your sad paten, that salver widowed of St John the Baptist's head!
I want to find a *lied*! to touch your feelings, and make you emigrate towards my mouth!

– But there aren't even any more rhymes for 'Moon'! Ah! what a deplorable lacuna!

Please Permit Me to Announce

Alas! Moons, Moons, to a little love-lucky tune . . . Alas! from one thing to another on the virtuosi's screeching strings!

Alas! To tease with a lily Isis's violet! Alas! To ceaselessly wear out my anomaly-flowered encephalon flesh-blossoming by garlands of anxiety! O Death, and then what?

Mais! j'ai peur de la vie
Comme d'un mariage!
Oh! vrai, je n'ai pas l'âge
Pour ce beau mariage! . . .

Oh! j'ai été frappé de CETTE VIE A MOI,
L'autre dimanche, m'en allant par une plaine!
Oh! laissez-moi seulement reprendre haleine,
Et vous aurez un livre enfin de bonne foi.

En attendant, ayez pitié de ma misère!
Que je vous sois à tous un être bienvenu!
Et que je sois absous pour mon âme sincère,
Comme le fut Phryné⁴ pour son sincère nu.

But! I'm just as scared of life as of getting married! Oh! true, I'm not old enough
for this fine marriage! . . .
I was struck by THIS LIFE OF MINE, the other Sunday, as I crossed a plain!
Simply let me get my breath back, and at last you'll have a book written in good
faith.
In the meantime, take pity on my misery! May I be to all of you a welcome
person! And may I be absolved for my sincere soul, as Phryne was for her sincere
nakedness.

DES FLEURS DE BONNE VOLONTÉ[1]

Some Flowers of Good Will

Avertissement

Mon père (un dur par timidité)
Est mort avec un profil sévère;
J'avais presque pas connu ma mère,
Et donc vers vingt ans je suis resté.

Alors, j'ai fait d'la littérature,
Mais le Démon de la Vérité
Sifflotait tout l'temps à mes côtés:
«Pauvre! as-tu fini tes écritures . . .»

Or, pas le cœur de me marier,
Etant, moi, au fond, trop méprisable!
Et elles, pas assez intraitables!!
Mais tout l'temps là à s'extasier! . . .

Warning

My father (stern out of shyness) died with a grim profile; I'd hardly known my mother, and so I was left at twenty or so.

So then, I did a spot of writing; but the Demon of Truth was whistling all the time at my elbow: 'Poor fool! have you done scribbling . . .'

Now, having no heart to marry, being, myself, basically too contemptible! And they not intractable enough!! But all the while going into ecstasies!

C'est pourquoi je vivotte, vivotte,
Bonne girouette aux trent'-six saisons,
Trop nombreux pour dire oui ou non . . .
– Jeunes gens! que je vous serv' d'Ilote![1]

Mettons le doigt sur la plaie

Que le pur du bonheur m'est bien si je l'escompte! . . .
Ou ne le cueille qu'en refrains de souvenance! . . .
O rêve, ou jamais plus! Et fol je me balance
Au-dessus du Présent en Ariel[1] qui a honte.

Mais, le cru, quotidien, et trop voyant Présent!
Et qui vous met au pied du mur, et qui vous dit:
«A l'instant, ou bonsoir!» et ne fait pas crédit,
Et m'étourdit le cœur de ses airs suffisants!

This is why I just keep rubbing along, faithful weathercock to the umpteen seasons, too numerous to decide on yes or no. – Young folks! Let me serve as a dreadful example!

Let's Get Down to Brass Tacks

How the purest happiness delights me when I anticipate it! . . . or when I taste it only in memory's refrains! . . . O dream, or nevermore! And madly I dangle above the Present like a shamefaced Ariel.

But the crude, everyday, and too garish Present! Which corners you with your back to the wall, and says: 'This very moment, or else it's all over!' and won't take your word for it, and stuns my heart with its self-important swanking!

Tout vibrant de passé, tout pâle d'espérance,
Je fais signe au Présent: «Oh! sois plus diaphane!»
Mais il me bat la charge et mine mes organes!
Puis, le bateau: parti, j'ulule «Oh! recommence . . .»

Et lui seul est bien vrai! – mais je me mords la main
Plutôt! (je suis trop jeune . . . ou, trop agonisant . . .)
Ah! rien qu'un pont entre mon Cœur et le Présent!
O lourd Passé, combien ai-je encor de demains?

> O cœur aride
> Mais sempiterne,
> O ma citerne
> Des Danaïdes! . . .²

Maniaque

POLONIUS (aside): Though this be madness, yet there is method in't.

Eh oui que l'on en sait de simples,
Aux matins des villégiatures,
Foulant les prés! et dont la guimpe
A bien quelque âme pour doublure . . .

All trembling with the past, all pale with hope, I hint to the Present, 'Oh! be more transparent!' But he sounds the charge and undermines my organs! Then, the same old story: The moment I've left, I wail 'Oh! start again . . .'

And he alone is real and true! but I'd sooner bite my own hand! (I'm too young . . . or too close to death . . .) Ah! if only I had a bridge between my Heart and the Present! O heavy-loaded Past, how many tomorrows have I left?

O arid but sempiternal heart, O my water tank of Danaïds!

Too Pernickety

Oh yes one knows of simple ones on mornings at holiday resorts, treading the meadows! and whose bodices have some sort of soul for a lining . . .

Mais, chair de pêche, âme en rougeurs!
Chair de victime aux Pubertés,
Ames prêtes, d'un voyageur
Qui passe, prêtes à dater![1]

Et Protées[2] valseurs[3] sans vergogne!
Changeant de nom, de rôle (d'âme!)
Sœurs, mères, veuves, Antigones,[4]
Amantes! mais jamais ma Femme.

Des pudeurs devant l'Homme? . . . – et si
J'appelle, moi, ces falbalas,
La peur d'examens sans merci?
Et si je ne sors pas de là!

Romance

HAMLET: To a nunnery, go.

J'ai mille oiseaux de mer d'un gris pâle,
Qui nichent au haut de ma belle âme,
Ils en emplissent les tristes salles
De rythmes pris aux plus fines lames . . .[1]

But peach-complexion, blushing soul! the complexion of a victim of the Puberties, souls ready, with any passing traveller, ready to make it a red-letter date,

And shameless Proteuses, keeping men on tenterhooks! changing your names, your roles (your souls!), sisters, mothers, widows, Antigones, lovers! but never My Wife.

Demureness in Man's company? And if I call all these fallals, a fear of merciless analysis? And if I stick to that opinion!

Sentimental Ballad

I've a thousand pale grey sea-birds nesting on the cliffs of my high-minded soul, they fill its mournful halls with rhythms borrowed from waves with the sharpest edges . . .

Or, ils salissent tout de charognes,
Et aussi de coraux, de coquilles;
Puis volent en ronds fous, et se cognent
A mes probes lambris de famille . . .

Oiseaux pâles, oiseaux des sillages!
Quand la fiancée ouvrira la porte,
Faites un collier de coquillages
Et que l'odeur de charogn's soit forte! . . .

Qu'Elle dise: «Cette âme est bien forte
«Pour mon petit nez . . . – je me r'habille.[2]
«Mais ce beau collier? hein, je l'emporte?
«Il ne lui sert de rien, pauvre fille . . .»

Esthétique

Je fais la cour à ma Destinée;
Et demande: «Est-ce pour cette année?»

Je la prends par la douceur, en Sage,
Tout aux arts, au bon cœur, aux voyages . . .

Now they soil everything with carrion, and also with corals and shells; then they fly around in mad circles, and knock into my respectable family wainscots.

Pale birds, birds following the wakes of ships! When my betrothed opens the door, prepare a necklace of shells, and may the stink of carrion be strong!

Let Her say, 'Your soul's a bit strong for my dainty nose. I'll make myself scarce. But this fine necklace? Hey! may I take it?' – It'll be no use to her, poor lass!

Aesthetic Principles

I court my Destiny; and ask: 'Will it be this year?'

I approach her in all gentleness like a Sage, devoted to the arts, to kindheartedness, to journeys . . .

Et vais m'arlequinant des défroques
Des plus grands penseurs de chaque époque . . .

Et saigne! en jurant que je me blinde
Des rites végétatifs de l'Inde . . .

Et suis digne, allez! d'un mausolée
En pleine future Galilée!

De la meilleure grâce du monde,
Donc, j'attends que l'Amour me réponde . . .

Ah! tu sais que Nul ne se dérange,
Et que, ma foi, vouloir faire l'ange . . .

Je ferai l'ange! Oh! va, Destinée,
Ta nuit ne m'irait pas chiffonnée!

Passe! et grâce pour ma jobardise . . .
Mais, du moins, laisse que je te dise,

Nos livres bons, entends-tu, nos livres
Seuls, te font ces yeux fous de Survivre[1]

and go harlequining myself with cast-offs of the greatest thinkers of every period . . .

and I bleed! swearing that I armour myself with the vegetative rites of India . . .

And am worthy, do admit it!, of a mausoleum in the midst of the Galilee of the future!

With the best grace in the world, therefore, I'm waiting for Love to respond . . .

Do you know – Nobody takes the trouble! and, my goodness, pretending to be good as gold . . .

I'll be good as gold! Oh! get away, Destiny, your night wouldn't suit me if it were rumpled!

So much for that! and forgive my gullibility . . . but at least let me tell you

Our books of quality, do you hear, it's only our books which make eyes at you, mad for Survival

Qui vers ta Matrice après déchaînent
Les héros du viol et du sans-gêne.[2]

Adieu. Noble et lent, vais me remettre
A la culture des Belles-Lettres.

Dimanches

O Dimanches bannis
De l'infini
Au delà du microscope et du téléscope,
Seuil nuptial où la chair s'affale en syncope . . .

Dimanches citoyens
Bien quotidiens
De cette école à vieux cancans, la vieille Europe,
Où l'on tourne, s'en tricotant des amours myopes . . .

which towards your Womb, later, unleash the heroes of rape and of 'I don't-give-a-damn.'

Farewell. Noble and dignified, I shall return to the grindstone of cultivating Great Literature.

Sundays

O Sundays exiled from the infinite, beyond microscope and telescope, marriage threshold where the body sinks in a swoon . . .

Sundays, who are everyday citizens of Europe, this school of old tittle-tattle, where we go round and round, knitting ourselves short-sighted loves . . .

Oh! tout Lois sans appel,
Je sais, ce Ciel,
Et non un brave toit de famille, un bon dôme
Où s'en viennent mourir, très-appréciés, nos psaumes!

C'est fort beau comme fond
A certains fronts,
Des Lois! et pas de plus bleue matière à diplômes . . .[1]
– Mais, c'est pas les Lois qui fait le bonheur, hein l'Homme?

Dimanches

Oh! ce piano, ce cher piano,
Qui jamais, jamais ne s'arrête,
Oh! ce piano qui geint là-haut
Et qui s'entête sur ma tête!

Ce sont de sinistres polkas,
Et des romances pour concierge,[1]
Des exercices délicats,
Et *La Prière d'une vierge*!

Oh! I know the Sky is all Laws from which there's no appeal, and it's not a strong family roof, a kindly dome where our psalms come to die, much applauded!

Laws! They're very fine as a background for certain foreheads, and there's no subject more apt for doctoral theses . . . But it's not Laws that make you happy, eh, Mankind?

Sundays

Oh! that piano, that dear piano, which never never stops, Oh! that piano moaning away up there, obstinately ringing in my head!

There are sinister polkas, romances for caretakers, delicate exercises, and *A Virgin's Prayer*!

Fuir? où aller, par ce printemps?
Dehors, dimanche, rien à faire . . .
Et rien à fair' non plus dedans . . .
Oh! rien à faire sur la Terre! . . .

Ohé, jeune fille au piano!
Je sais que vous n'avez point d'âme!
Puis pas donner dans le panneau
De la nostalgie de vos gammes . . .

Fatals bouquets du Souvenir,
Folles légendes décaties,
Assez! assez! vous vois venir,
Et mon âme est bientôt partie . . .

Vrai, un Dimanche sous ciel gris,
Et je ne fais plus rien qui vaille,
Et le moindre orgu' de Barbari
(Le pauvre!) m'empoigne aux entrailles!

Et alors, je me sens trop fou!
Marié, je tuerais la bouche
De ma mie! et, à deux genoux,
Je lui dirais ces mots bien louches:

Flee? Where shall I go, on this spring day? Out of doors, on Sunday, nothing to do . . . and nothing to do indoors either . . . Oh! nothing to do on Earth! . . .

Hey, young girl at the piano! I know you have no soul! So I mustn't fall into the trap of your nostalgic scales . . .

Fatal bouquets of Memory, mad decrepit legends, Enough! Enough! I can see what you're getting at, and my soul soon gets quite carried away . . .

True, a Sunday under a grey sky, and I'm doing nothing worthwhile, and the least barrel organ (poor thing!) grabs me by the guts!

And then I feel too wild! Married, I'd bruise my darling's mouth! and on my knees I'd speak these disreputable words:

«Mon cœur est trop, ah trop central!
«Et toi, tu n'es que chair humaine;
«Tu ne vas donc pas trouver mal
«Que je te fasse de la peine!»

Dimanches

HAMLET: Have you a daughter?
POLONIUS: I have, my lord.
HAMLET: Let her not walk in the sun: conception is a
    blessing; but not as your daughter may conceive.

Le ciel pleut sans but, sans que rien l'émeuve,
Il pleut, il pleut, bergère![1] sur le fleuve . . .

Le fleuve a son repos dominical;
Pas un chaland, en amont, en aval.

Les Vêpres carillonnent sur la ville.
Les berges sont désertes, sans idylles.

Passe un pensionnat (ô pauvres chairs!)
Plusieurs ont déjà leurs manchons d'hiver.

'My heart is too, ah too central! And you are only human flesh; so you're not going to object to me hurting your feelings!'

Sundays

The sky rains pointlessly, nothing affects it, it's raining, raining, shepherdess, on the river . . . The river's taking its Sunday rest; Not a barge, up or down stream.

The Vespers chime out over the town, the riverbanks are deserted, without idylls.

There passes a boarding school (poor creatures!) Several are already wearing their winter muffs.

Une qui n'a ni manchon, ni fourrures
Fait, tout en gris, une pauvre figure.

Et la voilà qui s'échappe des rangs,
Et court? ô mon Dieu, qu'est-ce qu'il lui prend?

Et elle va se jeter dans le fleuve.
Pas un batelier, pas un chien Terr'-Neuve.

Le crépuscule vient; le petit port
Allume ses feux. (Ah! connu, l'décor!).

La pluie continue à mouiller le fleuve,
Le ciel pleut sans but, sans que rien l'émeuve.

One, who has neither muff nor furs looks, all in grey, so wretched.

And look at her running out of the crocodile line, running! Oh goodness! What's come over her?

And she goes and throws herself into the river. No boatman, no Newfoundland dog.

Twilight falls; the little port lights its fires. (Yes, we all know the stage-setting!)

The rain continues to soak the river, the sky is raining pointlessly, nothing touches its feelings.

Cythère[1]

Quel lys sut ombrager ma sieste?
C'était (ah ne sais plus comme!) au bois trop sacré
Où fleurir n'est pas un secret.
Et j'étais fui comme la peste.
«Je ne suis pas une âme leste!»
Ai-je dit alors, et leurs chœurs m'ont chanté: «Reste!»

Et la plus grande, oh! si mienne! m'a expliqué
La floraison sans commentaires
De cette hermétique Cythère
Au sein des mers comme un bosquet,
Et comment quelques couples vraiment distingués
Un soir ici ont débarqué . . .

Non la nuit sait pas de pelouses,
D'un velours bleu plus brave que ses lents vallons!

Plus invitant au: dévalons!
Et déjoueur des airs d'épouse!
Et qui telle une chair jalouse,
En ses accrocs plus éperdument se recouse! . . .

Cythera

What lily knew so well how to shade my siesta? It was (ah I no longer know how!) in the too sacred wood where flowering is no secret. And people fled me like the plague. 'I'm not a lewd soul!' I said then, and their choirs chanted: 'Stay!'

And the tallest one, oh! so mine! explained to me the blossoming (untouched by slander) of this hermetic Cythera, like a grove in the bosom of the seas, and how several really refined couples disembarked here one evening . . .

No, the night knows no lawn of a finer blue velvet than its gentle valleys! more inviting to 'Let's run down the slope!' or more thwarting of wifely attitudes! or, like a jealous body, more frantic to sew up its rents.

Et la faune et la flore étant comme ça vient,
    On va comme ça vient; des roses
    Les sens, des floraisons les poses,
    Nul souci du tien et du mien;
Quant à des classements en chrétiens et païens,
    Ni le climat ni les moyens.

    Oui, fleurs de vies en confidences,
Mains oisives dans les toisons[2] aux gros midis,
    Tatouages des concettis;[3]
    L'un mimant d'inédites danses
    L'autre sur la piste d'essences . . .
– Eh quoi? Nouveau-venu, vos larmes recommencent!

– Réveil meurtri, je m'en irai je sais bien où;
    Un terrain vague, des clôtures,
    Un âne plein de foi pâture
    Des talons perdus sans dégoût,
Et brait vers moi (me sachant aussi rosse et doux)
    Que je desserre son licou.

And the flora and fauna being just as they come, one takes them as they come; of roses are the senses, of blossoms are the postures, no fuss about thine and mine; as for classification into Christians and Pagans, there's neither the climate nor the wherewithal.

Yes, the very flower of lives in private whispers, idle hands in the honeybush at high noon, tattooings of *concetti*, one of us miming hyper-inventive dances, another on the scent of essences . . . 'But what on earth? New arrival, you're starting to weep again!'

– Bruised awakening. I'll depart I know just where; a no man's land, some fences, a trustful donkey sniffing without disgust at a pair of lost high heels, who brays to me (knowing I'm good-for-nothing and gentle like himself) to undo his halter.

Dimanches

Je m'ennuie, natal! je m'ennuie,
  Sans cause bien appréciable,
Que bloqué par les boues, les dimanches, les pluies,
En d'humides tabacs ne valant pas le diable.

Hé là-bas, le prêtre sans messes![1]
  Ohé, mes petits sens hybrides! . . .
Et je bats mon rappel! et j'ulule en détresse,
Devant ce Moi, tonneau d'Ixion des Danaïdes.[2]

Oh! m'en aller, me croyant libre,
  Désattelé des bibliothèques,
Avec tous ces passants cuvant en équilibre
Leurs cognacs d'Absolu, leurs pâtés d'Intrinsèque! . . .

Messieurs, que roulerais tranquille,
  Si j'avais au moins ma formule,
Ma formule en pilules dorées, par ces villes
Que vont pavant mes jobardises d'incrédule! . . .

Sundays

Earth-born, I'm bored! I'm bored, for no apparent reason, except locked in by mires and Sundays and rains and wet tobaccos not worth the devil.

Hey you down there, you priest without masses! Heyup! my little hybrid senses! . . . And I call myself to arms! and howl in grief at What I Am, this Ixion's barrel of the Danaids.

Oh! to be off, believing myself free, unharnessed from libraries, with all those passers-by fermenting on an even keel their brandies of Absolute, their pâtés of Intrinsic! . . .

Gentlemen, how happily I'd roll along if I had at least my formula, my formula for sugaring the pill, through these towns which go paving my gullibilities with disbelief! . . .

    (Comment lui dire: «Je vous aime»?
    Je me connais si peu moi-même).
Ah! quel sort! Ah! pour sûr, la tâche qui m'incombe
M'aura sensiblement rapproché de la tombe.

Le bon apôtre

Nous avons beau baver nos plus fières salives,
Leurs yeux sont tout! Ils rêvent d'aumônes furtives!

O chairs de sœurs, ciboires[1] de bonheur! On peut
Blaguer, la paire est là; comme un et un font deux.

– Mais ces yeux, plus on va, se fardent de mystère!
– Eh bien, travaillons à les ramener sur Terre!

– Ah! la chasteté n'est en fleur qu'en souvenir!
– Mais ceux qui l'ont cueillie en renaissent martyrs!

Martyres mutuels! de frère à sœur sans Père![2]
Comment ne voit-on pas que c'est là notre Terre?

(How to tell her: 'I love you'? I know myself so little.) Ah! what a fate! Certainly the task I face will have brought me appreciably closer to the grave.

The Sanctimonious Fraud

It's no use drooling out our proudest salivas, their eyes are everything! They dream of furtive alms-giving!

O sister flesh, ciboria of happiness! You may joke about it, but there it is: the pair; just as one and one make two.

'But those eyes, the nearer you get, doll themselves up in mystery!' – 'All right then, let's work to bring them down to Earth!'

'Ah! chastity blossoms only in recollection!' – 'But those who've plucked it are reborn as martyrs!'

Mutual martyrdoms! of brother by sister without Father! How can people fail to see that this is how our World is?

Et qu'il n'y a que ça! que le reste est impôts
Dont nous n'avons pas même à chercher l'à-propos!

Il faut répéter ces choses! Il faut qu'on tette
Ces choses! jusqu'à ce que la Terre se mette,

Voyant enfin que Tout vivotte sans Témoin,
A vivre aussi pour Elle, et dans son petit coin!

Et c'est bien dans ce sens, moi, qu'au lieu de me taire,
Je persiste à narrer mes petites affaires.

Petites misères d'octobre

Octobre m'a toujours fiché dans la détresse;
Les Usines, cent goulots fumant vers les ciels . . .
                Les poulardes s'engraissent
                Pour Noël.

and that that is all there is! that the rest is tax-paying, whose aptness we're not supposed even to question!

We must repeat these things! We must suckle on these things! until the Earth gets down to the job

(seeing at last that everything struggles along without a Witness) of living Its Own life, in its own little nook!

And this is entirely the reason why, instead of shutting up, I persist in narrating my own trivial affairs.

Small October Miseries

October has always locked me in distress: Factories, a hundred gullets smoking at the skies . . . pullets, fattening for Christmas.

Oh! qu'alors, tout bramant vers d'albes atavismes,
Je fonds mille Icebergs vers les septentrions
      D'effarants mysticismes
         Des Sions! . . .

Car les seins distingués se font toujours plus rares;
Le légitime est tout, mais à qui bon ma cour?
      De qui bénir mes Lares[1]
         Pour toujours?

Je ferai mes oraisons aux Premières Neiges;
Et je crierai au Vent: «Et toi aussi, forçat!»
      Et rien ne vous allège
         Comme ça.

(Avec la neige tombe une miséricorde
D'agonie; on a vu des gens aux cœurs de cuir
      Et méritant la corde
         S'en languir.)

So then, belling towards white atavisms, I melt a thousand Icebergs towards the northern poles of the Zions with their terrifying mysticisms!

For breasts of true refinement grow ever scarcer; lawful wedlock is everything, but to whom is my courtship any good? With whom can I bless my Lares for ever?

I shall utter my prayers to the First Snows; and cry to the Wind, 'You too are a galley slave!' There's nothing like it for relieving the pain.

(With the snow there falls a dying breath's compassion; one has seen people with leathern hearts, who deserve hanging, pining away because of it.)

Mais vrai, s'écarteler les lobes, jeu de dupe . . .
Rien, partout, des saisons et des arts et des dieux,
      Ne vaut deux sous de jupe,
         Deux sous d'yeux.

Donc, petite, deux sous de jupe en œillet tiède,
Et deux sous de regards, et tout ce qui s'ensuit . . .
      Car il n'est qu'un remède
         A l'ennui.

Gare au bord de la mer

Kersœr. Côtes du Danemarck.
    Aube du 1er janvier 1886.

On ne voyait pas la mer, par ce temps d'embruns,
Mais on l'entendait maudire son existence:
«Oh! beuglait-elle, qu'il fût seulement Quelqu'Un!» . . .
Et elle vous brisait maint bateau pas-de-chance.

    But it's true, torturing one's cerebral lobes is a mug's game . . . Nothing anywhere, of seasons, arts or gods, is worth two ha'p'orth of skirt, two ha'p'orth of eyes.
    So, little one, two ha'p'orth of skirt made of warm carnation, and two ha'p'orth of glances, and everything that ensues . . . for there's only one cure for world-weariness.

Station by the Seaside

Kersoer, Danish coast.
Dawn on 1 January 1886.

You couldn't see the sea, in that weather full of spray, but you could hear it cursing its existence: 'Oh!' it bellowed, 'if only there were Someone!' . . . And it smashed up many an out-of-luck boat.

Et, ne pouvant mordre le steamer, les autans
Mettaient nos beaux panaches de fumée en loques
Et l'Homme renvoyait ses comptes à des temps
Plus clairs, et sifflotait: «Cet Univers se moque,

«Il raille! Et qu'il me dise où l'on voit Mon Pareil!
«Allez, déroulez vos parades sidérales,
«Messieurs! Un temps viendra que l'Homme, fou d'éveil,
«Fera pour les Pays Terre-à-Terre ses malles!

«Il crut à l'Idéal! Ah! milieux détraquants[1]
«Et bazars d'oripeaux! Si c'était à refaire,
«Chers madrépores,[2] comme on ficherait le camp
«Chez vous! Oh! même vers la Période Glaciaire! . . .

«Mais l'Infini est là, gare de trains ratés,
«Où les gens, aveuglés de signaux, s'apitoient
«Sur le sanglot des convois, et vont se hâter
«Tout à l'heure! et crever en travers de la voie . . .

And since they couldn't bite the steamer, the storm-winds tore our beautiful plumes of smoke to shreds, and Man postponed his financial calculations to finer weather, and whistled: This Universe doesn't care, it's scoffing!

Just let it tell me where it can find Another One Like Me! Come, unroll your parades of stars, gentlemen! A time will come when Man, mad to wake up, will pack his bags for the Down-to-Earth Countries!

Man used to trust in the Ideal! Ah! what disconcerting company, and what bazaars of tawdry frippery! If we could start all over again, how quickly, O dear madrepores, we'd rush back over to your place! Oh! even back to the Ice Age!

But the Infinite is there, that station for missed trains, where the inhabitants, blinded by signals, are moved to pity over the sobbing freight trains, and are going to hurry – in a moment! – and peg out across the tracks . . .

«– Un fin sourire (tel ce triangle d'oiseaux
«D'exil sur ce ciel gris!) peut traverser mes heures;
«Je dirai: passe, oh! va, ne fais pas de vieux os
«Par ici, mais vide au plus tôt cette demeure . . .»

Car la vie est partout la même. On ne sait rien!
Mais c'est la Gare! et faut chauffer qui pour les fêtes
Futures, qui pour les soi-disant temps anciens.
Oh, file ton rouet, et prie et reste honnête.

Impossibilité de l'infini en hosties

O lait divin! potion assurément cordiale
À vomir les gamelles de nos aujourd'huis!
Quel bon docteur saura décrocher ta timbale
Pour la poser sur ma simple table de nuit,
               Un soir, sans bruit?

'Occasionally a sarcastic smile (like that triangle of exiled birds flying across the grey sky!) accompanies my hours. I'll say: "Move on, oh indeed! don't make old bones in this place, but vacate these lodgings as quick as you can . . ."'

For life is everywhere the same. We know nothing! But here we are in the Railway Station! and must keep it warm, some for future celebrations, some for the so-called olden days. Oh turn your spinning-wheel, and pray, and do what's right.

The Impossibility of Tasting the Infinite in Wafers

O divine milk! O truly tonic potion to vomit out the mess tins of our todays! What kind doctor will know how to unhook your tin mug and put it on my simple bedside table, one evening, noiselessly?

J'ai appris, et tout comme autant de riches langues,
Les philosophies et les successives croix;
Mais pour mener ma vie au Saint-Graal[1] sans gangue,
Nulle n'a su le mot, le Sésame-ouvre-toi,
        Clef de l'endroit.

Oui, dilapidé ma jeunesse et des bougies
A regalvaniser le fond si enfantin
De nos plus immémoriales liturgies,
Et perdu à ce jeu de purs et sûrs instincts,
        Tout mon latin.

L'Infini est à nos portes! à nos fenêtres!
Ouvre, et vois ces Nuits Loin, et tout le Temps avec! . . .
Qu'il nous étouffe donc! puisqu'il ne saurait être
En une hostie, une hostie pour nos sales becs,
        Ah! si à sec! . . .

I've learnt, just like so many rich languages, philosophies and the stations of the cross; but to lead my life to the unadulterated Holy Grail, nobody has known the password, the Open-Sesame, the key to the place.

Yes, I've squandered my youth and many candles trying to regalvanize the childlike essence of our most immemorial rites, and, through playing this game of pure, sure instincts, I no longer know if I'm on my head or my heels.

The Infinite is at our doors! at our windows! Open, and see those Far-Off Nights and all Time with them! . . . Let it strangle us then! since it couldn't be in a holy wafer, a holy wafer for our dirty gobs which are, Ah! so parched! . . .

Ballade

OPHELIA: You are merry, my lord.
HAMLET: Who, I?
OPHELIA: Ay, my lord.
HAMLET: O God, your only jig-maker.
  What should a man do but be merry?

Oyez,[1] au physique comme au moral,
Ne suis qu'une colonie de cellules
De raccroc; et ce sieur que j'intitule
Moi, n'est, dit-on, qu'un polypier fatal!

De mon cœur un tel, à ma chair védique,[2]
Comme de mes orteils à mes cheveux,
Va-et-vient de cellules sans aveu,
Rien de bien solvable et rien d'authentique.

Quand j'organise une descente en Moi,
J'en conviens, je trouve là, attablée,
Une société un peu bien mêlée,
Et que je n'ai point vue à mes octrois.

Ballade

Oyez! Physically as well as spiritually, I am nothing but a colony of cells created by fluke; and this noble lord I entitle Myself, is merely, it is said, a fate-caused polyp.

From my Joe Bloggs heart to my Vedic flesh, as from my toes to my hair, a coming-and-going of vagrant cells, nothing very creditworthy and nothing authentic.

When I go pot- holing into Myself, I confess I find there, sitting round the table, a rather mixed company, whom I didn't see when I shared out the property rights.

Une chair bêtement staminifère,
Un cœur illusoirement pistillé,
Sauf certains jours, sans foi, ni loi, ni clé,
Où c'est précisément tout le contraire.

Allez, c'est bon. Mon fatal polypier
A distingué certaine polypière;
Son monde n'est pas trop mêlé, j'espère . . .
Deux yeux café, voilà tous ses papiers.

Petites Misères d'hiver

Vers les libellules
D'un crêpe si blanc des baisers
Qui frémissent de se poser,
Venus de si loin, sur leurs bouts cicatrisés,
Ces seins, déjà fondants, ondulent
D'un air somnambule . . .

A flesh which is stupidly stamen-bearing, a heart delusively wearing pistils, except on certain faithless, lawless, keyless evenings, when it's exactly the opposite.

Hey, here we go. My destined polyp has recognized a certain polypess; her company is not too mixed, I hope . . . Two coffee-coloured eyes, that's her only documentation.

Small Miseries of Winter

Towards the dragonflies of a crêpe so white, kisses which, come from so far, quiver to settle on their tips healed from suffering, these breasts, already melting, undulate as if sleepwalking . . .

Et cet air enlise
Dans le défoncé des divans
Rembourrés d'eiders dissolvants
Le Cygne[1] du Saint-Graal, qui rame en avant!
Mais plus pâle qu'une banquise
Qu'Avril dépayse . . .

Puis, ça vous réclame,
Avec des moues d'enfant goulu,
Du romanesque à l'absolu,
Mille Pôles plus loin que tout ce qu'on a lu! . . .
Laissez, laissez, le Cygne, ô Femme!
Qu'il glisse, qu'il rame,

Oh! que, d'une haleine,
Il monte, séchant vos crachats,
Au Saint-Graal des blancs pachas[2]
Et n'en revienne qu'avec un plan de rachat
Pour sa petite sœur humaine
Qui fait tant de peine . . .

And, in the bulginess of divans stuffed with enervating eiderdown, this air bogs down the Swan of the Holy Grail as he sculls onward! but paler than an ice-floe, exiled by April . . .

Then, making faces like a greedy child, the creature hypes up romanticism at its most absolute, a thousand Far Poles farther than anything one's ever read! Leave the Swan be, leave him be, O Woman! May he glide, may he scull,

And with a single breath may he climb, parching your spittle, to the Holy Grail the white nabobs, and never return till he has a redemption plan for his little human sister for whom we feel so sorry . . .

Le brave, brave automne!

Quand reviendra l'automne,
Cette saison si triste,
Je vais m'la passer bonne,
Au point de vue artiste.

Car le vent, je l'connais,
Il est de mes amis!
Depuis que je suis né
Il fait que j'en gémis . . .

Et je connais la neige,
Autant que ma chair même,
Son froment me protège
Contre les chairs que j'aime . . .

Et comme je comprends
Que l'automnal soleil
Ne m'a l'air si souffrant
Qu'à titre de conseil! . . .

The Oh So Wonderful Autumn!

When autumn comes round again, that season so dreary, I'm going to have an easy time from the artistic point of view.

For the wind, I know him, he's one of my friends! ever since I was born he's kept me groaning . . .

And I know the snow as well as I know my own body, its wheaten flour protects me against the bodies I love . . .

And how well I understand that the autumnal sun looks so sick only so as to advise me! . . .

Puis rien ne saurait faire
Que mon spleen ne chemine
Sous les spleens insulaires[1]
Des petites pluies fines . . .

Ah! l'automne est à moi,
Et moi je suis à lui,
Comme tout à «pourquoi?»
Et ce monde à «et puis?»

Quand reviendra l'automne,
Cette saison si triste,
Je vais m'la passer bonne
Au point de vue artiste.

Petites misères d'août

Oh! quelle nuit d'étoiles, quelles saturnales![1]
            Oh! mais des galas inconnus
                Dans les annales
                    Sidérales!
        Bref, un Ciel absolument nu!

Besides nothing could prevent my gloom following its course under the individual glooms of the fine drizzle . . .

Ah! autumn is mine, and I am autumn's, just as everything belongs to 'Why?' and this world belongs to 'So what?'

When autumn comes round again, that season so dreary, I'm going to have an easy time from the artistic point of view.

Small August Miseries

Ah! what a night of stars, what Saturnalias! Oh! but jubilees unknown in the annals of the stars! In short, a Sky that's absolutely naked!

O Loi du Rythme sans appel!
Que le moindre Astre certifie
Par son humble chorégraphie,
Mais nul spectateur éternel.

Ah! la Terre humanitaire
N'en est pas moins terre-à-terre!
Au contraire.

La Terre, elle est ronde
Comme un pot-au-feu,
C'est un bien pauv' monde
Dans l'Infini bleu.

Cinq sens seulement, cinq ressorts pour nos essors . . .
Ah! ce n'est pas un sort!
Quand donc nos cœurs s'en iront-ils en huit ressorts! . . .[2]

Oh! le jour, quelle turne!
J'en suis tout taciturne.
Oh! ces nuits sur les toits!
Je finirai bien par y prendre froid.

O inescapable Law of Rhythm! which the most humble Star confirms in its humble choreography – but no eternal spectator.

Ah! the humanitarian Earth does not thereby become less down-to-earth! On the contrary.

The Earth is round like a stewpot, it's a poor little world in the blue Infinite.

Five senses only, five springs for our soaring longings? Ah! this is no kind of life! When will our hearts fly off in a coach and four?

Oh! daytime, what a dump! It makes me all taciturn. Oh these nights on the tiles! I'll end up catching cold.

Tiens, la Terre,
Va te faire
Très lan-laire!

— Hé! pas choisi
D'y naître, et hommes!
Mais nous y sommes,
Tenons-nous-y.

La pauvre Terre, elle est si bonne! . . .
Oh! désormais je m'y cramponne
De tous mes bonheurs d'autochtone.

Tu te pâmes, moi je me vautre.
Consolons-nous les uns les autres.

Hey, Earth, go and get yourself taradiddled!
 — Hey, we didn't choose to be born here, and not as human beings either! But here we are, let's hold on for dear life!
Poor old Earth, she's so kind! . . . Oh from now on I'll cling to her with all my earth-born happinesses.
You swoon, I wallow. Let's console each other.

Dimanches

HAMLET: I have heard of your paintings too,
well enough. God hath given you one face,
and you make yourselves another; you jig,
you amble, and you lisp, and you nickname
God's creatures and make your wantonness
your ignorance. Go to; I'll no more on't; it
hath made me mad. To a nunnery, go.

N'achevez pas la ritournelle,
En prêtant au piano vos ailes,
O mad'moiselle du premier.
Ça me rappelle l'Hippodrome,
Où cet air cinglait un pauvre homme
Déguisé en clown printanier.

Sa perruque arborait des roses,
Mais, en son masque de chlorose,[1]
Le trèfle noir manquait de nez!
Il jonglait avec des cœurs rouges,
Mais sa valse trinquait aux bouges
Où se font les enfants mort-nés.

Sundays

Break off the refrain, as you lend the piano your wings, O young lady of the first-floor flat. It reminds me of the Hippodrome where that tune lashed a poor man disguised as a springtime clown.

His wig sported roses, but, in his mask of chlorosis, the black club hadn't a nose for things. He juggled with red hearts, but his waltz drank toasts in the hovels where still-born babies are made.

Et cette valse, ô mad'moiselle,
Vous dit les Roland,[2] les dentelles
Du bal qui vous attend ce soir!
– Ah! te pousser par tes épaules
Décolletées, vers de durs pôles
Où je connais un abattoir!

Là, là, je te ferai la honte!
Et je te demanderai compte
De ce corset cambrant tes reins,
De ta tournure et des frisures
Achalandant contre nature
Ton front et ton arrière-train.[3]

Je te crierai: «Nous sommes frères!
«Alors, vêts-toi à ma manière,
«Ma manière ne trompe pas;
«Et perds ce dandinement louche
«D'animal lesté de ses couches,
«Et galopant par les haras!»

And that waltz, Mademoiselle, speaks to you of Rolands and of the lace you'll wear at the ball which awaits you this evening! – Ah! to push you by your two bare shoulders, towards the hard poles where I know of an abattoir!

There, there I'll shame you! And shall call you to account for that corset curving your haunches, your get-up and the curls unnaturally adorning your forehead and your hindquarters.

I'll cry to you, 'We're brothers! So dress my way! My way doesn't deceive; and get rid of that indecent hip-swagger of an animal ballasted with childbirth, and galloping through the stud-farms!

Oh! vivre uniment autochtones
Sur cette terre (où nous cantonne
Après tout notre être tel quel!)
Et sans préférer, l'âme aigrie,
Aux vers luisants de nos prairies
Les lucioles des prés du ciel;

Et sans plus sangloter aux heures
De lendemains, vers des demeures
Dont nous nous sacrons les élus.
Ah! que je vous dis, autochtones!
Tant la vie à terre elle est bonne,
Quand on n'en demande pas plus.

L'Aurore-promise

Vois, les Steppes stellaires
Se dissolvent à l'aube . . .
La lune est la dernière
A s'effacer, badaude.

Oh! to live harmoniously belonging to this earth (where after all our nature unceremoniously billets us) and not to prefer, with bitterness in one's soul, the fireflies of the fields of heaven to the glow-worms of our meadows;

And without grieving for tomorrows' hours, for dwellings of which we consecrate ourselves the chosen ones. Ah! as I say, earth-born! Life down-to-earth is so good, when one asks for nothing more.

The Affianced Dawn

See, the stellar Steppes dissolve at dawn . . . the moon is the last to vanish, snooper that she is.

Oh! que les cieux sont loin, et tout! Rien ne prévaut!
Contre cet infini; c'est toujours trop nouveau! . . .

> Et vrai, c'est sans limites! . . .
> T'en fais-tu une idée,
> O jeune Sulamite[1]
> Vers l'aurore accoudée?

L'Infini à jamais! comprends-tu bien cela!
Et qu'autant que ta chair existe un au-delà?

> Non; ce sujet t'assomme.
> Ton Infini; ta sphère,
> C'est le regard de l'Homme,
> Patron de cette Terre.

Il est le Fécondeur, le Galant Chevalier
De tes couches, la Providence du Foyer!

> Tes yeux baisent Sa Poigne,[2]
> Tu ne te sens pas seule!
> Mais lui bat la campagne
> Du ciel, où nul n'accueille! . . .

Oh how far off the skies are, and all that! Nothing prevails against this infinity; it's always far too new!

And true, it's limitless! Have you any notion of it, young Shulamite, leaning on your elbows, gazing at the dawn?

The Infinite for ever! can you take that in? And how a beyond exists just as much as your body does?

No: this subject bores you rigid. Your Infinite – your sphere – is the admiration of the Male, who's boss of this Earth.

He's the Fecundator, the Gallant Knight of your childbirths, the Providence of the Home!

Your eyes embrace His Grip, you don't feel lonely! But he reconnoitres the Sky, where nothing offers him hospitality!

Nulle Poigne vers lui, il a tout sur le dos;
Il est seul; l'Infini reste sourd comme un pot.

> O fille de la Terre,
> Ton dieu est dans ta couche!
> Mais lui a dû s'en faire,
> Et si loin de sa bouche! . . .[3]

Il s'est fait de bons dieux, consolateurs des morts,
Et supportait ainsi tant bien que mal son sort,

> Mais bientôt, son idée,
> Tu l'as prise, jalouse!
> Et l'as accommodée
> Au culte de l'Épouse!

Et le Déva[4] d'antan, Bon Cœur de l'Infini
Est là . . . – pour que ton lit nuptial soit béni!

> Avec tes accessoires,
> Ce n'est plus qu'une annexe
> Du Tout-Conservatoire
> Où s'apprête Ton Sexe.

No Grip extended towards him, everything's on his shoulders; he's alone; the Infinite stays as deaf as a doorpost.

O daughter of Earth, your god is in your marriage bed! But he has had to go to lots of trouble, and so far from her [pretty] mouth!

He has made himself kind gods, comforters of the dead, and so endured his lot as best he may,

but soon you stole his idea, jealous woman! and adapted it to the cult of the Wife!

And the Deva of yesteryear, the Kind Heart of the Infinite is there . . . to bless your marriage bed!

With your equipment, it's no longer any more than an annex of the All-Conservatory where Your Sex does its training.

Et ces autels bâtis de nos terreurs des cieux
Sont des comptoirs où tu nous marchandes tes yeux!

> Les dieux s'en vont. Leur père
> S'en meurt. – O Jeune Femme,
> Refais-nous une Terre
> Selon ton corps sans âme!

Ouvre-nous tout Ton Sexe! et, sitôt, l'Au-delà
Nous est nul! Ouvre, dis? tu nous dois bien cela . . .

Dimanches

J'aurai passé ma vie à faillir m'embarquer
> Dans de bien funestes histoires,
> Pour l'amour de mon cœur de Gloire! . . .[1]
> – Oh! qu'ils sont chers, les trains manqués
> Où j'ai passé ma vie à faillir m'embarquer! . . .

And those altars built out of our dread of the heavens are the cash-desks where you haggle with us over the price of your eyes!

The gods are leaving us. Their father is dying. – O Young Woman, make us a new Earth according to your soulless body!

Open to us Your Sex! and at once, the Beyond is nothing to us! Open, say! you owe us that at least!

Sundays

I'll have spent my life nearly embarking on disastrous entanglements for my heart's love of Glory! . . . Oh! how I cherish them, the missed trains on which I've spent my life nearly embarking!

Mon cœur est vieux d'un tas de lettres déchirées,
      Oh! Répertoire en un cercueil
      Dont la Poste porte le deuil! . . .
      – Oh! ces veilles d'échauffourées
Où mon cœur s'entraînait par lettres déchirées! . . .

Tout n'est pas dit encor, et mon sort est bien vert.
      O Poste, automatique Poste,
      O yeux passants fous d'holocaustes,[2]
      Oh! qu'ils sont là, vos airs ouverts! . . .
Oh! comme vous guettez mon destin encor vert!

      (Une, pourtant, je me rappelle,
          Aux yeux grandioses
          Comme des roses,
          Et puis si belle! . . .
          Sans nulle pose.
Une voix me criait: «C'est elle! Je le sens;
«Et puis, elle te trouve si intéressant!»
– Ah! que n'ai-je prêté l'oreille à ses accents! . . .

My heart is aged by a pile of torn-up letters, Oh! portfolio in a coffin whose mourning black is worn by the Post! – Oh! those eves of angry scenes for which my heart practised by tearing up letters!

All is not yet said, and my destiny is quite green. O Post, automatic Post, O passing eyes mad with holocausts, Oh! how present it is, your frank and open look! . . . Oh! how closely you watch my still green destiny!

(One, however, I remember, with eyes as awe-inspiring as roses, and besides she was so beautiful! . . . and without affectation. A voice cried to me: 'It is she! I sense it; besides, she finds you so interesting!' Ah! why didn't I lend an ear to its words! . . .)

La vie qu'elles me font mener

Pas moi, despotiques Vénus
Offrant sur fond d'or le Lotus
Du Mal,[1] coiffées à la Titus![2]
Pas moi, Circées[3]
Aux yeux en grand deuil violet comme des pensées!
Pas moi, binious
Des Papesses[4] des blancs Champs-Élysées[5] des fous,
Qui vous relayez de musiques
Par le calvaire de techniques
Des sacrilèges domestiques!

Le mal m'est trop! tant que l'Amour
S'échange par le temps qui court.
Simple et sans foi comme un bonjour,
Des jamais franches
A celles dont le Sort vient le poing sur la hanche,
Et que s'éteint

The Life They Make Me Lead

It's not my sort of thing, despotic Venuses offering on a golden background the Lotus of Evil, and their hair done in Titus fashion! Not my sort of thing, Circes with your eyes in full mourning, as violet as pansies! Not my sort of thing, bagpipes of the Popesses of the madmen's white Elysian Fields, who (with different sorts of music, through the calvary of techniques) pass to and fro among yourselves those domestic sacrileges!

It hurts me too much that Love is exchanged the way it is these days. Simple and faithless as a 'hello', from those who are never straight to those whose Fate comes with arms akimbo;

La Rosace du Temple,[6] à voir, dans le satin,
     Ces sexes livrés à la grosse
     Courir, en valsant, vers la Fosse
     Commune des Modernes Noces.

     O Rosace! leurs charmants yeux
     C'est des vains cadrans d'émail bleu
     Qui marquent l'heure que l'on veut,
         Non des pétales,
De ton Soleil des Basiliques Nuptiales!
         Au premier mot,
Peut-être (on est si distinguée à fleur de peau!)
     Elles vont tomber en syncope
     Avec des regards d'antilope; –
     Mais tout leur être est interlope!

     Tu veux pas fleurir fraternel?
     C'est bon, on te prendra tel quel,
     Petit mammifère usuel!
         Même la blague
Me chaut peu de te passer au doigt une bague.

I can't bear the Temple Rose-Window turning its light off, when it sees sexes in satin delivered by the gross and running in three-four time towards the Common Grave of Modern Marriage.

O Rose-Window! their charming eyes are empty sundials of blue enamel which show any time you like – and not the time of petals – of your Sun of the Marital Basilicas! at the first word, perhaps (one is so refined at skin level!) they'll fall in a faint, all antelope-eyed; – but their very nature is suspect!

You don't wish to blossom into brotherhood? Okay, we'll take you as you are, little commonplace mammal! Even the joke of putting a ring on your finger doesn't strike my fancy.

– Oh! quel grand deuil,
Pourtant, leur ferait voir leur frère d'un autre œil!
      Voir un égal d'amour en l'homme
      Et non une bête de somme
      Là pour lui remuer des sommes![7]

      Quoi? vais-je prendre un air géant,
      Et faire appeler le Néant?
      Non, non; ce n'est pas bienséant.
          Je me promène
Parmi les sommités des colonies humaines;
          Du bout du doigt
Je feuillette les versions dé l'Unique Loi.
      Et je vivotte et m'inocule
      Les grands airs gris du crépuscule,
      Et j'en garrule! et j'en garrule!

– Oh what deep mourning, however, would make them see their brother from a different angle! To see man as an equal in love and not a beast of burden who's there to play the Stock Exchange!

What? Am I going to swell up into a giant and order Nothingness to be summoned? No, no, that wouldn't be well-bred. I stroll among the leading lights of the human colonies; with a finger-end I leaf through versions of the One Law. And I struggle along, and inoculate myself with the great grey airs of twilight, and I blether about it, blether on and on!

Dimanches

Mon Sort est orphelin, les vêpres ont tu leurs cloches . . .
Et ces pianos qui ritournellent, jamais las! . . .
Oh! monter, leur expliquer mon apostolat!
Oh! du moins, leur tourner les pages, être là,
Les consoler! (J'ai des consolations plein les poches) . . .

Les pianos se sont clos. Un seul, en grand deuil,
    s'obstine . . .
Oh! qui que tu sois, sœur! à genoux, à tâtons,
Baiser le bas de ta robe dans l'abandon! . . .
Pourvu qu'après, tu me chasses, disant: «Pardon!
«Pardon, m'sieu, mais j'en aime un autre, et suis sa cousine!»

Oh! que je suis bien infortuné sur cette Terre! . . .
Et puis si malheureux de ne pas être Ailleurs!
Ailleurs, loin de ce savant siècle batailleur: . . .
C'est là que je m'créerai un petit intérieur,
Avec Une dont, comme de Moi, Tout n'a que faire.

Sundays

My Destiny is an orphan, the vespers have silenced their bells . . . and those pianos which strum away tirelessly! . . . Oh! to climb the stairs, and explain my apostolic task! Oh! at least to turn their pages, to be there, and comfort them! (My pockets are stuffed full of consolations!)

    The pianos have shut. One, in full mourning, still persists . . . Oh! whoever you are, sister! on my knees, hesitantly, to kiss the hem of your dress in frantic emotion! . . . Provided that afterwards, you show me the door, saying, 'Sorry, so sorry, sir, but I love another, and I'm his cousin!'

    Oh! how truly unlucky I am on this Earth! . . . and then so unlucky not to be Elsewhere! Elsewhere, far from this clever argumentative century . . . It's there that I'll create for myself a little home from home, with One who, like Me, the All has no business with.

Une maigre qui me parlait,
Les yeux hallucinés de Gloires virginales,
De rendre l'âme, sans scandale,
Dans un flacon de sels anglais . . .

Une qui me fit oublier
Mon art et ses rançons d'absurdes saturnales,
En attisant, gauche vestale,
L'Aurore dans mes oreillers . . .

Et que son regard
Sublime
Comme ma rime
Ne permît pas le moindre doute à cet égard.

A thin girl who spoke to me, her eyes hallucinated with virginal Glories, of giving up her soul, without fuss, in a bottle of English smelling salts . . .

One who made me forget my art and the price I pay for it in absurd saturnalia, by kindling – gauche vestal virgin! – Dawn among my pillows . . .

And would that her gaze, as sublime as my rhyme, might not allow the faintest doubt in that respect.

Petites misères d'automne

HAMLET: Get thee to a nunnery; why wouldst thou
be a breeder of sinners? I am myself indifferent
honest; but yet I could accuse me of such things
that it were better, my mother had not borne me.
I am very proud, revengeful, ambitious; with more
offences at my beck than I have thoughts to put
them in etc . . . to a nunnery.

Je me souviens, – dis, rêvé ce bal blanc?
Une, en robe rose et les joues en feu,
M'a tout ce soir-là dévoré des yeux,
Des yeux impérieux et puis dolents,
        (Je vous demande un peu!)

Car vrai, fort peu sur moi d'un en vedette,
Ah! pas plus ce soir-là d'ailleurs que d'autres,
Peut-être un peu mon natif air d'apôtre,
Empêcheur de danser en rond sur cette
        Scandaleuse planète.

Small Autumn Miseries

I remember – say, did I dream that ball in white? One, in a pink dress, her cheeks
on fire, devoured me with her eyes all evening long, her imperious and then doleful
eyes (I ask you, how absurd!)

    For it's true not much about me belongs to the headlines, Ah! no more that
evening than any other, or perhaps a little because of my air of being a born apostle,
a preventer of dancing round in circles on this scandal of a planet.

Et, tout un soir, ces grands yeux envahis
De moi! Moi, dos voûté sous l'A quoi Bon?
Puis, partis, comme à jamais vagabonds!
(Peut-être en ont-ils peu après failli? . . .)
  Moi quitté le pays.

Chez nous, aux primes salves d'un sublime,
Faut battre en retraite. C'est sans issue.
Toi, pauvre, et t'escomptant déjà déçue
Par ce cœur (qui même eût plaint ton estime)
  J'ai été en victime,

En victime après un joujou des nuits!
Ses boudoirs pluvieux mirent en sang
Mon inutile cœur d'adolescent . . .
Et j'en dormis. A l'aube je m'enfuis . . .
  Bien égal aujourd'hui.

And all evening long those big eyes taken up with me! Me, with my back bowed under What's-the-Point? Then gone, footloose as always! (Perhaps shortly afterwards it sent them blind? . . .) I, gone from the country.

With my sort, at the first salvoes of a sublime experience, we beat a retreat. There's no way out. You, poor thing, already expecting to be deceived by my heart (which might even have been sorry you thought well of me). I played the victim's role,

night-time plaything, then victim! Her rainy boudoirs rubbed raw my futile adolescent's heart . . . and sent me to sleep. At dawn I fled . . . Makes no difference now.

Sancta Simplicitas[1]

Passants, m'induisez point en beautés d'aventure,
     Mon Destin n'en saurait avoir cure;
Je ne peux plus m'occuper que des Jeunes Filles,
     Avec ou sans parfum de famille.

Pas non plus mon chez moi, ces précaires liaisons,
     Où l'on s'aime en comptant par saisons;
L'Amour dit légitime est seul solvable! car
     Il est sûr de demain, dans son art.

Il a le Temps, qu'un grand amour toujours convie;
     C'est la table mise pour la vie;
Quand demain n'est pas sûr, chacun se gare vite!
     Et même, autant en finir tout de suite.

Oh! adjugés à mort! comme qui concluraient:
     «D'avance, tout de toi m'est sacré,
«Et vieillesse à venir, et les maux hasardeux!
     «C'est dit! Et maintenant, à nous deux!»

Sancta Simplicitas

Passers-by, tempt me not to adventitious beauties, my Destiny could take no interest in them; no more can I busy myself but with Young Ladies, with or without a family fragrance.

Nor any more 'my own place', those precarious liaisons, where one times a love-affair by the seasons; so-called legitimate Love is the only one that's creditworthy! for, in its artfulness, it's sure of tomorrow.

It has Time, which a great love always invites; it's a table set for life; when tomorrow's unsafe, everyone steers clear! and even, you might as well plump for it at once.

O you who are assigned to death! who might conclude: 'In advance everything of you is sacred to me, both old age to come, and the risks of suffering! It's said! Now, it's up to the two of us!'

Vaisseaux brûlés! et, à l'horizon, nul divorce!
　　　C'est ça qui vous donne de la force!
O mon seul débouché! – O mon vatout nubile!
　　　A nous nos deux vies! Voici notre île.

Notre petite compagne

Si mon air vous dit quelque chose,
Vous auriez tort de vous gêner;
Je ne la fais pas à la pose;
Je suis la Femme, on me connaît.

Bandeaux plats ou crinière folle,
Dites? quel Front vous rendrait fou?
J'ai l'art de toutes les écoles,
J'ai des âmes pour tous les goûts.

Cueillez la fleur de mes visages,
Buvez ma bouche et non ma voix,
Et n'en cherchez pas davantage . . .
Nul n'y vit clair; pas même moi.

Burnt boats! and, on the horizon, no divorce! That's what gives you the strength!
O my only way out! O my nubile stake-my-all! Ours are our two lives! Here is
our island.

Our Little Companion

If my Look appeals to you, don't stand on ceremony; I'm not putting it on; I'm
Woman, everyone knows me.

Flat headbands or wild hair flying, tell me – which Hair-Do will drive you insane?
I know the art of every school, I have souls for every taste.

Pluck the flower of my various faces, drink my mouth and not my words, and
don't ask for more . . . Nobody ever saw it straight; not even I.

Nos armes ne sont pas égales,
Pour que je vous tende la main.
Vous n'êtes que de naïfs mâles,
Je suis l'Éternel Féminin!

Mon But se perd dans les Étoiles!
C'est moi qui suis la Grande Isis![1]
Nul ne m'a retroussé mon voile.
Ne songez qu'à mes oasis . . .

Si mon Air vous dit quelque chose,
Vous auriez tort de vous gêner;
Je ne la fais pas à la pose:
Je suis La Femme! on me connaît.

Complainte des crépuscules célibataires

C'est l'existence des passants . . .
Oh! tant d'histoires personnelles! . . .
Qu'amèrement intéressant
De se navrer de leur kyrielle!

Your weapons and mine are not equally matched, for me to offer you my hand. You are merely naïve males, I'm the Eternal Feminine!

My Purpose fades from view among the Stars! . . . I'm the Great Isis! No one has lifted my veil. Just think of my oases . . .

If my Look appeals to you, don't stand on ceremony; I'm not putting it on; I'm Woman, everyone knows me.

Complaint of Bachelor Twilights

The existences of people passing in the street . . . Oh! so many private stories! . . . What a bitter pastime it is, to be grief-struck by their torrents of abuse!

Ils s'en vont flairés d'obscurs chiens,
Ou portent des paquets, ou flânent . . .
Ah! sont-ils assez quotidiens,
Tueurs de temps et monomanes,

Et lorgneurs d'or comme de strass
Aux quotidiennes devantures! . . .
La vitrine allume son gaz,
Toujours de nouvelles figures . . .

Oh! que tout m'est accidentel!
Oh! j'ai-t-y[1] l'âme perpétuelle! . . .
Hélas, dans ces cas, rien de tel
Que de pleurer une infidèle! . . .

Mais qu'ai-je donc laissé là-bas?
Rien. Eh! voilà mon grand reproche!
O culte d'un Dieu qui n'est pas,
Quand feras-tu taire tes cloches! . . .

Je vague depuis le matin
En proie à des loisirs coupables,
Epiant quelque grand destin
Dans l'œil de mes douces semblables . . .[2]

They go their way sniffed at by stray dogs, or they carry parcels, or they stroll
. . . Ah! how could they be more commonplace, time-killing and obsessional,
  and gawpers at gold and at fake jewellery in the commonplace shop-windows!
. . . the window ignites its gas-light, new faces all the time . . .

Oh! how random I find everything! Oh! how perpetual is my soul! . . . Alas, in
these cases, nothing makes you feel more like this, than weeping for a faithless lover!

So what did I leave behind? Nothing. Ah! that's my great sin! O worship of a
God who does not exist, when will you silence your bells? . . .

I've been wandering since morning, a prey to sinful leisures, on the look-out for
some great destiny in the eyes of my sweet fellow-creatures . . .

Oh! rien qu'un lâche point d'arrêt
Dans mon destin qui se dévide! . . .
Un amour pour moi tout exprès
En un chez nous de chrysalide! . . .

Un simple cœur, et des regards
Purs de tout esprit de conquête,
Je suis si exténué d'art!
Me répéter, oh! mal de tête! . . .

Va, et les gouttières de l'ennui!
Ça goutte, goutte sur ma nuque . . .
Ça claque, claque à petit bruit . . .
Oh! ça claquera[3] jusque . . . jusque? . . .

Ève, sans trêve

Et la Coiffure, l'art du Front,
Cheveux massés à la Néron
Sur des yeux qui, du coup, fermentent;
Tresses, bandeaux, crinière ardente;
Madone ou caniche ou bacchante;[1]
Mes frères, décoiffons d'abord! puis nous verrons.

Oh! if only I could have a cowardly halt in my unwinding destiny! . . . A love intended for me in a chrysalis-like place-of-our-own! . . .

A straightforward heart, and eyes innocent of all spirit of conquest, I'm so tired of pretending! Repeating myself, Oh! what a headache! . . .

Get away with you, and gutterful of worldweariness! It drips, drips down my neck . . . It quietly clicks and clacks . . . oh! it'll go on till . . . till when?

Eve As Ever

And Coiffure, the art of the Forehead, hair piled up Nero-style over eyes which, instantly, ferment; tresses, headbands, tresses like flames; Madonna or poodle or bacchante; my brothers, let her hair down first! then we'll see.

Ah! les ensorcelants Protées![2]
Et suivez-les décolletées
Des épaules; comme, aussitôt,
Leurs yeux, les plus durs, les plus faux,
Se noient, l'air tendre et comme il faut,
Dans ce halo de chair en harmonies lactées! . . .

Et ce purgatif:[3] Vierge hier,
Porter aujourd'hui dans sa chair,
Fixe, un œil mâle, en fécondée!
L'âme doit être débordee!
Oh! nous n'en avons pas idée!
Leur air reste le même, avenant et désert . . .

Avenant, Promis et Joconde!
Et, par les rues, et dans le monde,
Qui saurait dire de ces yeux
Réfléchissant tout ce qu'on veut
Voici les vierges, voici ceux
Où la Foudre finale a bien jeté la sonde.

Ah! the bewitching Proteuses! And follow them with their shoulders bare; how at once their eyes, even the hardest, the falsest, melt with an air of tenderness, just right, in this halo of flesh with milky harmonies! . . .

And this purgative: a Virgin yesterday, to carry today in her body, fixed, a male Eye, fertilized! Her soul must be brimming over! Oh! we haven't the faintest idea! Their look remains the same, attractive and forsaken . . .

Attractive, Promised and Mona Lisa! And in the streets and everywhere, who could say of those eyes, which reflect all and anything, 'Here are virgins, here are those into whom the Final Thunderbolt has cast its sounding.'

Ah! non, laissons, on n'y peut rien.
Suivons-les comme de bons chiens,
Couvrons de baisers leurs visages
Du moment, faisons bon ménage
Avec leurs bleus, leurs noirs mirages,
Cueillons-en, puis chantons: merci c'est bien, fort bien . . .

La mélancolie de Pierrot

Le premier jour, je bois leurs yeux ennuyés . . .
            Je baiserais leurs pieds,
            A mort. Ah! qu'elles daignent
            Prendre mon cœur qui saigne!
Puis on cause . . . et ça devient de la Pitié,
Et enfin je leur offre mon amitié.

No, let's drop the subject, we can't help ourselves. Let's follow them like faithful dogs, let's cover with kisses their faces of the moment, let's accommodate ourselves to their blue and black mirages, let's take a sample, then let's sing, 'Thank you, that's nice, very nice . . .'

Pierrot's Melancholy

On the first day, I drink in their bored eyes . . . I would kiss their feet – to death. Ah! If they would only deign to accept my bleeding heart! Then, we chat . . . – and it turns to Pity; and at last I offer them my friendship.

C'est de pitié, que je m'offre en frère, en guide;
        Elles, me croient timide,
        Et clignent d'un œil doux:
        «Un mot, je suis à vous!»
(Je te crois.) Alors, moi, d'étaler les rides
De ce cœur, et de sourire dans le vide . . .

Et soudain j'abandonne la garnison,
        Feignant de trahisons!
        (Je l'ai échappé belle!)
        Au moins, m'écrira-t-elle?
Point. Et je la pleure toute la saison . . .
– Ah! j'en ai assez de ces combinaisons!

Qui m'apprivoisera le cœur! belle cure . . .
        Suis si vrai de nature!
        Ai la douceur des sœurs!
        Oh viens! suis pas noceur,
Serait-ce donc une si grosse aventure
Sous le soleil? dans toute cette verdure . . .

It's out of pity I offer myself as brother, as guide; *they* think I'm shy, and wink with a gentle eye: 'One word, and I'm yours!' (I can believe you.) Then I start displaying the frown-marks of my heart, and smiling into the void . . .

And suddenly I abandon the garrison, pretending treachery! (I've had a narrow escape!) At least will she write to me? No. And I weep for her all season long . . .
– Ah! I've had enough of these machinations!

Who'll tame my heart! a fine vocation . . . I'm so true by nature! I have the gentleness of nuns! Oh come! I'm not a roué, would it be such an alarming venture in the sunlight? among all these green leaves . . .

Cas rédhibitoire

(Mariage)

Ah! mon âme a sept facultés![1]
Plus autant qu'il est de chefs-d'œuvre,
Plus mille microbes ratés
Qui m'ont pris pour champ de manœuvre.

Oh! le suffrage universel
Qui se bouscule et se chicane,
A chaque instant, au moindre appel,
Dans mes mille occultes organes ! . . .

J'aurais voulu vivre à grands traits,[2]
Le long d'un classique programme
Et m'associant en un congrès
Avec quelque classique femme.

Mais peut-il être question
D'aller tirer des exemplaires
De son individu si on
N'en a pas une idée plus claire? . . .

A Case of Returning a Faulty Article
(Marriage)

Ah! my soul has seven faculties! Plus as many as there are masterpieces, plus a thousand failed microbes who've taken me for their field of operations.

Oh! the universal suffrage which hustles and wrangles with itself, every moment, at the least outcry, in my thousand secret organs!

I'd have liked to live drinking life down like wine, following a classic masterplan, associating myself in congress with some classic woman.

But can there be a question of producing copies of one's person, if one hasn't a clearer idea of what that person is?

Les chauves–souris

C'est qu'elles m'ont l'air bien folles, ce soir,
Les cloches du couvent des carmélites!
Et je me demande au nom de quels rites . . .
              Allons, montons voir.

Oh! parmi les poussiéreuses poutrelles,
Ce sont de jeunes chauves-souris
Folles d'essayer enfin hors du nid
              Leurs vieillottes ailes!

– Elles s'en iront désormais aux soirs,
Chasser les moustiques sur la rivière,
A l'heure où les diurnes lavandières
              Ont tu leurs battoirs.[1]

– Et ces couchants seront tout solitaires,
Tout quotidiens et tout supra-Védas,[2]
Tout aussi vrais que si je n'étais pas,
              Tout à leur affaire.

The Bats

It's because they sound quite mad, this evening, the bells of the Carmelite convent! and I ask in the name of what rites . . . Let's climb the hill and see.

Oh! among the dusty beams, it's a pack of young bats crazy to try out at last outside the nest their quaint old-fashioned wings!

From now on they'll wing off every evening to hunt the mosquitoes on the river, at the hour when the daily laundresses have stilled their pestles.

And these sunsets will be utterly lonely, utterly everyday and utterly supra-Vedic, just as utterly true as if I did not exist, utterly wrapped up in themselves.

Ah! ils seront tout aussi quotidiens
Qu'aux temps où la planète à la dérive
En ses langes de vapeur primitives
   Ne savait rien d'rien.

Ils seront tout aussi à leur affaire
Quand je ne viendrai plus crier bravo!
Aux assortiments de mourants joyaux
   De leur éventaire,

Qu'aux jours où certain bohême filon
Du commun néant n'avait pas encore
Pris un accès d'existence pécore
   Sous mon pauvre nom.

Ah! they'll be just as everyday as when the planet drifting in its primeval swaddling-clothes of vapour knew sweet nothing.

They'll be just as busy with themselves when I no longer come to cry: 'Bravo!' at the assortments of dying jewels on their market-stall,

As they were in the days when a certain bohemian stratum of common-or-garden nothingness hadn't yet had a fit of impertinent existence under my dreary name.

Signalement

Chair de l'Autre Sexe! Élément non-moi!
Chair, vive de vingt ans poussés loin de ma bouche! . . .
L'air de sa chair m'ensorcelle en la foi
Aux abois
Que par Elle, ou jamais, Mon Destin fera souche . . .
Et, tout tremblant, je regarde, je touche . . .

Je me prouve qu'Elle est! – et puis, ne sais qu'en croire . . .
Et je revois mes chemins de Damas[1]
Au bout desquels c'était encor les balançoires
Provisoires . . .
Et je me récuse, et je me débats!
Fou d'un art à nous deux! et fou de célibats . . .

Et toujours le même Air! me met en frais
De cœur, et me transit en ces conciliabules . . .
Deux grands yeux savants, fixes et sacrés
Tout exprès.

Descriptive Particulars

Flesh of the Other Sex! Alien essence! Flesh, alive with all its twenty years of growing far from my lips! The look of her flesh bewitches me in my last-ditch faith that by Her – or never – My Destiny will found its family line . . . and, trembling, I gaze, I touch . . .

I prove to myself that She is! – and then, I don't know what to think . . . and I remember my roads to Damascus – at the ends there were always temporary seesaws . . . and I declare myself incompetent to judge, and I flounder! Mad for an art which is yours and mine, and mad for celibacy . . .

And always the same Look! puts my heart out of pocket, and paralyses me in these confabulations . . . two big knowing eyes, intent and worshipful, intentionally.

Là, pour garder leur sœur cadette, et si crédule,
    Une bouche qui rit en campanule! . . .

(O yeux durs, bouche folle!) – ou bien Ah! le contraire:
    Une bouche toute à ses grands ennuis,
Mais l'arc tendu! sachant ses yeux, ses petits frères
             Tout à plaire,
    Et capables de rendez-vous de nuit
Pour un rien, pour une larme qu'on leur essui'! . . .

        Oui, sous ces airs supérieurs,
        Le cœur me piaffe de génie
        En labyrinthes d'insomnie! . . .
        Et puis, et puis, c'est bien ailleurs
            Que je communie . . .

Air de biniou

Non, non, ma pauvre cornemuse,
Ta complainte est pas si oiseuse;
Et Tout est bien une méprise,
Et l'on peut la trouver mauvaise;

They're there to keep her mouth, their younger sister, safe – for she's so gullible!
– she laughs like a campanula! . . .

    (O eyes so hard, O mouth so mad!) – or else Ah! the opposite! a mouth obsessed by its tribulations (but its bow is at the ready!) knowing her eyes, her little brothers, are devoted to giving pleasure, and capable of assignations in the dark for a trifle, for a tear wiped easily away! . . .

    Yes, though I adopt these superior airs, my heart prances with genius through mazes of insomnia! . . . Besides, besides, it's very far from here that I take communion.

Bagpipe Tune

No, no my poor bagpipe, your complaint ain't so superfluous; Everything is certainly a misunderstanding, and one may well find it a bad joke;

Et la Nature est une épouse
Qui nous carambole d'extases,
Et puis, nous occit, peu courtoise,
Dès qu'on se permet une pause.

Eh bien! qu'elle en prenne à son aise,
Et que tout fonctionne à sa guise!
Nous, nous entretiendrons les Muses,
Les neuf immortelles Glaneuses!

(Oh! pourrions-nous pas, par nos phrases,
Si bien lui retourner les choses,
Que cette marâtre jalouse
N'ait plus sur nos rentes de prise?)

And Nature is a wife who cannons us off from ecstasy to ecstasy, and then slays us, very discourteously, as soon as we take a breather.

Well, let her do as she fancies, and let everything be ruled by her whims! *We'll* entertain the Muses, the nine immortal Gleaners!

(Oh! if only, by our phrases, we could turn the tables on her, so that this jealous stepmother no longer controls our revenues.)

DERNIERS VERS

Last Verse

I have not art to reckon my groans [. . .] Thine evermore,
Most dear lady, whilst this machine is to him.
                                        J. L.

OPHELIA: He took me by the wrist, and held me hard;
        Then goes he to the length of all his arm,
        And, with his other hand thus o'er his brow,
        He falls to such perusal of my face,
        As he would draw it. Long stay'd he so:
        At last, – a little shaking of mine arm,
        And thrice his head thus waving up and down,
        He rais'd a sigh so piteous and profound,
        That it did seem to shatter all his bulk,
        And end his being. That done he lets me go,
        And with his head over his shoulder turn'd
        He seem'd to find his way without his eyes;
        For out o'doors he went without their help,
        And to the last bended their light on me.
POLONIUS: This is the very ecstasy of love.

(I) L'hiver qui vient

Blocus sentimental![1] Messageries du Levant! . . .[2]
Oh! tombée de la pluie! Oh! tombée de la nuit,
Oh! le vent! . . .
La Toussaint, la Noël, et la Nouvelle Année,
Oh, dans les bruines, toutes mes cheminées! . . .
D'usines . . .[3]

On ne peut plus s'asseoir, tous les bancs sont mouillés;
Crois-moi, c'est bien fini jusqu'à l'année prochaine,
Tous les bancs sont mouillés, tant les bois sont rouillés,
Et tant les cors ont fait ton ton, ont fait ton taine! . . .

Ah! nuées accourues des côtes de la Manche,
Vous nous avez gâté notre dernier dimanche.

(I) The Onset of Winter

Sentimental blockade! Levantine packet-boats! . . . Oh, falling of the rain! Oh falling of the night, Oh, the wind! All-Saints, Christmas and New Year, Oh, in the drizzle, all my hearthfires! All my factory chimneys!

By now you can't sit down, all the benches are wet. Believe me, it's quite over till next year, all the benches are wet, the woods are so rusty, and the horns have sounded tantivvy, have sounded tantara!

Ah! clouds running up from the coasts of the Channel, you've spoiled our last Sunday.

Il bruine;
Dans la forêt mouillée, les toiles d'araignées
Ploient sous les gouttes d'eau, et c'est leur ruine.
Soleils plénipotentiaires des travaux en blonds Pactoles[4]
Des spectacles agricoles,
Où êtes-vous ensevelis?
Ce soir un soleil fichu gît au haut du coteau,
Gît sur le flanc, dans les genêts, sur son manteau.
Un soleil blanc comme un crachat d'estaminet
Sur une litière de jaunes genêts,
De jaunes genêts d'automne.
Et les cors lui sonnent!
Qu'il revienne . . .
Qu'il revienne à lui!
Taïaut! Taïaut! et hallali!
O triste antienne, as-tu fini! . . .
Et font les fous! . . .
Et il gît là, comme une glande arrachée dans un cou,
Et il frissonne, sans personne! . . .

It's drizzling. In the wet forest, the spiders' webs sway under the drops of water, and it's their ruin. Suns, you plenipotentiaries of the labours (golden as Pactoluses) of agricultural festivals, where are you buried? This evening a clapped-out sun lies on the hilltop, lies on his side, in the gorse, on his cloak. A sun as white as a gobbet of pub-spit, on a litter of young gorse, young autumn gorse. And the horns ring out to him! Let him come back! Let him come round! Tallyho, tallyho, and view halloo! O sad refrain, are you finished yet? And what a mad noise they make! And he lies there, like a gland torn out of a neck, and he quivers, all alone!

Allons, allons, et hallali!
C'est l'Hiver bien connu qui s'amène;
Oh! les tournants des grandes routes,
Et sans petit Chaperon Rouge qui chemine! . . .
Oh! leurs ornières des chars de l'autre mois,
Montant en don quichottesques rails
Vers les patrouilles des nuées en déroute
Que le vent malmène vers les transatlantiques bercails! . . .
Accélérons, accélérons, c'est la saison bien connue, cette fois.
Et le vent, cette nuit, il en a fait de belles!
O dégâts, ô nids, ô modestes jardinets!
Mon cœur et mon sommeil: ô échos des cognées! . . .

Tous ces rameaux avaient encor leurs feuilles vertes,
Les sous-bois ne sont plus qu'un fumier de feuilles mortes;
Feuilles, folioles, qu'un bon vent vous emporte
Vers les étangs par ribambelles,
Ou pour le feu du garde-chasse,
Ou les sommiers des ambulances
Pour les soldats loin de la France.

Off and away and view halloo! It's our old friend Winter coming; Oh! the bends of the main roads, and no Little Red Riding Hood on her way! . . . Oh! last month's wagon-ruts, climbing in Don Quixote-like rails towards the patrols of clouds in rout hustled off by the wind towards transatlantic sheepfolds! Faster, faster, it's the well-known season, this time. And the wind last night wrought a fine destruction! O ravages, O nests, O modest little gardens! In my heart and in my sleep: O echoes of the woodsman's axe! . . .

All those boughs still had their green leaves, the underwoods are no more now than a midden of dead leaves; leaves, little leaves, may a good wind carry you off towards the ponds in droves, or the gamekeeper's fire, or the ambulance mattresses for soldiers far from France.

C'est la saison, c'est la saison, la rouille envahit les masses,[5]
La rouille ronge en leurs spleens kilométriques
Les fils télégraphiques des grandes routes où nul ne passe.

Les cors, les cors, les cors – mélancoliques! . . .
Mélancoliques! . . .
S'en vont, changeant de ton,
Changeant de ton et de musique,
Ton ton, ton taine, ton ton! . . .
Les cors, les cors, les cors! . . .
S'en sont allés au vent du Nord.

Je ne puis quitter ce ton: que d'échos! . . .
C'est la saison, c'est la saison, adieu vendanges! . . .
Voici venir les pluies d'une patience d'ange,
Adieu vendanges, et adieu tous les paniers,
Tous les paniers[6] Watteau des bourrées sous les marronniers,
C'est la toux dans les dortoirs du lycée qui rentre,
C'est la tisane sans le foyer,
La phtisie pulmonaire attristant le quartier,
Et toute la misère des grands centres.

It's the season, it's the season, rust invades the surfaces, rust gnaws at the telegraph wires in their kilometric boredom, [strung out along] the highways where no one passes.

The horns, the horns, the melancholy horns! . . . melancholy! . . . away they go, changing tone, changing tone and tune, tan-tan, tantivy, tan-tan! The horns, the horns, the horns! . . . have been borne away in the North Wind.

I cannot throw off this mood: how many echoes! . . . It's the season, the season, farewell to the vine-harvests! . . . Here come the rains of angelic patience, farewell vine-harvests, and farewell all the baskets, all the Watteau crinolines of the dances under the chestnut-trees. It's the coughing in the dormitories at the start of a new school term, it's tea away from home, tuberculosis saddening the neighbourhood, and all the poverty of the great conurbations.

Mais, lainages, caoutchoucs,[7] pharmacie, rêve,
Rideaux écartés du haut des balcons des grèves
Devant l'océan de toitures des faubourgs,
Lampes, estampes, thé, petits-fours,
Serez-vous pas mes seules amours! . . .
(Oh! et puis, est-ce que tu connais, outre les pianos,
Le sobre et vespéral mystère hebdomadaire
Des statistiques sanitaires
Dans les journaux?)

Non, non! c'est la saison et la planète falote!
Que l'autan, que l'autan
Effiloche les savates que le Temps se tricote!
C'est la saison, oh déchirements! c'est la saison!
Tous les ans, tous les ans,
J'essaierai en chœur d'en donner la note.

But woollens, waterproofs, chemist's shop, dreams, curtains drawn back above riverside balconies before the ocean of suburban roofs, lamps, prints, tea, petits-fours, won't you be my only loves! (Oh! and also do you know, besides the pianos, the sober, vesperal weekly mystery of the medical statistics in the newspapers?)

No, no! It's the season and the quaint old planet! Let the storm wind, the storm wind fray away the down-at-heel slippers that Time knits for herself! It's the season, oh heartbreak! it's the season! Every year, every year I'll try in chorus to sound its note.

(II) Le mystère des trois cors

Un cor dans la plaine
Souffle à perdre haleine,
Un autre, du fond des bois,
Lui répond;
L'un chante ton taine
Aux forêts prochaines,
Et l'autre ton ton
Aux échos des monts.

Celui de la plaine
Sent gonfler ses veines,
Ses veines du front;
Celui du bocage,
En vérité, ménage
Ses jolis poumons.

— Où donc tu te caches,
Mon beau cor de chasse?
Que tu es méchant!

— Je cherche ma belle,
Là-bas, qui m'appelle
Pour voir le Soleil couchant.

(II) The Mystery of the Three Horns

A horn on the plain is blowing fit to bust, another deep in the woods answers him; one sings tarantara to the nearby forests, the other sings tantivvy to the mountains' echoing.

The one from the plain feels his veins swelling, the veins of his forehead; the one in the woodland, to tell the truth, is sparing his pretty lungs.

'Where are you hiding, my handsome hunting horn? What a mischief you are!'
'I'm seeking my lady over there, who calls me to see the setting Sun.'

– Taïaut! Taïaut! Je t'aime!
Hallali! Roncevaux![1]

– Être aimé est bien doux;
Mais, le Soleil qui se meurt, avant tout!

Le soleil dépose sa pontificale étole,
Lâche les écluses du Grand-Collecteur[2]
En mille Pactoles[3]
Que les plus artistes
De nos liquoristes
Attisent de cent fioles de vitriol oriental! . . .
Le sanglant étang, aussitôt s'étend, aussitôt s'étale,
Noyant les cavales du quadrige[4]
Qui se cabre, et qui patauge, et puis se fige
Dans ces déluges de bengale et d'alcool! . . .

Mais les durs sables et les cendres de l'horizon
Ont vite bu tout cet étalage de poisons.

'Tallyho, tallyho! I love you! View halloo! Roncevaux!'
'To be loved is sweet; but first we must view the Sun dying!'
The Sun lays aside his papal stole, opens the sluices of the Great Collector in a thousand Pactoluses that the most arty of our wine merchants set blazing with a hundred phials of oriental vitriol! . . . The blood-filled pond at once spreads out, at once displays itself, drowning the nags of the four-horse chariot, which rears and flounders and then congeals in these floods of Bengal fire and alcohol! . . .

But the horizon's hard sands and ashes have quickly drunk this whole shop-window of poisons.

Ton ton ton taine, les gloires! . . .

Et les cors consternés
Se retrouvent nez à nez;

Ils sont trois;
Le vent se lève, il commence à faire froid.

Ton ton ton taine, les gloires![5]

«— Bras dessus, bras dessous,
«Avant de rentrer chacun chez nous,
«Si nous allions boire
«Un coup?»

Pauvres cors! pauvres cors!
Comme ils dirent cela avec un rire amer!
(Je les entends encor.)

Le lendemain, l'hôtesse du *Grand-Saint-Hubert*[6]
Les trouva tous trois morts.

On fut quérir les autorités
De la localité,

Qui dressèrent procès-verbal
De ce mystère très immoral.

Tan-tan, tantivvy, the glory! . . .
And the horns to their consternation find themselves face to face.
There are three of them; the wind is rising, it's beginning to get cold.
Tan-tan, tantivvy, the glory!
'Arm in arm, before we each go home, why don't we have a drink?'
Poor horns! Poor horns! With what a bitter laugh they spoke! (I hear them still.)
Next morning, the landlady of the Great Saint Hubert found them dead, all three.
They sent for the local authorities,
who drew up an official report on this most immoral mystery.

(III) Dimanches

Bref, j'allais me donner d'un «Je vous aime»
Quand je m'avisai non sans peine
Que d'abord je ne me possédais pas bien moi-même.

(Mon Moi, c'est Galathée[1] aveuglant Pygmalion!
Impossible de modifier cette situation.)

Ainsi donc, pauvre, pâle et piètre individu
Qui ne croit à son Moi qu'à ses moments perdus
Je vis s'effacer ma fiancée
Emportée par le cours des choses.
Telle l'épine voit s'effeuiller,
Sous prétexte de soir sa meilleure rose.

Or, cette nuit anniversaire, toutes les Walkyries[2] du vent
Sont revenues beugler par les fentes de ma porte:
Væ soli![3]
Mais, ah! qu'importe?
Il fallait m'en étourdir avant!
Trop tard! ma petite folie est morte!
Qu'importe *Væ soli!*
Je ne retrouverai plus ma petite folie.

(III) Sundays

In short, I was going to give myself with an 'I love you', when I realized with some chagrin that, for one thing, I wasn't firmly in possession of myself.

(My Self – it's Galatea dazzling Pygmalion! Impossible to modify this situation.)

And so, poor, pale and paltry person, believing in my Self only at idle moments, I saw my betrothed vanish, carried off by the course of events, as the thorn sees the petals plucked from its finest rose on the pretext that it's evening.

Now on this anniversary night, all the Valkyries of the wind have returned bellowing through the crannies of my door: *Væ soli!* but ah! what does it matter? They should have deafened me before! Too late! my little flight of fancy is dead! What matter *Væ soli!* I'll never find my little flight of fancy again.

Le grand vent bâillonné,
S'endimanche enfin le ciel du matin.
Et alors, eh! allez donc, carillonnez,
Toutes cloches des bons dimanches!
Et passez layettes et collerettes et robes blanches
Dans un frou-frou de lavandes et de thym
Vers l'encens et les brioches!
Tout pour la famille, quoi! *Væ soli!* C'est certain.

La jeune demoiselle à l'ivoirin paroissien
Modestement rentre au logis.
On le voit, son petit corps bien reblanchi
Sait qu'il appartient
A un tout autre passé que le mien!

Mon corps, ô ma sœur, a bien mal à sa belle âme . . .

Oh! voilà que ton piano
Me recommence, si natal maintenant!
Et ton cœur qui s'ignore s'y ânonne
En ritournelles[4] de bastringues à tout venant,
Et ta pauvre chair s'y fait mal! . . .
A moi, Walkyries!
Walkyries des hypocondries et des tueries!

The high wind has been gagged, the morning sky at last puts on its Sunday best.
So, then, ring out, all you good Sunday bells, and put on baby-clothes and lace
collars and white dresses in a rustle of lavender and thyme towards the incense and
the brioches! The family's what counts, eh! *Vae soli!* That's for sure.

The young lady with the ivory-bound prayer-book is modestly walking home.
It's obvious, her well-laundered little body knows it belongs to a quite different
past from mine!

My body, O my sister, has an ache in its high-minded soul . . .

Oh! and now your piano sets me off again, so birth-like now! And your heart,
unselfaware, blunders along in cheap dance-hall refrains to all and sundry, and it
makes your poor body ache! Gather round, Valkyries! Valkyries of hypochondrias
and massacres!

Ah! que je te les tordrais avec plaisir,
Ce corps bijou, ce cœur à ténor,
Et te dirais leur fait, et puis encore
La manière de s'en servir
De s'en servir à deux.
Si tu voulais seulement m'approfondir ensuite un peu!

Non, non! C'est sucer la chair d'un cœur élu,
Adorer d'incurables organes
S'entrevoir avant que les tissus se fanent
En monomanes, en reclus!

Et ce n'est pas sa chair qui me serait tout.
Et je ne serais pas qu'un grand cœur pour elle,
Mais quoi s'en aller faire les fous
Dans des histoires fraternelles!

L'âme et la chair, la chair et l'âme,
C'est l'esprit édénique et fier
D'être un peu l'Homme avec la Femme.

Ah! how I'd torment them with pleasure, that gem of a body, that virtuoso heart, and would tell you what they're for, and then again how they're meant to be used, used by a couple. If afterwards you only wanted to get just a little deeper into me!

No, no! That would be gnawing the flesh of a Chosen Heart, worshipping incurable organs, glimpsing each other, before the tissues fade, as monomaniacs, as recluses!

And it isn't her flesh which would be everything to me, and I wouldn't be just a big darling for her, but – guess what! – fooling about at playing brother and sister!

Soul and body, body and soul, it's the proud spirit of Eden – just trying to be Man and Woman together.

En attendant, oh! garde-toi des coups de tête,
Oh! file ton rouet et prie et reste honnête.

– Allons, dernier des poètes,
Toujours enfermé tu te rendras malade!
Vois, il fait beau temps, tout le monde est dehors,
Va donc acheter deux sous d'ellébore,[5]
Ça te fera une petite promenade.

(IV) Dimanches

C'est l'automne, l'automne, l'automne,
Le grand vent et toute sa séquelle
De représailles! et de musiques! . . .
Rideaux tirés, clôture annuelle,
Chute des feuilles, des Antigones, des Philomèles:[1]
Mon fossoyeur, *Alas poor Yorick*![2]
Les remue à la pelle! . . .

In the meantime, oh! beware the headstrong impulse, oh! turn your spinning-wheel, and pray, and do what's right.

'Look here, you worst of poets, always shut indoors like this, you'll make yourself ill! See, the weather's fine, everyone's out of doors, go and buy two ha'p'orth of hellebore, it'll stretch your legs.'

(IV) Sundays

It's autumn, autumn, autumn, the gale and all its sequel of reprisals! and of musics! Curtains drawn, the season's end, the fall of the leaves, of Antigones, of Philomelas: My grave-digger, *Alas poor Yorick!* stirs them with his spade! . . .

Vivent l'Amour et les feux de paille! . . .[3]

Les Jeunes Filles inviolables et frêles
Descendent vers la petite chapelle
Dont les chimériques cloches
Du joli, joli dimanche
Hygiéniquement et élégamment les appellent.

Comme tout se fait propre autour d'elles!
Comme tout en est dimanche!

Comme on se fait dur et boudeur à leur approche! . . .

Ah! moi, je demeure l'Ours Blanc![4]
Je suis venu par ces banquises
Plus pures que les communiantes en blanc . . .
Moi, je ne vais pas à l'église,
Moi je suis le Grand Chancelier de l'Analyse,
Qu'on se le dise.

Pourtant! pourtant! Qu'est-ce que c'est que cette anémie?
Voyons, confiez vos chagrins à votre vieil ami . . .

Vraiment! Vraiment!
Ah! Je me tourne vers la mer, les éléments
Et tout ce qui n'a plus que les noirs grognements!

Long live Love and flashes-in-the-pan!

The frail inviolable Young Ladies descend towards the little chapel whose delusory bells this pretty pretty Sunday hygienically and elegantly summon them.

How clean everything becomes around them! How Sundayish is everything to do with it!

How stiff and sulky one becomes as they approach!

Ah! I'm still the Polar Bear! I've come past ice-floes purer than the communicants in white . . . I don't go to church, I'm the Lord High Chancellor of Analysis, you've been warned.

And yet, and yet! What's this anaemia? Come, confide your woes to your old friend . . .

Really! Really! Ah! I turn towards the sea, the elements, and things which have nothing to offer but black lamentations!

Oh! que c'est sacré![5]
Et qu'il y faut de grandes veillées!

Pauvre, pauvre, sous couleur d'attraits! . . .

Et nous, et nous,
Ivres, ivres, avant qu'émerveillés . . .
Qu'émerveillés et à genoux! . . .

Et voyez comme on tremble,
Au premier grand soir
Que tout pousse au désespoir
D'en mourir ensemble!

O merveille qu'on n'a su que cacher!
Si pauvre et si brûlante et si martyre!
Et qu'on n'ose toucher
Qu'à l'aveugle, en divin délire!

O merveille.
Reste cachée, idéale violette,
L'Univers te veille,
Les générations de planètes te tettent.
De funérailles en relevailles! . . .[6]

Ah! how sacred it is! and what long evenings you need to devote to it!
Meagre, meagre, though outwardly attractive!
And we, and we, frantic, frantic, before being wonderstruck, wonderstruck and
on our knees! . . .
And see how one trembles, on the first long evening how everything urges
towards the despair of dying of it together!
O marvel – what could they do with it, but keep it hidden! So meagre, so ardent,
so self-sacrificial! Which one daren't touch save blindly, in divine delirium!
O marvel. Stay hidden, ideal violet, the Universe is watching over you, the
generations of planets suckle you, from funerals to churchings! . . .

Oh! que c'est plus haut
Que ce Dieu et que la Pensée!
Et rien qu'avec ces chers yeux en haut,
Tout inconscients et couleur de pensée![7]

Si frêle, si frêle!
Et tout le mortel foyer
Tout, tout ce foyer en elle! . . .

Oh, pardonnez-lui si, malgré elle,
Et cela tant lui sied,
Parfois ses prunelles clignent un peu
Pour vous demander un peu
De vous apitoyer un peu!

O frêle, frêle et toujours prête
Pour ces messes dont on a fait un jeu,
Penche, penche ta chère tête, va,
Regarde les grappes des premiers lilas,
Il ne s'agit pas de conquêtes, avec moi,
Mais d'au-delà!

Oh, how much higher it is than God and Thought itself! And with nothing more than those dear eyes on high, all unconscious and thought-coloured! So frail, so frail! And all the mortal hearth-home, all that, all within her!

Oh, forgive her if, despite herself – and how pretty it makes her look! – sometimes her pupils flicker a little, so as to ask you a little, to please relent a little!

O frail, frail and always ready for those Masses which we've made light of, bend, bend your darling head – come, look at the bunches of the first lilacs. In my case, it's nothing to do with 'conquests' – but with the Great Beyond!

Oh! puissions-nous quitter la vie
Ensemble dès cette Grand'Messe,
Ecœurés de notre espèce
Qui bâille assouvie
Dès le parvis! . . .

(V) Pétition

Amour absolu, carrefour sans fontaine;
Mais, à tous les bouts, d'étourdissantes fêtes foraines.

Jamais franches,
Ou le poing sur la hanche:
Avec toutes, l'amour s'échange
Simple et sans foi comme un bonjour.

Oh! if we could only depart this life together, at the end of this Grand Mass, sickened by our species, which yawns with relief the moment they get out of church into the square.

(V) Petition

True love is a crossroads without a fountain; but at the far end of every street, deafening funfairs.

They're never straight with you; or arms akimbo: with all of them, love is a deal, straightforward and faithless as a 'Hey there!'

O bouquets d'oranger cuirassés de satin,
Elle s'éteint, elle s'éteint,
La divine Rosace[1]
A voir vos noces de sexes livrés à la grosse
Courir en valsant vers la fosse
Commune! . . . Pauvre race!

Pas d'absolu; des compromis;
Tout est pas plus, tout est permis.

Et cependant, ô des nuits, laissez-moi, Circés[2]
Sombrement coiffés à la Titus,[3]
Et les yeux en grand deuil comme des pensées!
Et passez,
Béatifiques Vénus
Étalées et découvrant vos gencives comme un régal,
Et bâillant des aisselles au soleil
Dans l'assourdissement des cigales!
Ou, droites, tenant sur fond violet le lotus
Des sacrilèges domestiques,
En faisant de l'index: *motus!*

Oh orange-blossom bouquets breastplated in satin, the divine Rose-Window's light is fading, fading, when she sees your sex-weddings served up by the gross, waltzing at a run towards the common grave! Poor doomed folk!

No absolute; just compromises; everything's 'no further than that!', everything's allowed.

Yet, Oh! some nights, leave me alone, you Circes, your hair arranged darkly in Titus style, and your eyes in deep mourning like pansies! Pass by, beatific Venuses, sprawled out, uncovering your gums like a present, your armpits yawning in the sun in the deafening din of the cicadas! Or upright, bearing on a violet background the lotus of domestic desecrations, signalling with your forefingers: *hush!*

Passez, passez, bien que les yeux vierges
Ne soient que cadrans d'émail bleu,
Marquant telle heure que l'on veut,
Sauf à garder pour eux, pour Elle,
Leur heure immortelle.
Sans doute au premier mot,
On va baisser ces yeux,
Et peut-être choir en syncope,
On est si vierge à fleur de robe
Peut-être même à fleur de peau,
Mais leur destinée est bien interlope, au nom de Dieu!

O historiques esclaves!
Oh! leur petite chambre!
Qu'on peut les en faire descendre
Vers d'autres étages,
Vers les plus frelatées des caves,
Vers les moins ange-gardien des ménages!

Et alors, le grand Suicide, à froid,
Et leur *Amen* d'une voix sans Elle,
Tout en vaquant aux petits soins secrets,

Pass by, pass by, although virgin eyes are merely blue enamel sundials, marking any hour you like, though reserving the right to preserve for those men, for Her, their immortal hour. Doubtless at the first word, they'll lower those eyes of theirs, and perhaps fall down in a swoon, they are so virgin at dress-level! and perhaps even at skin-level, but, God knows, their destiny is pretty shady!

O slaves throughout history! Oh! Their little bedrooms! from which you can make them descend to other floors, to the most adulterated cellars, to the least guardian-angel of households!

And then, the big Suicide, played cold, and their *Amen* in a voice without Her, while all the time preoccupied with little secret concerns,

Et puis leur éternel air distrait
Leur grand air de dire: «De quoi?[4]
«Ah! de quoi, au fond, s'il vous plait?»

Mon Dieu, que l'Idéal
La dépouillât de ce rôle d'ange!
Qu'elle adoptât l'homme comme égal
Oh! que ses yeux ne parlent plus d'Idéal
Mais simplement d'humains échanges!
En frères et sœurs par le cœur,
Et fiancés par le passé,
Et puis unis par l'Infini!
Oh! simplement d'infinis échanges
A la fin de journées
A quatre bras moissonnées,
Quand les tambours, quand les trompettes,
Ils s'en vont sonnant la retraite,
Et qu'on prend le frais sur le pas des portes,
En vidant les pots de grès
A la santé des années mortes
Qui n'ont pas laissé de regrets,
Au su de tout le canton
Que depuis toujours nous habitons,
Ton ton, ton taine, ton ton.

and then their everlasting absent-minded look, their lofty look of saying, 'What on earth? What on earth, really, I ask you!'

My God, if only the Ideal would strip her of this angel's rôle! If only she'd adopt man as her equal! Oh, let her eyes no longer speak of the Ideal, but simply of human interchange! Like brothers and sisters by the heart, and fiancés by the past, and finally united by the Infinite! Oh simply infinite interchanges at the end of days harvested by four arms, when the drums, when the trumpets march off sounding the retreat, and when we sit in the evening's cool on the doorstep, emptying stoneware jugs to the health of dead years which have left no regrets, as the whole district knows, where we've lived for ever, tan-tan, tantivvy, tantara.

(VI) Simple agonie

O paria! – Et revoici les sympathies de mai.
Mais tu ne peux que te répéter, ô honte!
Et tu te gonfles et ne crèves jamais.
Et tu sais fort bien, ô paria,
Que ce n'est pas du tout ça.

Oh! que
Devinant l'instant le plus seul de la nature,
Ma mélodie, toute et unique, monte,
Dans le soir et redouble, et fasse tout ce qu'elle peut
Et dise la chose qu'est la chose,
Et retombe, et reprenne,
Et fasse de la peine,
O solo de sanglots,
Et reprenne et retombe
Selon la tâche qui lui incombe.
Oh! que ma musique
Se crucifie,
Selon sa photographie
Accoudée et mélancolique! . . .

(VI) Simple Agony

Pariah! – And the sympathies of May are back again. But you can only repeat yourself, O shame! And you puff yourself up and never burst. And you know very well, pariah, that that's not the real point.

Oh! If only it could happen that – guessing the most solitary instant in nature, my melody, entire and unique, might ascend into the evening, and redouble, and do its utmost, and say the thing which the thing really is, and die away, and start up again, and arouse pity, O aria of sobbing, and start up again and die away as its task requires. Oh! let my music be spreadeagled on a cross, according to her photograph, leaning on her elbows, brooding!

Il faut trouver d'autres thèmes,
Plus mortels et plus suprêmes.
Oh! bien, avec le monde tel quel,
Je vais me faire un monde plus mortel!

Les âmes y seront à musique,
Et tous les intérêts puérilement charnels,
O fanfares dans les soirs,
Ce sera barbare,
Ce sera sans espoir.

Enquêtes, enquêtes,
Seront l'unique fête!
Qui m'en défie?
J'entasse sur mon lit, les journaux, linge sale,
Dessins de mode, photographies quelconques,
Toute la capitale,
Matrice sociale.
Que nul n'intercède,
Ce ne sera jamais assez,
Il n'y a qu'un remède,
C'est de tout casser.

I must find other themes, more mortal and more ultimate. Oh! really? Out of so shoddy a world, am I going to make me a world more mortal?

Souls, there, will be set to music, and every interest childishly carnal. O fanfares in the evenings, it'll be barbarous, it'll be hopeless.

Interrogation, interrogation, will be the only celebration! Who defies me to think so? I pile up on my bed, newspapers, dirty linen, fashion prints, nondescript photographs, the whole of the capital, womb of society! Please, nobody intercede, it'll never be enough, there's only one remedy, to smash up everything.

O fanfares dans les soirs!
Ce sera barbare,
Ce sera sans espoir.
Et nous aurons beau la piétiner à l'envi.
Nous ne serons jamais plus cruels que la vie,
Qui fait qu'il est des animaux injustement rossés,
Et des femmes à jamais laides . . .
Que nul n'intercède,
Il faut tout casser.

Alléluia, Terre paria.
Ce sera sans espoir,
De l'aurore au soir,
Quand il n'y en aura plus il y en aura encore,
Du soir à l'aurore.
Alléluia, Terre paria!
Les hommes de l'art
Ont dit: «Vrai, c'est trop tard.»
Pas de raison,
Pour ne pas activer sa crevaison.

Aux armes, citoyens! Il n'y a plus de RAISON:[1]

O evening fanfares! It'll be barbarous, it'll be hopeless. And it'll be no good our trampling on life, outvying each other. We'll never be crueller than life, which ensures that there are always animals unjustly thrashed and women for ever ugly . . . Let no one intercede, we must smash up everything.

Alleluyah, Pariah Earth. It'll be hopeless from dawn to dusk; when there are no more, the more there'll be, from dusk to dawn. Alleluyah, Pariah Earth! The experts have said: 'Truly it's too late.' No reason for not activating its termination.

To arms! citizens! there's no more REASON:

Il prit froid l'autre automne,
S'étant attardé vers les peines des cors,
Sur la fin d'un beau jour.
Oh! ce fut pour vos cors, et ce fut pour l'automne,
Qu'il nous montra qu'«on meurt d'amour»!
On ne le verra plus aux fêtes nationales,
S'enfermer dans l'Histoire et tirer les verrous,
Il vint trop tôt, il est reparti sans scandale;
O vous qui m'écoutez, rentrez chacun chez vous.[2]

(VII) Solo de lune

Je fume, étalé face au ciel,
Sur l'impériale[1] de la diligence,
Ma carcasse est cahotée, mon âme danse
Comme un Ariel;[2]
Sans miel,[3] sans fiel, ma belle âme danse,
O routes, coteaux, ô fumées, ô vallons,
Ma belle âme, ah! récapitulons.

He caught a chill last autumn, staying out late towards the sorrows of the horns, towards the end of a fine day. Oh! it was for your hunting horns, it was for the autumn, that he showed you 'One dies of love'! We'll never see him again on Bank Holidays, locking himself up behind History and drawing the bolts, he came too soon, he's departed without scandal; 'O you who hear me, get yourselves home!'

(VII) Moonlight Aria

I'm smoking, sprawled out gazing at the sky, on the roof of the stage-coach, my carcass is being jolted about, my soul is dancing like an Ariel; without honey, without malice, my high-minded soul is dancing, O roads, hills, smoking chimneys, valleys, my high-minded soul, ah! let's go over it again.

Nous nous aimions comme deux fous,
On s'est quitté sans en parler,
Un spleen me tenait exilé,
Et ce spleen me venait de tout. Bon.

Ses yeux disaient: «Comprenez-vous?
«Pourquoi ne comprenez-vous pas?»
Mais nul n'a voulu faire le premier pas,
Voulant trop tomber *ensemble* à genoux.
(Comprenez-vous?)

Où est-elle à cette heure?
Peut-être qu'elle pleure . . .
Où est-elle à cette heure?
Oh! du moins, soigne-toi, je t'en conjure!

O fraîcheur des bois le long de la route,
O châle de mélancolie, toute âme est un peu aux écoutes,
Que ma vie
Fait envie!
Cette impériale de diligence tient de la magie.

We loved each other like two lunatics, we parted without mentioning it, a melancholy kept me exiled, and this melancholy came to me from everything. Oh well.

Her eyes said: 'Do you understand? Why don't you understand?' But neither wished to take the first step, wanting too much to fall to our knees *at the same moment*. (Do you understand?)

Where is she at this hour? Perhaps she's weeping . . . Where is she at this hour? Ah, at least look after your health, I implore you!

O coolness of the woods along the roadside, O shawl of melancholy, every soul is a little on the *qui-vive*. How envious they are of my life! The roof of this stage-coach holds magic.

Accumulons l'irréparable!
Renchérissons sur notre sort!
Les étoiles sont plus nombreuses que le sable
Des mers où d'autres ont vu se baigner son corps;
Tout n'en va pas moins à la Mort.
Y a pas de port.[4]

Des ans vont passer là-dessus,
On s'endurcira chacun pour soi,
Et bien souvent et déjà je m'y vois,
On se dira: «Si j'avais su . . .»
Mais mariés de même, ne se fût-on pas dit
«Si j'avais su, si j'avais su! . . .»?
Ah! rendez-vous maudit!
Ah! mon cœur sans issue! . . .
Je me suis mal conduit.

Maniaques de bonheur,
Donc, que ferons-nous? Moi de mon âme,
Elle de sa faillible jeunesse?
O vieillissante pécheresse,
Oh! que de soirs je vais me rendre infâme
En ton honneur!

Let's pile up the irreparable! Let's embellish our fate! The stars are more numerous than the sands of the seas where other men have seen her bathing her body; Everything goes no less towards Death, there ain't no haven.

Years will pass over it, we'll become harder, each of us separately, and very often – already I see myself doing it – we'll say to ourselves, 'If only I'd known . . .' But married, wouldn't we have said just the same, 'If I'd known, if I'd only known! . . .'? Ah! cursed rendez-vous! Ah! my heart with no way out! . . . I've behaved badly.

Maniacs for happiness, therefore, what shall we do? I with my soul, she with her fallible youth? You ageing sinner, Oh! how many evenings I'll defame myself in your honour!

Ses yeux clignaient: «Comprenez-vous?
«Pourquoi ne comprenez-vous pas?»
Mais nul n'a fait le premier pas
Pour tomber ensemble à genoux. Ah! . . .

La Lune se lève,
O route en grand rêve! . . .

On a dépassé les filatures, les scieries,
Plus que les bornes kilométriques,
De petits nuages d'un rose de confiserie,
Cependant qu'un fin croissant de lune se lève,
O route de rêve, ô nulle musique . . .
Dans ces bois de pins où depuis
Le commencement du monde
Il fait toujours nuit,
Que de chambres propres et profondes!
Oh! pour un soir d'enlèvement!
Et je les peuple et je m'y vois,
Et c'est un beau couple d'amants,
Qui gesticulent hors la loi.

Her eyes signalled: 'Do you understand? Why don't you understand?' But no one took the first step to fall to our knees together. Ah! . . .

The Moon is rising, O road of high reverie!

We've passed the cotton mills, the sawmills, there's nothing left but milestones, little clouds of sweetshop pink, while the slender crescent of the moon rises, O road of dream, O non-existent music . . . In these pinewoods where since the beginning of the world it's always been dark, how many clean, deep-hidden bedrooms! Oh for an evening of elopement! And I fill them with people and see myself there, and it's a handsome pair of lovers with lawless gestures.

Et je passe et les abandonne,
Et me recouche face au ciel.
La route tourne, je suis Ariel,
Nul ne m'attend, je ne vais chez personne.
Je n'ai que l'amitié des chambres d'hôtel.

La lune se lève,
O route en grand rêve.
O route sans terme,
Voici le relais,
Où l'on allume les lanternes,
Où l'on boit un verre de lait,
Et fouette postillon,
Dans le chant des grillons,
Sous les étoiles de juillet.

O clair de Lune,
Noce de feux de Bengale noyant mon infortune,
Les ombres des peupliers sur la route . . .
Le gave qui s'écoute, . . .
Qui s'écoute chanter . . .
Dans ces inondations du fleuve du Léthé . . .[5]

And I pass and leave them behind, and lie down again my face to the sun, the road swings round, I am Ariel, nobody awaits me, I'm going to no address, I have only the friendship of hotel bedrooms.

The moon is rising, O road of high reverie! O endless road, here is the coaching house where they light the lanterns, where we drink a glass of milk, and 'Drive on, coachman!' through the crickets' song, under the stars of July.

O Moonlight, wedding of Bengal light drowning my misfortune, the shadows of the poplars on the road . . . the mountain torrent listening to itself . . . listening to itself singing . . . in those floodings of the river of Lethe . . .

O Solo de lune,
Vous défiez ma plume,
Oh! cette nuit sur la route;
O Étoiles, vous êtes à faire peur,
Vous y êtes toutes! toutes!
O fugacité de cette heure . . .
Oh! qu'il y eût moyen
De m'en garder l'âme pour l'automne qui vient! . . .

Voici qu'il fait très, très frais,
Oh! si à la même heure,
Elle va de même le long des forêts,
Noyer son infortune
Dans les noces du clair de lune! . . .
(Elle aime tant errer tard!)
Elle aura oublié son foulard,
Elle va prendre mal, vu la beauté de l'heure!
Oh! soigne-toi, je t'en conjure!
Oh! je ne veux plus entendre cette toux!

Ah! que ne suis-je tombé à tes genoux!
Ah! que n'as-tu défailli à mes genoux!
J'eusse été le modèle des époux!
Comme le frou-frou de ta robe est le modèle des frou-frou.

Moonlight Aria, you defy my pen, oh! that night on the road; Stars, you're enough to terrify, you're all there! every one! O the fleetingness of that hour, Oh! if only there'd been a way of preserving its soul for the coming autumn! . . .

And now it's become very chilly, Oh! if at this same hour, she too goes through the forests, to drown her unhappiness in the moonlight wedding! . . . (She loves so much to wander late!) She'll have forgotten her scarf, she'll catch cold, on account of the beauty of the hour! Oh! look after your health, I beseech you! Oh! I can't bear to hear that cough any more!

Ah! why didn't I fall at your knees! Ah! why didn't you faint at my knees! I would have been the ultimate in husbands! As the rustle of your dress is the ultimate in rustling.

(VIII) Légende

Armorial d'anémie!
Psautier d'automne!
Offertoire de tout mon ciboire[1] de bonheur et de génie
A cette hostie si féminine,
Et si petite toux sèche maligne,
Qu'on voit aux jours déserts, en inconnue,
Sertie en de cendreuses toilettes qui sentent déjà l'hiver,
Se fuir le long des cris surhumains de la Mer.

Grandes amours, oh! qu'est-ce encor? . . .

En tout cas, des lèvres sans façon,[2]
Des lèvres déflorées,
Et quoique mortes aux chansons,
Après encore à la curée.
Mais les yeux d'une âme qui s'est bel et bien cloîtrée.

Enfin, voici qu'elle m'honore de ses confidences.
J'en souffre plus qu'elle ne pense.

(VIII) Legend

Heraldry of anæmia! Psalm-book of autumn! Offertory of all my ciborium of happiness and genius to this communion-host so feminine, with her little dry malignant cough, whom you see on forsaken days, incognito, clad in ash-grey dresses that already smack of winter, fleeing past the more-than-human cries of the Sea.

Grand passions, oh! and what else?

In any case, lips without fuss, deflowered lips, and although dead to songs, still hot for the chase. But the eyes of a soul which is utterly cloistered.

At last, here she is, honouring me with her confidences. This hurts me more than she thinks.

– «Mais, chère perdue, comment votre esprit éclairé
«Et le stylet d'acier de vos yeux infaillibles,
«N'ont-ils pas su percer à jour la mise en frais
«De cet économique et passager bellâtre?»

– «Il vient le premier; j'étais seule près de l'âtre;
«Son cheval attaché à la grille
«Hennissait en désespéré . . .»

– «C'est touchant (pauvre fille)
«Et puis après?
«Oh! regardez, là-bas, cet épilogue sous couleur de
      couchant;
«Et puis, vrai,
«Remarquez que dès l'automne, l'automne!
«Les casinos,
«Qu'on abandonne
«Remisent leur piano;
«Hier l'orchestre attaqua
«Sa dernière polka,
«Hier, la dernière fanfare
«Sanglotait vers les gares . . .»

'But dear fallen one, how could your enlightened mind and the steel stiletto of your infallible eyes not have seen through the outlay of this penny-pinching passer-by, this smoothie?'

'He was there first; I was alone by the hearth; his horse tied to the gate was neighing like a lost soul . . .'

'How touching (poor lass) and what of it? Oh! look, over there, at that epilogue pretending it's a sunset! After all, it's worth noting that when autumn comes, it's autumn! The abandoned casinos pack away their pianos; yesterday the orchestra struck up its last polka, yesterday the last fanfare sobbed away towards the railway stations.'

(Oh! comme elle est maigrie!
Que va-telle devenir?
Durcissez, durcissez,
Vous, caillots de souvenir!)

— «Allons, les poteaux télégraphiques
«Dans les grisailles de l'exil
«Vous serviront de pleureuses de funérailles;
«Moi, c'est la saison qui veut que je m'en aille,
«Voici l'hiver qui vient.
«Ainsi soit-il.
«Ah! soignez-vous! Portez-vous bien.

«Assez! assez!
«C'est toi qui as commencé!

«Tais-toi! Vos moindres clins d'yeux sont des parjures.
«Laisse! Avec vous autres rien ne dure.
«Va, je te l'assure,
«Si je t'aimais, ce serait par gageure.

«Tais-toi! tais-toi!
«On n'aime qu'une fois!»

Ah! voici que l'on compte enfin avec Moi!

(Oh! how thin she's got! What will become of her? Set harder, harder, blood-clots of memory!)

'Come, the telegraph poles in the greynesses of exile will act as your mourners at the funeral. As for me, it's the season which compels me to leave, here's winter on its way. So be it. Ah! look after your health! Keep well.

'Quiet! Quiet! It was you who began it!

'Be quiet! The slightest winks of your eye are perjuries. Drop the subject! With your sex nothing lasts. Look, I assure you, if I loved you, it would be for a dare.

'Shut up! Shut up! Nobody loves more than once!'

Ah! at last she has to reckon with Me!

Ah! ce n'est plus l'automne, alors,
Ce n'est plus l'exil.
C'est la douceur des légendes, de l'âge d'or,
Des légendes des Antigones,[3]
Douceur qui fait qu'on se demande:
«Quand donc cela se passait-il?»

C'est des légendes, c'est des gammes perlées,
Qu'on m'a tout enfant enseignées,
Oh! rien, vous dis-je, des estampes,
Les bêtes de la terre et les oiseaux du ciel
Enguirlandant les majuscules d'un Missel,
Il n'y a pas là tant de quoi saigner?

Saigner? moi pétri du plus pur limon de Cybèle![4]
Moi qui lui eusse été dans tout l'art des Adams
Des Édens aussi hyperboliquement fidèle
Que l'est le Soleil chaque soir envers l'Occident! . . .

Ah! it's no longer autumn, so it's no longer exile. It's the gentleness of legends
– the Golden Age – of legends of Antigones, a gentleness which makes one wonder:
'How long ago did that happen?'

It's legends, it's pearly scales that they taught me as a child, Oh! nothing, I tell
you, prints – the beasts of the earth and the birds of the sky, garlanding the capitals
of a Missal, there's not enough in that to make you bleed?

Bleed? I, moulded in Cybele's purest clay! I, who would have been in all the art
of the Adams of the Edens as far-fetchedly faithful to her as is the Sun every evening
to the West!

(IX)

Oh! qu'une, d'Elle-même, un beau soir, sût venir
Ne voyant plus que boire à mes lèvres, ou mourir! . . .

Oh! Baptême!
Oh! baptême de ma Raison d'être!
Faire naître un «Je t'aime!»
Et qu'il vienne à travers les hommes et les dieux,
Sous ma fenêtre,
Baissant les yeux!

Qu'il vienne, comme à l'aimant la foudre,
Et dans mon ciel d'orage qui craque et qui s'ouvre,
Et alors, les averses lustrales jusqu'au matin,
Le grand clapissement des averses toute la nuit! Enfin

Qu'Elle vienne! et, baissant les yeux
Et s'essuyant les pieds
Au seuil de notre église, ô mes aïeux
Ministres de la Pitié,
Elle dise:

(IX)

Oh! if one, of Her own free will, one fine evening, could come, seeking nothing but to drink at my lips, or die!

Oh! Baptism! baptism of my *raison d'être*! To evoke an 'I love you!' – and may it come past men and gods, under my window, lowering its eyes!

May it come, like lightning to the magnet, through my stormy sky which cracks and opens, and then, lustral downpours till morning, loud shrieking of the showers all night long! At last

may She come! and, casting down her eyes and wiping her feet on the threshold of our church, O my ancestors, Ministers of Pity, may she say:

«Pour moi, tu n'es pas comme les autres hommes,
«Ils sont ces messieurs, toi tu viens des cieux.
«Ta bouche me fait baisser les yeux
«Et ton port me transporte
«Et je m'en découvre des trésors!
«Et je sais parfaitement que ma destinée se borne
«(Oh! j'y suis déjà bien habituée!)
«A te suivre jusqu'à ce que tu te retournes,
«Et alors t'exprimer comment tu es!

«Vraiment je ne songe pas au reste; j'attendrai
«Dans l'attendrissement de ma vie faite exprès.

«Que je te dise seulement que depuis des nuits je pleure,
«Et que mes sœurs ont bien peur que je n'en meure.

«Je pleure dans les coins, je n'ai plus goût à rien;
«Oh! j'ai tant pleuré dimanche dans mon paroissien!

«Tu me demandes pourquoi toi et non un autre.
«Ah! laisse, c'est bien toi et non un autre.

'I find you're not like other men, they're "those gentlemen", but you come from the heavens. 'Your mouth makes me lower my eyes, and your bearing transports me and I find all sorts of delights in it! and I know for sure that my destiny is confined (Oh, to this I'm already quite resigned!) to following you till you turn round, and then describing you to yourself!

'Really I think of nothing else; I shall wait in the tender passion of my life, which was made specially for this.

'Let me tell you merely that I've been weeping for nights, and that my sisters are very afraid I may die.

'I weep in corners, I've lost interest in everything; oh! I wept so much last Sunday into my prayer-book!

'You ask me why it's you and not another, Ah, never mind! it *is* you and not another.

«J'en suis sûre comme du vide insensé de mon cœur
«Et comme de votre air mortellement moqueur.»

Ainsi, elle viendrait, évadée, demi-morte,
Se rouler sur le paillasson que j'ai mis à cet effet devant ma
    porte
Ainsi, elle viendrait à Moi avec des yeux absolument fous,
Et elle me suivrait avec ses yeux-là partout, partout!

(X)

O géraniums diaphanes, guerroyeurs sortilèges,
Sacrilèges monomanes![1]
Emballages,[2] dévergondages, douches! O pressoirs
Des vendanges des grands soirs!
Layettes aux abois,
Thyrses[3] au fond des bois!

'I'm as sure of it as I am of the senseless emptiness of my heart, and of your look
of deadly mockery.'

So, she would come, like a fugitive, half-dead, to roll upon the doormat which
I have put for this very purpose outside my door. So, she would come to Me with
eyes absolutely insane, and she would follow me with those eyes everywhere,
everywhere!

(X)

O diaphanous geraniums, warring enchantments, obsessive blasphemies! Cycle-
sprints, spurts of shamelessness, cold showers! O wine-presses of the wine-harvests
of long evenings! Baby clothes at bay, thyrsi deep in the woods!

Transfusions, représailles,
Relevailles, compresses et l'éternelle potion,
Angelus! n'en pouvoir plus
De débâcles nuptiales! de débâcles nuptiales! . . .

Et puis, ô mes amours,
A moi, son tous les jours
O ma petite mienne, ô ma quotidienne,
Dans mon petit intérieur,
C'est-à-dire plus jamais ailleurs!
O ma petite quotidienne! . . .

Et quoi encore? Oh du génie!
Improvisations aux insomnies!

Et puis? L'observer dans le monde,
Et songer dans les coins:
«Oh! qu'elle est loin! Oh! qu'elle est belle!
«Oh! qui est-elle? A qui est-elle?
«Oh! quelle inconnue! Oh! lui parler! Oh! l'emmener!»
(Et, en effet, à la fin du bal,
Elle me suivrait d'un air tout simplement fatal.)

Transfusions, reprisals, churching of women, cold compresses and the everlasting potion, Angelus! I've had it up to here with nuptial breakdowns! nuptial breakdowns!

And then, O my darling love, mine is her every day, O my little mine, O my everyday one, in my little indoors, that's to say never anywhere else! O my little everyday one!

And what else? Oh what genius! Improvisations during insomnia!

And then? Seeing her about the world, and musing in corners, 'How unobtainable she is! How beautiful! Oh who is she? Whose is she? Oh what a beautiful stranger! Oh to speak to her! Oh to go off with her!' (And, in fact, at the end of the ball, she'd follow me with an air of pure destiny.)

Et puis, l'éviter des semaines
Après lui avoir fait de la peine,
Et lui donner des rendez-vous,
Et nous refaire un chez nous.

Et puis, la perdre des mois et des mois,
A ne plus reconnaître sa voix! . . .

Oui, le Temps salit tout,
Mais, hélas! sans en venir à bout.

Hélas! hélas! et plus la faculté d'errer,
Hypocondrie et pluie,
Et seul sous les vieux cieux,
De me faire le fou,
Le fou sans feux ni lieux
(Le pauvre, pauvre fou sans amours!)
Pour, alors, tomber bien bas
A me purifier la chair,
Et exulter au petit jour
En me fuyant en chemin de fer,
O Belles-Lettres, ô Beaux-Arts,
Ainsi qu'un Ange à part!

And next, avoiding her for weeks after hurting her feelings, and giving her rendez-vous and rebuilding a place of our own.

And next, losing her for months upon months, till I no longer knew her voice! . . .

Yes, time soils everything, but, alas! it never completes the job.

Alas! alas! and no longer able to stray, hypochondria and rain, alone under the aged skies, to play the fool, fool without hearth or home (poor, poor loveless fool!) and then to fall so low as to purify my flesh, and exulting at dawn as I run away from myself on a train, O Literature, O Fine Arts, like an Angel set apart.

J'aurai passé ma vie le long des quais
A faillir m'embarquer
Dans de bien funestes histoires,
Tout cela pour l'amour
De mon cœur fou de la gloire d'amour.

Oh! qu'ils sont pittoresques les trains manqués! . . .

Oh! qu'ils sont «A bientôt! à bientôt!»
Les bateaux
Du bout de la jetée! . . .

De la jetée charpentée
Contre la mer,
Comme ma chair
Contre l'amour.

(XI) Sur une défunte

Vous ne m'aimeriez pas,[1] voyons,
Vous ne m'aimeriez pas plus,
Pas plus, entre nous,
Qu'une fraternelle Occasion? . . .

I shall have spent my life on railway platforms, almost embarking on quite disastrous entanglements, all for the love of my heart mad with love's glory.

Missed trains! Oh, how picturesque they are! . . .

Oh! how 'See you soon! We'll soon be back!' are the boats at the end of the jetty!

Of the jetty, firmly timbered against the sea, like my body against love.

(XI) On a Dead Woman

Is it really true you don't love me, for goodness' sake? 'Between you and me' you 'don't love me any more than for a brotherly Encounter?'

– Ah! elle ne m'aime pas!
Ah! elle ne ferait pas le premier pas
Pour que nous tombions ensemble à genoux.

Si elle avait rencontré seulement
A, B, C ou D, au lieu de Moi,
Elle les eût aimés uniquement!

Je les vois, je les vois . . .

Attendez! Je la vois
Avec les nobles A, B, C ou D.
Elle était née pour chacun d'eux.
C'est lui, Lui, quel qu'il soit,
Elle le reflète;
D'un air parfait, elle secoue la tête
Et dit que rien, rien ne peut lui déraciner
Cette étonnante destinée.[2]

C'est Lui; elle lui dit:
«Oh! tes yeux, ta démarche!
«Oh! le son fatal de ta voix!
«Voilà si longtemps que je te cherche!
«Oh! c'est bien Toi cette fois! . . .»

– Ah! she doesn't love me! Ah! she'd not take the first step for us both to fall to our knees together!

If she'd only met A, B, C or D, instead of Me, she'd have loved them uniquely! I can see them, I can see them . . .

Wait! I can see her with the noble A, B, C or D. She was born for each of them. Each is he, He, whichever he may be, she reflects him; looking perfected, she shakes her head and says that nothing, nothing can uproot from her this astounding destiny.

It's He: she tells him: 'Oh, your eyes, your bearing! Oh, the destiny-laden sound of your voice! How long I've been seeking you! Oh, it's really You, this time! . . .'

Il baisse un peu sa bonne lampe,
Il la ploie, Elle, vers son cœur,
Il la baise à la tempe
Et à la place de son orphelin cœur.

Il l'endort avec des caresses tristes,
Il l'apitoie avec de petites plaintes,
Il a des considérations fatalistes,
Il prend à témoin tout ce qui existe,
Et puis voici que l'heure tinte.

Pendant que je suis dehors
A errer avec elle au cœur,
A m'étonner peut-être
De l'obscurité de sa fenêtre.

Elle est chez lui, elle s'y sent chez elle.
Et, comme on vient de le voir,
Elle l'aime, éperdument fidèle,
Dans toute sa beauté des soirs! . . .

Je les ai vus! Oh! ce fut trop complet!
Elle avait l'air trop fidèle
Avec ses grands yeux tout en reflets
Dans sa figure toute nouvelle!

He turns down the light of his trusty lamp a little, he sways her, Her, towards his heart, he kisses her on the temple and at the place of her orphan heart.

He lulls her to sleep with sad caresses, he moves her to pity with his little grumbles, he pronounces destiny-laden thoughts, he calls to witness the world and everything in it, and then, goodness! there's the clock striking.

Meanwhile I'm out of doors, wandering, with her in my heart, surprised perhaps at the darkness of her window.

She's at his place, feeling quite at home. And as we've just seen, she loves him, frantically faithful, in all her evening beauty! . . .

I saw them! Oh, it was too much! She had that all too faithful look, with her big eyes shining bright in her brand new face!

Et je ne serais qu'un pis-aller,

Et je ne serais qu'un pis-aller,
Comme l'est mon jour dans le Temps,
Comme l'est ma place dans l'Espace;
Et l'on ne voudrait pas que je m'accommodasse
De ce sort vraiment dégoûtant! . . .

Non, non! pour Elle, tout ou rien!
Et je m'en irai donc comme un fou,
A travers l'automne qui vient,
Dans le grand vent où il y a tout!

Je me dirai: Oh! à cette heure,
Elle est bien loin, elle pleure,
Le grand vent se lamente aussi,
Et moi je suis seul dans ma demeure,
Avec mon noble cœur tout transi,
Et sans amour et sans personne,
Car tout est misère, tout est automne,
Tout est endurci et sans merci.

Et, si je t'avais aimée ainsi,
Tu l'aurais trouvée trop bien bonne! Merci!

And I'd be nothing but second best,
    And I'd be nothing but second best, like my day in Time, like my place in Space. And you wouldn't really want me to settle for this truly disgusting fate! . . .
    No, no! for Her, all or nothing! And so I'll stride off like a madman, through the approaching Autumn, in the high wind which says it all!
    I'll tell myself: 'Oh! at this hour, she's far away, she's weeping, the high wind's mourning too,' and I'm alone in my lodgings, my noble heart ice-cold, loveless and all alone, for everything is misery, everything is autumn, everything is callous and merciless.
    And, if I'd loved you so, your reaction would have been, 'You're having me on!' Thank you!

(XII)

Get thee to a nunnery: why wouldst thou be a
    breeder of sinners? I am myself indifferent
    honest; but yet I could accuse me of such
    things, that it were better my mother had
    not borne me. We are arrant knaves, all;
    believe none of us. Go thy ways to a
    nunnery.

                                        HAMLET.

Noire bise, averse glapissante,
Et fleuve noir, et maisons closes,
Et quartiers sinistres comme des Morgues,
Et l'Attardé qui à la remorque traîne
Toute la misère du cœur et des choses,
Et la souillure des innocentes qui traînent,
Et crie à l'averse. «Oh? arrose, arrose
«Mon cœur si brûlant, ma chair si intéressante!»

Oh! elle, mon cœur et ma chair, que fait-elle? . . .

Oh! si elle est dehors par ce vilain temps,
De quelles histoires trop humaines rentre-t-elle?
Et si elle est dedans,
A ne pas pouvoir dormir par ce grand vent,

(XII)

Black North Wind, yelping downpour, and black river, and closed-up houses, and
neighbourhoods as sinister as Morgues, and the Latecomer towing behind him all
the wretchedness of his heart and of things in general, and the besmirching of
innocent girls who lag behind – and cry to the downpour, 'Oh! bathe, bathe my
burning heart, my so interesting flesh!'

Oh, she, my heart and my flesh, what is she doing?

Oh! if she's out of doors in this foul weather, from what all too human goings-on
is she returning? And if she's indoors, unable to sleep in this high wind,

Pense-t-elle au Bonheur,
Au bonheur à tout prix
Disant: tout plutôt que mon cœur reste ainsi incompris?

Soigne-toi, soigne-toi! pauvre cœur aux abois.

(Langueurs, débilité, palpitations, larmes,
Oh! cette misère de vouloir être notre femme!)

O pays, ô famille!
Et l'âme toute tournée[1]
D'héroïques destinées
Au delà des saintes vieilles filles,
Et pour cette année!

Nuit noire, maisons closes, grand vent,
Oh! dans un couvent, dans un couvent!

Un couvent dans ma ville natale
Douce de vingt mille âmes à peine,
Entre le lycée et la préfecture
Et vis à vis la cathédrale,

is she thinking of Happiness, happiness at any price, saying: 'Anything, sooner than this – that my heart should remain so misunderstood!'?

Take care of your health, poor heart at bay.

(Languors, debility, palpitations, tears, Oh, the misery of wanting to be our wife!)

O nation, O family! And the soul quite turned with destinies more heroic than those of holy old maids, that's it, all over for this year!

Black night, closed-up houses, high wind, Oh, to a nunnery, to a nunnery!

A convent in my native town, sweet with barely twenty thousand souls, between the grammar school and the prefecture and facing the cathedral, with

Avec ces anonymes en robes grises,
Dans la prière, le ménage, les travaux de couture;
Et que cela suffise . . .
Et méprise sans envie
Tout ce qui n'est pas cette vie de Vestale
Provinciale,
Et marche à jamais glacée,
Les yeux baissés.

Oh! je ne puis voir ta petite scène fatale à vif,
Et ton pauvre air dans ce huis-clos,
Et tes tristes petits gestes instinctifs,
Et peut-être incapable de sanglots!

Oh! ce ne fut pas et ce ne peut être,
Oh! tu n'es pas comme les autres,
Crispées aux rideaux de leur fenêtre
Devant le soleil couchant qui dans son sang se vautre!
Oh! tu n'as pas l'âge,
Oh! dis, tu n'auras jamais l'âge,
Oh! tu me promets de rester sage comme une image? . . .

La nuit est à jamais noire,
Le vent est grandement triste,
Tout dit la vieille histoire

those grey-robed anonymous women, at prayer, doing housework, needlework; and let that suffice . . . and despise without envy all that isn't this provincial Vestal Virgin's life, and walk for ever frozen, eyes on the ground.

Ah! I can't bear to see your doom-laden, nerve-jangling little scene, and how wretched you look behind those closed doors, and your sad little instinctive gestures, and not perhaps even able to sob!

Oh! it was not and it cannot be, Oh! you're not like others, clenching the curtains of their windows before the setting sun wallowing in its own blood! Oh! you're not old enough, Oh, tell me, you'll never be old enough, Oh, you promise me to stay as good as gold? . . .

The night is for ever black, the wind is vastly sad, everything tells the old story

Qu'il faut être deux au coin du feu,
Tout bâcle un hymne fataliste,
Mais toi, il ne faut pas que tu t'abandonnes,
A ces vilains jeux! . . .

A ces grandes pitiés du mois de novembre!
Reste dans ta petite chambre,
Passe, à jamais glacée,
Tes beaux yeux irréconciliablement baissés.

Oh! qu'elle est là-bas, que la nuit est noire!
Que la vie est une étourdissante foire!
Que toutes sont créature, et que tout est routine!

Oh! que nous mourrons!

Eh bien, pour aimer ce qu'il y a d'histoires
Derrière ces beaux yeux d'orpheline héroïne,
O Nature, donne-moi la force et le courage[2]
De me croire en âge,
O Nature, relève-moi le front!
Puisque, tôt ou tard, nous mourrons . . .

that one must be a couple in the chimney-corner, everything cobbles together a fatalistic hymn, but *you* mustn't give yourself up to these sordid games! . . .

to these great griefs of the month of November! Stay in your little bedroom, pass, for ever frozen, with your beautiful eyes for ever on the ground.

Oh, how far off she is, how black the night is! what a dizzying circus is life! how creaturely all women are, how pedestrian everything is!

Oh, that we all shall die!

And so, to love whatever goings-on there may be behind this orphan heroine's beautiful eyes, O Nature, give me the strength and the courage to think I'm old enough. O Nature, raise up my head! Since, sooner or later, we shall die . . .

NOTES

LE SANGLOT DE LA TERRE and Other Early Poems

Ballade de retour [Ballad of Home-coming]
1. *ritournelles*: a ritornello is a repeated musical phrase, or a musical phrase too often repeated.

Nuage [Cloud]
1. *Agent*: the Agent is the Unconscious, manipulating man and woman behind the scenes. *Nuage* suggests a cloud over their relationship, or a kind of smoke-screen – behind which this Agent lurks.
2. *pauvres Bourreaux*: because our sexual drives make us obey the Unconscious – in creating living creatures, all of whom are doomed to death.

Complainte du libre-arbitre [Lament of Free Will]
1. *responsableu*: the popular-song pronunciation of *responsable* shows us that Laforgue is guying free will.
2. *l'Golgotha*: the Mount of Golgotha was the place where Christ was crucified.

Complainte de l'Organiste de Notre-Dame de Nice [Lament of the Organist of Notre-Dame de Nice]
1. *Miserere*: 'Have pity . . .' The opening words of the 51st Psalm.

La Chanson du Petit hypertrophique [The Song of the Hypertrophic Child]
1. *hypertrophique*: hypertrophy is a medical term signifying an over-enlargement of the heart, or of some other organ. Laforgue also uses it to mean over-enlarged emotion.

2. *Tir-lan-laire!*: Laforgue suppresses the mute e's, and inserts meaningless refrains, as in folk and popular song.

Hypertrophie [Hypertrophy]

1. *pantoum*: a form of poem, originally from Malaya, in which the second and fourth lines of each verse become the first and third of the next. It thus suggests the endless repetitiveness of Nature.

La Première nuit [The First Night]

1. *chlorotique*: suffering from Chlorosis, or Green Sickness, a form of anaemia which, in the nineteenth century, used to afflict young women.

LES COMPLAINTES

A Paul Bourget [To Paul Bourget]

1. *cent pur-sang*: an excruciating pun on '*cent pour cent*' ('100 per cent').
2. *Armide*: in Tasso's *Jerusalem Delivered*, the gardens of Armida are where she put a spell on Rinaldo so as to keep him from the Crusades. Doubtless the Metaphysical Armida is an image for the failure to engage in action.
3. *chalumeau*: the deeper of the two registers of the clarinet.
4. *Nom de Lac*: Lake-Name – because the name of Bourget, Laforgue's great friend, is also the name of a lake in the Alps.
5. *feuilleteurs du quai*: a reference to the second-hand booksellers along the *quais de la Seine*.
6. *AVEUX*: Bourget's *Les Aveux* (*Confessions*) had been published in 1882.

Préludes autobiographiques [Autobiographical Preamble]

1. *Noël gras*: an invention based on *Mardi gras*, a time of carnival.
2. *Où je . . . réel*: his tears burn the handkerchief, because they're 'hot tears', as the old cliché puts it. (Hiddleston)
3. *cobalt sourd*: the 'deaf cobalt' is the blue Heavens, from which no God replies.
4. *hypertrophique*: see note 1 to 'La Chanson du Petit hypertrophique' (*Sanglot*).
5. *Jourdain*: Paris's 'bourgeois River Jordan' is the Seine, but he is punning

on Molière's Monsieur Jourdain, who was the eponymous *Bourgeois gentilhomme*.

6. *bébé*: formed on the analogy of 'bon enfant/bon garçon' which mean naïvely easy-going.

7. *vers quand*: written instead of *à qui* ('to whom'), and meaning perhaps 'to whose when-ness'.

8. *lamasabaktani*: Jesus's words on the Cross: 'My God, my God, why hast thou forsaken me?' (Matthew XXVII:34).

9. *les cercles du Cercle*: it is likely that Laforgue picked up this phrase from Pascal who notes that God is described as 'a sphere whose centre is everywhere and whose circumference nowhere' in Hermes Trismegistus, pseudonymous 'author' of a variety of ancient mystical and gnostic writings. This beautiful idea is probably Pythagorean.

10. *géhenne*: Gehenna is the ancient Hebrew hell.

11. *Draguant . . . abrutis*: *Draguer* is to dredge for, and hence to chat up or pick up. I have thus written 'cruise'. '*Impôts*' (taxes) and '*sols*' (ground-floors) are common Laforguian metaphors for the suffering our poor Earth has to undergo.

12. *soirs d'exil*: in Psalm 137 the exiled Jews in Babylon accompany with harps their songs to God.

13. *Galathée*: see note 1 to 'Dimanches' ('Bref, j'allais . . .') (*DV*).

14. *fugues douces*: a combination of *fugue* with *taille-douce*, which means copperplate engraving or etching.

15. *Psalmiste*: i.e. the preacher who cries, in Ecclesiastes I:2, that all is vanity.

16. *Soif à trucs*: i.e. the Universe creates insatiably, but with total indifference to the quality of *what* it creates!

17. *Songe d'une nuit d'août*: *Songe d'une nuit d'été* is the customary French for *A Midsummer Night's Dream*.

18. *tes soeurs*: i.e. the Earth's sister planets.

19. *Et . . . Amen*: an ironic quotation from the Doxology.

20. *mon Sacré-Cœur*: Laforgue always capitalises *Sacré-Coeur*, as if it referred to the Sacred Heart of Jesus. But his tone is always bitter, and *Sacré* is also a swear-word in French, hence my translation.

21. *du cèdre à l'hysope*: this means 'from the biggest to the smallest', and is a favourite expression of Laforgue's.

22. *qui m'aime me suive!*: Philippe VI King of France (1328–50) shouted these words during a battle in Flanders, but was as it were mutilated of all but one of his knights – the only one who followed him!

23. *Ninive*: the reference must be to the prophet Jonah, who was told by God to preach destruction against the city of Nineveh for its sins. The people of Nineveh repented (Jonah III:10), and were saved.

24. *Nirvâna*: the Buddhist after-life, an ultimate reality inexpressible in words, but often equated by nineteenth-century Europeans with Nothingness.

25. *vermis . . . es*: the first was said by the psalmist (XXII:6), the second by God when he condemned Adam to death in Genesis III:19.

26. *Tout-Un en soi*: a Hartmannian expression for the Ultimate, Brahma being the ultimate reality in Hinduism, identical with the Atman.

27. *O Robe . . . doriques*: pleated like the fluting on the Doric temple pillars of Greece.

28. *O Robe de Maïa*: the veil of the Goddess, i.e. an Indian term for this illusory world of appearances.

29. *Danaïdes*: the Danaids are proverbial of futility. Having murdered their husbands, they were punished in Hades by being forced to draw water in sieves. We often find Laforgue complaining that literary activity is similarly futile and endless.

30. *Sainte Piscine*: in churches, the place where water, used to wash the holy vessels, is emptied. The word is however the same as 'swimming bath' in French, and here Laforgue is committing suicide in it – in noble Roman fashion, emptying his veins – a Schopenhauerian suicide, abandoning life for Nirvana.

31. *s'il en reste un pour toi*: Laforgue (addressing himself as 'toi') has cried out too much; but will anyone utter a cry for him?

Complainte propitiatoire à l'Inconscient [Propitiatory Complaint to the Unconscious]

1. this is the Lord's Prayer, done according to the Laforguian faith.

2. *Aditi*: Vedic mythology. Aditi is the Infinite, a sky-goddess, and the mother of the Aditya, i.e. the gods Indra, Mitra, Varuna, Vishnu and others.

3. *Que . . . l'Éternité*: although 'Thy Will be done' echoes the Lord's Prayer, the reference is also to Schopenhauer, in whose philosophy Will is the invincible inner drive of the Universe.

4. *sans salaires*: 'without wages' because 'the wages of sin is death' (Romans VI:23).

5. *Mourir . . . Montagne*: to be crucified on the Hill of Golgotha. It is Christ speaking in this verse.

6. *scapulaires*: scapular: a monastic garment, worn over the shoulders.

7. *zones*: *la zone* means the *bidonville* (shanty town) around a city.

8. *Radeau du Mal*: Géricault's horrifying *Radeau de la Méduse* (*Raft of the Medusa*) (1819), in the Louvre, was based on a contemporary event, and is a depiction of cannibalism, and of human brutishness and selfishness in general.

Complainte-Placet de Faust Fils [Plea-Complaint of Faust the Younger]

1. *Je*: there is little that can be done with Laforgue's ironic capital letter for I, since, in English, we have it already – and unfortunately quite without irony.

2. *Si . . . Panurge*: *faire une boulette* is 'to put your foot in it'; *Moutons de Panurge* are folk who mindlessly follow the mob.

Complainte à Notre-Dame des Soirs [Complaint to Our Lady of the Evenings]

1. *bizarrants*: this invented word combines *bizarre* and *bigarrant* (striped black and white).

2. *in articulo mortis*: at the critical moment of death.

3. *Lune . . . puits*: the echoes are the holy-wafer-shaped reflexions of the Moon in the water of wells. These, the eyes of portraits (reputed to follow the spectator) and the Moon's apparent movement due to parallax (two verses later) show the consciously subjective nature of the poet's view.

4. *Reposoirs*: the moon is identified here with Our Lady the Virgin Mary, whose wayside altars can be found all over Catholic countries.

5. *l'oasis . . . rendez-vous*: i.e. is the oasis a mere Saharan mirage?

6. *O . . . Mecque*: the Crescent Moon is a Muslim symbol.

Complainte de cette bonne Lune [Ballad of the Dear Old Moon]

1. *On . . . rond*: the rhythm exactly echoes 'Sur le pont d'Avignon'.

2. *médaillon*: i.e. the Earth, her 'sister planet' being the Sun.

3. *rosière enfarinée*: *la Rosière* was the maiden awarded a wreath of roses and

a dowry by her village for her virtuous behaviour. *Enfarinée* signifies the white-floured face of the clown. As the next three lines make clear, the Moon is a hypocrite, for see what she presides over!

Complainte des pianos qu'on entend dans les quartiers aisés [Complaint of the Pianos Overheard in Prosperous Districts]

1. *Tu . . . vas*: these words are the refrain of a popular song.

2. *bonne blessure*: the blood of defloration, proof of 'white' virginity.

3. *Roland*: a reference both to Roland, the legendary paladin of Charlemagne, killed at Roncevaux, and to Ariosto's romantic hero in the poem *Orlando Furioso* (1516).

4. *Sulamites*: there is no finer love-poetry than the 'Song of Solomon' in the Old Testament, addressed to 'the Shulamite'. These lines express the beauty, and the repressed sexuality, of the young women being educated in the convent.

5. *Fatales . . . apparues*: i.e. menstruation. In the old days, girls were often not warned in advance.

6. *essais sans fond*: *essais sans fin* ('endless experiments') would be more usual. But here it implies young bourgeois ladies have had no sexual training.

7. *hôte . . . chiffons*: the bourgeois male's 'host' is his wife, whose function is to flatter him and dress *à la mode*.

8. *bohême*: Bohemian, i.e. the unconventional world of artists.

9. *ritournelles*: i.e. the sexual rhythms of love-making.

Complainte de l'orgue de Barbarie [Lament of the Barrel Organ]

1. *postiches*: the hairpieces, like the other images in this line, are signs of mortality.

2. *Sulamites*: see note 4 to 'Complainte des pianos' (*Complaintes*).

3. *Brûlée* (normally, 'burnt') derives here from *se brûler* 'to succumb to temptation' and *être brûlé* 'to have lost one's good name'.

4. Precisely what is going on in this poem seems obscure, as other critics have noted. My guess is that *brûle*, *guérir* and *cicatrice* are wilful mystification, and conceal a sexual meaning. *Guérir* (to heal) and *cicatriser* (to scar over) both signify the assuagement of suffering. But *cicatrice* (scar) is slang for *vulve* or for *clitoris* (which it resembles in sound); and 'healing one's suffering' can have a sexual meaning, as in 'Complainte des pianos qu'on entend . . .'.

As for the *hospice* (workhouse), young women of immoral life might end up there.

Complainte d'un certain Dimanche [Lament for a Particular Sunday]

1. *Quadrige*: ('quadriga') the four horses which haul a chariot.
2. *confidence*: evening confides in us, but we cannot understand its message.
3. *ogive*: a pointed Gothic arch, either the niche from where a saint looks down, or the central arch of a church where a crucified Christ hangs, with His watchful eye upon the worshippers. A favourite image of Laforgue, which stands sometimes for apotheosis, but also suggests guilt and reproach.
4. *madrépores*: the creatures which build coral reefs. A variety of polyp. Laforgue often sighs to return to a more primitive stage of evolution.

Complainte d'un autre Dimanche [Lament for Another Sunday]

1. *glabre*: 'clean-shaven' because the trees have lost their leaves.
2. *scaphandre*: because plunging always into his own inner self.

Complainte de la fin des Journées [Ballad for the End of Time]

1. *ciboires*: ('ciborium') a chalice-shaped vessel, in which the communion host is deposited. This image is astonishing. It equates failure with the supreme Christian rite.
2. *Lemnos*: a prophecy stated that the Achaeans could not conquer Troy without Philoctetes' bow. But he had been marooned on Lemnos, suffering from an incurable, painful and stinking wound. He is a symbol of the suffering and social pariah-hood which go hand-in-hand with genius.
3. *Passeport*: i.e. are we mere visitors here, our real home being Eternity?
4. *orpheline*: John XIV:18; Christ's promise in the French version reads: 'I will not leave you orphans.'
5. *Faites . . . moi*: Matthew XXVI:39; Christ is in the Garden of Gethsemane praying, as his Crucifixion approaches: 'O Father, if it be possible, let this cup pass from me.' We are reminded of the TB of which Laforgue died, for this allusion is not so much blasphemous as tragic.
6. *Vomitoire*: a huge door through which a large crowd is let out. And no crowd is larger than that which exits to Death. Note the facetious, desperate rhythm, like a nursery rhyme.

Complainte de la Vigie aux minuits polaires [Lament of the Vigil at Polar Midnights]

1. *O . . . sanglots*: *côte* could mean ribs. But the sea is often described by Laforgue as suffering or 'sobbing' from its waves beating in on to the shore.
2. *L'Ex-Voto*: thank-offering for a granted prayer.

Complainte de la Lune en province [Complaint of the Provincial Moon]

1. *province*: these particular 'provinces' are no doubt Berlin, so provincial compared with Paris!

Complainte des Printemps [Complaint for the Springtimes]

1. *système*: i.e. the System of the Universe, with all its chemistry.
2. *Du . . . naine*: i.e. from the biggest to the smallest, and not excluding the grotesque.
3. *Elyséennes*: doubtless the night-life of Paradise as experienced on the Champs-Elysées in Paris!
4. *Nous . . . bois*: the folksong 'Nous n'irons plus au bois,/ Les lauriers sont coupés.' – which has hints, as here, of illicit love-making in the woods, and also of the tragedy of passing time.
5. *missel*: in the Roman Catholic Church, a book containing, for every day of the year, the prayers used in Mass.

Complainte de l'Automne monotone [Complaint of Monotonous Autumn]

1. *Regards levants*: a pun on *soleil levant* which means 'Dawn'.
2. *Antigone*: loyal daughter of Oedipus. After her father's death, her brother Polyneices was killed while attacking his own city, Thebes. When, disobeying King Creon's orders, she buried her brother out of family and religious duty, the king ordered her to be buried alive. Her name is used because she is a particularly tragic case of an *orphan*.
3. *Bateaux . . . d'or*: half-sunken boats rotting in a lake full of autumn leaves?
4. *Paris . . . voiles*: this is difficult. 'Taking the veil' normally means entering a nunnery. But of course brides wear veils too, and the nun is marrying God. *Grasseyer* means pronouncing the 'r' in Parisian fashion. But Laforgue

is using the word inventively, for *rire gras* is to laugh at dirty jokes. It therefore makes the best sense of the lines to suppose that 'taking the veil' means both becoming a nun and becoming a bride, and that dirty jokes are being told. This is made still more probable by the play on Paris/*paris* ('bets'). People are taking bets at a wedding on whether the bride will keep her vows.

5. *Roses ouvertes*: girls in nunnery schools were instructed to cross their arms when going to sleep and to beware of committing any sexual sin.

Complainte de l'Ange incurable [Complaint of the Incurable Angel]

1. *Je . . . Cœurs*: 'to puff out breath' and 'to expire' are both contained in this image. The 'Hearts' are his dead loves, and the ashes a sign of mourning.
2. *rames d'antan*: cf. *Mais où sont les neiges d'antan* ('Where are the snows of yesteryear?'), from Villon's fifteenth-century *Ballade des dames du temps jadis*. One of the most famous lines in French.

Complainte des Nostalgies préhistoriques [Complaint of Feeling Home-Sick for Primeval Times]

1. *délèvrant*: another Laforguian invention, formed from *lèvres* ('lips') and *délivrer* ('to free').

Autre Complainte de l'orgue de Barbarie [Another Lament from the Barrel Organ]

1. *créatures*: critters (a nineteenth-century term) are creatures, nature's products, who by definition endlessly live and die.
2. *camélias*: allusion to Dumas *fils*'s play, *La Dame aux camélias* (1852), still famous today in its adaptation as *La Traviata* by Verdi.

Complainte du pauvre Chevalier-Errant [Complaint of the Poor Knight Errant]

1. *Instincts-levants*: another invention based on *soleil-levant* ('sunrise').
2. *Ma . . . crachats*: his bark is worse than his bite. Some snakes spit poison, but *his* literary spittle will hurt nobody.
3. *frêle . . . monde*: this ideal union of him and her is like the most delicate of births.

4. *sens encensoirs*: the first three syllables ('săsăsăs') sound like '*sens sans sens*', i.e. senseless senses.

5. *roulis*: literally the rolling of a ship.

6. *sandwiche*: a sandwich-man is a walking hoarding, sandwiched between his advertisements, two of which are carried by a framework on his back, the third being supported above his head. He has an *armoured* look, hence Laforgue's Knight Errant.

Complainte des Consolations [Complaint of the Consolations]

1. *sans . . . toile*: 'keyless' and so without any way in, or 'clueless' and so insoluble. The painting he pretends to insult by not remembering it is his favourite enigma, the Mona Lisa. See note 5 to 'Locutions des Pierrots' (*N-D*).

2. *cant*: i.e. the English word meaning 'hypocrisy, or a pretentious pose'.

3. *Je . . . compte*: this is ironic, of course. Laforgue doesn't assert he'll get what he wants, but only what he deserves.

4. Who is speaking in this poem is not always clear. But at this point certainly Woman suddenly intervenes – identical with the Universal Fate of the World – summing up everything, from Woman to Silence – for that is just about all there is for Laforgue. But certainly, she is not merely 'his happiness'. She's bigger than that. When she says she's 'too much a thing' this means she's too fundamental. As for the 'scale', which ranges all the way from Woman to Silence, well, what else is there?

5. *s'y mirer*: I don't suppose Laforgue knew this, but, in Hittite art, the mirror is the symbol of the female divinity, and the door to wisdom. She reflects nature and consciousness, and is the mirror of the soul. It is also interesting that Eluard the great surrealist poet says of his lover: '*Tu es la ressemblance.*' (You are likeness itself.)

6. Woman is nature, and her enigma is that of nature itself.

Complainte de Lord Pierrot [Lord Pierrot's Complaint]

1. *Au . . . zéro*: the refrain is sarcastically modelled on the old children's song which begins with these identical two lines.

2. *Agiter . . . servir*: cf. the instructions on a medicine bottle.

3. *le Régent*: a huge diamond in the Royal Crown of France.

4. *Corybanthe*: corybantes are wild dancers associated with various Greek deities, particularly the Great Goddess Cybele.

5. *Après . . . Déluge*: said – rather accurately – by Louis XIV and Mme de Pompadour.

6. *Léda*: in Greek myth, Zeus turned himself into a swan to seduce her.

7. *Pierrot . . . mène*: Hiddleston quotes Fénelon, *Sermon pour la fête de l'Épiphanie*, '*L'homme s'agite, mais Dieu le mène.*' Man bustles to and fro, but God controls him.

8. *pleut . . . bergères*: quoted from the old French children's song, '*Il pleut, il pleut, bergère!*'

9. *(Bis)*: the repetition, as in a sung refrain, has a curious effect. It deliberately sends up the feeling. (Nor must we be taken in by Laforgue's assertion, earlier in the poem, that he would be Woman's finest conquest!)

Autre Complainte de Lord Pierrot [Another Complaint from Lord Pierrot]

1. *Dieu . . . siens*: an allusion to the Crusade against the Albigensians. When asked by the crusaders at the sack of Béziers in 1209 how they were to recognize the Catholics in the city so as to spare them, the ecclesiastic in charge of the Crusade replied, 'Kill them all, God will recognize his own.' Everyone, duly, was massacred.

2. *yeux*: women don't have just two eyes, for Laforgue, but a whole battery of searchlights.

3. *Après . . . plaît*: it's polite to permit the woman, if she tires first, to withdraw first, as through a door. This does not prevent him feeling resentment, of course.

Complainte sur certains ennuis [Complaint about Certain Annoyances]

1. *du . . . souvienne*: Hiddleston points out that this is modelled on *du plus loin qu'on se souvienne* ('as far back as one can remember').

Complainte des noces de Pierrot [The Ballad of Pierrot's Wedding]

1. *Où . . . corybante*: God has a small letter here, deliberately, for it means 'the divine'. For *corybante*, see note 4 to 'Complainte de Lord Pierrot' (*Complaintes*).

2. *calices*: two meanings: chalice, with all its holy connexions, but also simply the calyx of a flower.

3. *Isis*: Isis, the Egyptian Great Goddess, certainly knows everything!

4. *Pythie*: the Pythia was the priestess who gave oracles at ancient Delphi, drugged with fumes from the Underworld, and seated on a tripod.

5. *tout . . . n'existe*: there is a textual problem here. But since, according to Laforgue, everything which exists doesn't really exist(!), I prefer to print this half negative.

6. *Introïbo*: solemn words from the Mass, here used in a sexual sense: *Introïbo ad altare Dei*, I shall go in to the altar of God.

7. *ut*: do, the base note of the scale.

8. *baptême*: i.e. the sweat of sexual initiation.

Complainte du Vent qui s'ennuie la nuit [Complaint of the Wind Which Gets Bored at Night]

1. *Toison-d'Or*: in Greek legend, Jason with his Argonauts went in heroic search of the Golden Fleece; but *toison* is also the usual word for pubic hair.

2. *sans retour*: both 'irrevocably' and 'unrequitedly'.

3. *hypogée*: an underground place, often a tomb, but more positively a prehistoric cave or shelter. As an adjective – more positively still – it refers to plants which bud and become green underground before bursting through into the light. Then again, it also means 'the nadir'!

Complainte du pauvre corps humain [Ballad of the Wretched Human Body]

1. *ressorts*: springs, i.e. suspension, as in a coach or carriage, or, these days, in a motor car.

2. *chlorose*: see note 1 to 'La Première nuit' (*Sanglot*). 'It' in this translation refers to the human body.

3. *Mais . . . conscience*: the Great All (Substance) stirs us back into the mindless soup of the Universe.

Complainte du Roi de Thulé [Ballad of the King of Thulé]

1. In *There was a King of Thulé* by Goethe, the King drinks every day from a goblet given to him by his dead lover, and flings it in the sea when he is at the point of death. It was set to music by Gounod.

2. *palais*: 'palace' or 'palate', so equally, 'What taste! What a gourmet!'

3. *Soleil-crevant*: pun on *soleil-levant* ('rising sun'). *Crever* is the best-known slang term in French for 'dying'.

4. *holocaustes vivipares*: sexual activity (viviparous means 'born live') brings about the deaths of spermatozoa in their millions (holocausts) – but also of offspring and their descendants in their millions, for those who are born must in their turn die. See note 9 to 'Locutions des Pierrots' (*N-D*).

5. *Alcôve*: (1) a place of literary discussions; (2) a recess containing a bed; (3) a place of love-making.

Complainte des Cloches [Ballad of the Bells]

1. *Chansons*: (1) songs, (2) nonsense.

2. *Globe . . . pourchas*: as we all know, the human quest on this Earth is for Meaning!

3. *les lys . . . pas*: Jesus advised his followers to 'Consider the lilies of the field, how they grow; they toil not, neither do they spin.' Matthew VI:28.

4. *Bohême*: see note 8 to 'Complainte des pianos' (*Complaintes*).

5. *Témoin*: people would like to shake hands with an imaginary Witness in the Sky, such as God, or any supernatural observer who might give our lives meaning.

6. *Et ailleurs*: Laforgue's own dry note adds 'And elsewhere.' For Liège is not in Brabant. But does that matter?

Complainte des grands Pins dans une villa abandonnée
[Complaint of the Tall Pines in an Abandoned Villa]

1. *œil sacré*: the eye of Ra, in Egyptian mythology, is the Sun.

2. *paquets de bitume*: i.e. the rain-clouds.

3. *chaos . . . posthume*: the universe, according to several religions, started in chaos. Unfortunately, according to Laforgue, it ends in chaos too.

4. *Misérérés*: see note 1 to 'Complainte de l'Organiste' (*Sanglot*).

5. *Memnon*: the Greeks misnamed the colossal statue of Amenhotep III at Thebes as 'Memnon'. It seems to be a fact that, for some centuries in ancient times, it used to utter a strange 'music' when struck by the rays of the rising sun.

6. *Misérérés*: refers back to the sun five lines before. The poem is a self-interrupting structure of different voices.

7. *Labarum*: the Roman military standard, to which Constantine I added

Gaulish solar symbols which were later interpreted as Christian (see *Grand Larousse*).

8. *Nox irae*: 'Night of Wrath' based on *Dies Irae*, the Last Day, or Day of Judgement.

9. *cinquième classe*: i.e. he'll be given a cut-price, fifth-class funeral.

10. *Alsace*: but Laforgue's parents were not buried in Alsace. Hiddleston suggests that this image deepens the emotions of death, by alluding to war, to dead soldiers, to the loss of Alsace to Prussia in 1871.

Complainte de l'oubli des Morts [Complaint for the Forgetting of the Dead]

1. *Pauvres . . . villes*: traditionally, graveyards were outside the town walls.

2. *O gué*: a quotation from the folksong in Molière's *Le Misanthrope*, 'J'aime mieux ma mie au gué.' 'Au gué' should mean 'at the ford', but here it seems to be one of those meaningless refrains.

Complainte de l'Époux outragé [Ballad of the Outraged Husband]

1. *chaise . . . sous*: apparently people used to have to pay for seats in church.

Complainte du Temps et de sa commère l'Espace [Ballad of Time and of his Old Crony, Space]

1. *songe . . . d'été*: see note 17 to 'Préludes autobiographiques' (*Complaintes*).

2. *Ver solitaire*: the tapeworm.

3. *Sulamite*: see note 4 to 'Complainte des pianos' (*Complaintes*).

4. *azur . . . pendule*: the Azure is a poetic synonym for the Heavens. Meter and pendulum are scientific measures of the Universe – and appear to be part of its nature, though this is ironic considering its lack of meaning.

5. *l'automate*: I translate this by the word 'robot'. I admit this is an anachronism, but the idea isn't, since the Universe in the poem is a mindless machine.

6. *éther*: in the nineteenth century all orthodox scientists agreed that the Universe could not be empty space, but must be filled with a 'medium', namely ether, via which vibrations of light and so on could pass.

Complainte-Litanies de mon Sacré-Cœur [Complaint-Litanies of My Damned Sacred Heart]

1. *Sacré-Cœur*: see note 20 to 'Préludes autobiographiques' (*Complaintes*).

2. *Prométhée et Vautour*: Prometheus was punished for the blasphemous theft of fire from the Gods by being bound to a rock and having his liver gnawed by a vulture.

3. *Histoire-Corbillard*: for History is everyone's funeral.

4. *Styx*: the River of Death across which one passed to Hades.

5. *danaïdes*: see note 29 to 'Préludes autobiographiques' (*Complaintes*).

Complainte des Débats mélancoliques et littéraires [Complaint of Mournful Literary Debates]

1. *Corinne ou l'Italie*: by Mme de Staël (Book 1, Ch. 4).

2. *crépusculâtre*: *crépusculâtre*, *angéluser* and *exilescent* are all inventions of Laforgue.

3. *Jourdains blasés*: see note 5 to 'Préludes autobiographiques' (*Complaintes*). To cross the Jordan is to traverse death, and achieve rebirth.

Complainte d'une Convalescence en mai [Complaint of a Convalescence in May]

1. *auscultant*: as if she were a doctor using a stethoscope.

2. *chosé*: the verb *choser* is another invention. To 'thing' you, i.e. to turn you into senseless matter.

3. *Ganges*: sacred river of the Hindus.

Complainte du sage de Paris [Lament of the Wise Man of Paris]

1. *Éxecuteur . . . œuvres*: executioner.

2. *ut*: see note 7 to 'Complainte des noces' (*Complaintes*).

3. *air de tête*: a term in art criticism for the attitude of a head, or the way in which it is drawn.

4. *ballons*: presumably because balloons climb to airless heights.

5. *Créature*: Laforgue avoids calling himself a *Créateur*, for we are all 'creature' rather than 'creator'.

6. *Brennus*: a Celtic chief who led a victorious invasion of Italy about 390 BC. When the Romans complained that false weights were being used to weigh their ransom money, Brennus threw his sword into the scale, crying 'Vae victis!' ('Woe to the defeated!').

7. *la Loi . . . siens*: see note 1 to 'Autre Complainte de Lord Pierrot' (*Complaintes*).

8. *anguilles . . . roche*: *il y a anguille sous roche* means 'I smell a rat'.

9. *Geysers*: i.e. fountains of bird-shit!

10. *titubent . . . génitoires*: under the weight of their heredity.

11. *l'Amour . . . siens*: see note 1 to 'Autre Complainte de Lord Pierrot' (*Complaintes*).

12. *l'Eden-Levant*: again formed from *soleil-levant* ('the rising sun').

13. *divines sélections*: i.e. Darwinian natural selection.

14. *Mancenilier*: the Manchineel tree has poisonous fruit and sap, and lying in its shadow was reputed to induce the sleep of death.

15. *Lévite*: a Jewish priest. Used here, I presume, as an example of unquestioning orthodoxy.

16. *choser*: see note 2 to 'Complainte d'une Convalescence' (*Complaintes*).

Complainte des Complaintes [Complaint for these Complaints]

1. *ivraie*: tares, a valueless crop, hence 'worthless from a religious point of view'. See Matthew XIII:25 ff. Cf. the biblical images of 'separating the wheat from the chaff' or 'the sheep from the goats'.

2. *Sisyphes*: like the Danaids, a figure in Greek mythology who was punished by being given an endless and futile task. In his case it was to roll a stone up to the top of a hill; after which the stone would always bound back to where it had started.

L'IMITATION DE NOTRE-DAME LA LUNE

Epigraph

1. *Île de la Mainau*: Laforgue was with the Empress Augusta's entourage on this island in July 1884.

Un mot au Soleil pour commencer [An Opening Word to the Sun]

1. *soudard*: a contemptuous word for a soldier. There is no exact equivalent in English.

2. *Vestales*: the Vestal Virgins had charge of the Sacred Flame at Rome. For one to lose her virginity was a sacrilege punishable by death, since she had imperilled the supernatural safety of the City.

3. *œil-de-chat*: a kind of quartz crystal jewel.

4. *rosace*: the rose-window, in Laforgue, is the image of a (disapproving) Virgin Mary, and also of the Moon, because, leaning out of the night, she resembles a rose-window in a darkened cathedral.

5. *Gomorrhe*: this and Sodom were the Cities of the Plain, destroyed by God for their sins. In both French and English, they are bywords for sexual immorality.

6. *Ombilicale*: I suggest that Laforgue is seeing the sunset as a very bloody childbirth.

7. *Phoebus*: a pretentious literary term for the sun.

8. *Déva*: Hindu word for a god.

9. *Port-Royal*: abbey near Chevreuse which, in the seventeenth century, became the intellectual centre of Jansenism, a Catholic heresy.

10. *au frais*: 'in jug', or 'in the cooler'. Mind you, you don't only put prisoners 'au frais' you also put wine there! The tale-tellers of Boccaccio's *Decameron* were locked away, escaping from a plague – but with lots of wine to drink.

11. *l'Agrégat inorganique*: i.e. that lifeless agglomeration of rocks, the Moon.

12. *PHŒBUS*: a contemptuous term for someone who talks obscurely and pretentiously.

13. *Crescite et multiplicamini*: advice from Genesis IX:1, when God, having just drowned the whole population of the Earth save Noah and his children, advises the latter to 'Be fruitful and multiply!'

Litanies des premiers quartiers de la Lune [Litanies of the First Two Quarters of the Moon]

1. *Endymions*: Endymion fathered fifty daughters on Selene, the Greek moon-goddess. Tiring of all this fruitfulness, she kissed him into a dreamless sleep from which he has never yet woken. He continues however to possess immortal youth.

2. *Salammbô*: the heroine of Flaubert's novel of that name, set in ancient Carthage. She dies for having touched the veil of the moon-goddess Tanith.

3. *Diane-Artémis*: Diana is the Roman name for Artemis, the Greek moon-goddess and huntress, famous for her savage protection of her own virginity – but also (by a contradiction typical of mythology) to be identified with the Great Goddess of Fertility worshipped in Ephesus.

4. *Sainte Vigie*: punningly modelled on Sainte-Virginie.

5. *baccarats*: a card game used in gambling.

6. *œil-de-chat*: see note 3 to 'Un mot au Soleil' (*N-D*).

Au Large [On the Deep Ocean]

1. *Grand Dynamique*: presumably the Sun, whose light and warmth sustains life on Earth. More widely, the whole Mystery of the Universe!

Clair de lune [Music by Moonlight]

1. *Icares*: Icarus was the son of Daedalus the inventor, who made wings for them both. In their joint escape from Crete, Icarus flew too near the Sun. The joints of his wings melted, he fell into the sea, and drowned. He has therefore a terrible grudge against the Sun, but for more than 3,000 years has been an awful warning against 'flying too high'. Here we have whole flights of Icaruses falling to death on the surface of the Moon, and this image plainly connects with that of the moths, see note 3 to 'Jeux' (*N-D*).

2. *dorique*: the Dorians were one of the Ancient Greek dialect groups, of whom the Spartans were the most notable. The chlamys was the short cloak of the active person. Diana/Artemis was depicted in a short skirt, and I imagine that the more Doric the chlamys, the shorter it was!

Guitare [Piece for Guitar]

1. *Astre*: any heavenly body, here the Moon.

2. *sans reproche*: sarcastic allusion to Pierre du Terrail de Bayard (1473–1524), the supreme model of French chivalry, who entered into legend as 'le chevalier sans peur et sans reproche' (the knight without fear and without reproach).

3. *Maintenon*: supplanted Mme de Montespan as Louis XIV's mistress, married him secretly, and became famous for her prudish bigotry.

4. *Port-Royal*: see note 9 to 'Un mot au Soleil' (*N-D*).

5. *Circée*: a witch in the *Odyssey* who turns Odysseus's companions into animals, but becomes his mistress.

6. *roseau qui jase*: Blaise Pascal (1623–62), scientist and thinker (who spent some years of his life at Port-Royal), said of man that he is 'un roseau pensant' (a reed that thinks).

7. *Philippe de Champaigne*: de Champaigne (1602–74) painted the portraits of some of the famous Jansenists of Port-Royal.

8. *scapulaire*: see note 6 to 'Complainte propitiatoire' (*Complaintes*).

Pierrots [Pierrots]

1. *en-allé*: an invention of Laforgue's.

2. *trèfle*: the trefoil is the shape of a club on playing cards.

3. *scarabée*: the Egyptian dung-beetle, symbol of the sun which is continually reborn from itself. Apparently, the word for scarab in Ancient Egyptian means something like 'to come to existence by taking a particular form'. How well this fits Laforgue's Hartmannian philosophy!

4. *mi-carême*: a festival at the mid-point of the fast of Lent. Note the echo of Pangloss's optimistic philosophy, guyed by Voltaire in *Candide*: 'All is for the best in the best of all possible worlds.'

5. *Evohé*: a wild, joyous, but threatening Bacchantian exclamation. See note 1 to 'Ève, sans trève' (*FBV*).

6. *lange à cicatriser*: This rather enigmatic image is based on a slang term for the vulva, namely *cicatrice* (scar). The skirt is seen as a bandage covering this so-called 'wound'.

7. *Prise . . . lune*: relevant associations may be: *demander/promettre la lune* ('to ask for/promise someone the moon'); *être dans la lune* ('to be in the clouds'); *être dans une bonne/mauvaise lune* ('to be in a good/bad mood'); and even *lune* ('backside').

8. *d'abandon*: not *à l'abandon* (which would mean 'neglectfully, in a slapdash way'), nor *avec abandon* (which would mean 'without restraint'), but 'using forlornness as a disguise'.

9. *lunologues*: i.e. scientists who study the Moon.

Pierrots (On a des principes) [Pierrots: One has principles]

1. *capitaliste Idéal*: the capitalist's ideal would be that the devotees of the Ideal, namely the artists of the 'Art for Art's Sake' movement (talk of the town in the late nineteenth century), would get no pay at all. Laforgue is not going to get anything out of this young woman, either!

2. *Zaïmph*: veil of the goddess Tanith, who was the moon-goddess of the Carthaginians, see note 2 to 'Litanies des premiers quartiers' (*N-D*).

Pierrots (Scène courte, mais typique) [Pierrots: A short, but typical scene]

1. *Væ soli*: woe to the lonely one.

2. *sans reproche*: see note 2 to 'Guitare' (*N-D*).

Locutions des Pierrots [The Things that Pierrots Say]

1. *Voilà tantôt*: Laforgue's phraseology has a comically antiquated tone.

2. *Cydalise*: spelt thus, this Greek name means 'famous' or 'glorious'. Its origin is obscure, but the French of the seventeenth and eighteenth centuries had a taste for classical-sounding names, and it was sometimes used in the eighteenth century as a *nom de guerre* for a woman of the theatre. But Laforgue is most probably thinking of Gérard de Nerval, who always uses the name (e.g. in his famous poem *Les Cydalises*) to signify a poet's Muse or Mistress. Nerval spells it *Cidalise* in his *La Bohême galante*; I am inclined to suspect that this reveals the origin of the name in Fragment 244(136) of Pindar: Kidalia (or Akidalia) was 1) a spring of Orchomenus in Bœotia, sacred to Aphrodite and the Graces, or 2) the nymph of that spring. No name could be more suitable for a poet's Muse!

3. *faculté-maîtresse*: Hippolyte Taine's phrase – more or less the central and controlling essence of a person, from whom all his or her other abilities flow.

4. *nuits blanches*: a sleepless night is a 'white night' in French, which prettily fails to echo the absence of the Moon.

5. *Joconde*: the Gioconda or Mona Lisa. This most famous of all paintings (by Leonardo da Vinci) is in the Louvre. The reason for its fame is that it has been incorporated into the Eve myth. The Mona Lisa's smile has been seen as enigmatic, but is really an irresistible 'come-on', meaning: 'Can *you*, sir, overcome my immortal irony at the expense of men?'

6. *Dalila*: the biblical traitress who cut off Samson's flowing hair and thereby magically took his strength from him. A figure of black disapproval to believing Christians, she remains, to Laforgue and to most men, the archetypal temptress, archetypally attractive.

7. *ogive*: the ogive and the circumflex accent have the same shape. See note 3 to 'Complainte d'un certain Dimanche' (*Complaintes*).

8. *trois hémisphères*: the third hemisphere (thus giving him one-and-a-half brains!) must be the half-brain of some writer whom he's plagiarizing.

9. *Limbes*: in a curious rejection of orthodox Christianity, this was long reputed to be the place not only where the souls of unbaptized babies *went*, but also from which the souls of new-born children *came*.

10. *holocaustes*: Hiddleston says this refers to contraception, in which millions of spermatozoa die. However, as Laforgue is well aware, so they do even when contraception is not being practised.

11. *Je te vas dire*: a popular form of words, which indicates complete down-to-earth straightforwardness.

12. *védique*: belonging to the Veda, i.e. the sacred texts of the ancient Hindus.

13. *j'en . . . char*: what part of them I submit to your control.

14. *cétacé*: whale-like, i.e. fishy. But *rire comme une baleine* means to laugh like a drain, so feeling is being sent up even more rudely.

15. *silhouettes . . . écran*: the image has to do with the nineteenth-century hobby of making portrait silhouettes.

16. *chercher . . . heures*: *Chercher midi à 14 heures* means to find difficulties where there are none.

17. *la Cruche cassée*: a picture by J.-B. Greuze (1725–1805).

18. *du . . . l'hysope*: see note 21 to 'Préludes autobiographiques' (*Complaintes*).

19. *Houri*: houris are beautiful women who, the Koran tells us, are 'loving companions', 'dark-eyed', and 'chaste as hidden pearls', and who attend the Muslim in Paradise (*Al-Waqi'a*, Chapter 56).

20. *memento mori*: something which reminds one of mortality.

21. *Ave Paris stella*: 'Hail, star of Paris!' From *Ave maris stella!* ('Hail, star of the Sea!'), an address to the Virgin from a ninth-century hymn for Vespers.

22. *saluts*: there was much of this at the German court.

23. *l'Inclusive Sinécure*: i.e. death. Since then indeed you have no more cares in the world.

24. *l'Hymette*: Mount Hymettus (overlooking Athens) was famous in Ancient Greece for its honey.

25. *Sacré-Cœur*: see note 20 to 'Préludes autobiographiques' (*Complaintes*).

26. *Pan*: ancient Greek god whose upper half was human and whose lower half was a goat. His name seems to mean 'Everything'. His pipes symbolize the innocent but by no means unsexual pleasures of natural life.

27. *ronds*: the rings made by his tears, or the stones he casts into the ponds, or by the Pierrot himself were he to commit suicide.

28. *Mais . . . d'antan*: see note 2 to 'Complainte de l'Ange incurable' (*Complaintes*).

Petits Mystères [Small Mysteries]

1. *au frais*: either 'in the cool' or 'in the cooler'.

Nuitamment [Nightly]

1. *Delos*: Laforgue compares the Moon to Delos, which, according to Greek legend, had floated about the Mediterranean – until it became the birthplace of Artemis the Moon and Apollo the Sun, when it became stationary like more commonplace islands.

2. *Putiphars*: Potiphar's wife tried to seduce Joseph, but he fled, leaving his cloak behind. She then accused him of rape. Genesis XXXIX:12.

La Lune est stérile [The Moon is Sterile]

1. *Paphos*: the Kings of Paphos in Cyprus were also, in ancient times, hereditary priests of the Paphian Nature Goddess. As Priest-Kings, therefore, they resembled Popes.

2. *logique . . . fœtus*: embryos are 'logical' because they follow causally from the act of sex. Pregnancy, Laforgue claims, 'blocks off' promiscuity. Embryos are an 'excrement' in a literal Latin sense. Emotionally repulsive? Yes, and this is merely a pseudo-medical dirty joke.

3. *Carguez . . . but*: the succession of subordinate constructions and clauses gives a bewildering impression which is quite deliberate – for the plan of the Unconscious is to confuse us!

4. *Tantales*: Tantalus committed the crimes of stealing the divine ambrosia, and of offering the gods his own son Pelops as a meal. Zeus punished him by imprisoning him in a lake where the water vanishes underground the moment the thirsty man bends to drink it. Hence the verb 'tantalize'. But how beautifully this figure fits Laforgue's philosophy.

5. *bons sens*: not 'good sense' but, ironically, 'good senses', i.e. our senses are interested only in the 'tantalizing stimulants' of sensation.

6. *Après . . . déluge*: see note 5 to 'Complainte de Lord Pierrot' (*Complaintes*).

7. *centre . . . part*: see note 9 to 'Préludes autobiographiques' (*Complaintes*).

8. *stylite*: St Simeon Stylites (AD 390–459), one of the most celebrated ascetics of Christian Egypt, spent thirty-seven years on the top of a series of pillars, the last and tallest of which was sixty feet high. He claimed he was trying to get away from the sightseers, but the higher he built his pillars, the more the tourists came!

9. *Or . . . locaux*: most of this stanza is ferociously obscure. Laforgue is a master of, or slave to, mixed metaphor. *Passer au peigne fin* means 'to pass through a fine-tooth comb'. *Peigner* means 'to comb', but also 'to cultivate land with due care'. It was traditionally believed that sperm came from the spinal column. *Cru* usually means 'vintage' or 'the land from which vintages come'; but the phrase *de mon cru* means 'truly my own'. I have consequently translated *cru* as 'heartland'. As for the violin bows, a nineteenth-century café orchestra suddenly appears to serenade the young couple – this being part of the Unconscious's conspiratorial sexual plotting. But Laforgue had read the medical books of his time, and I suggest that these romantic fiddles stand also for the vibrant erectile tissue of both sexes.

10. *l'abattoir*: see note 10 to 'Locutions des Pierrots' (*N-D*).

11. *la faim . . . moyens*: the usual phrase is *La fin justifie les moyens* ('The end justifies the means'). A pun on *fin/faim* and *infini*. Here 'Hunger for the Infinite justifies the means.'

12. *baobab*: the baobab can be seen as a sort of temple of poetry, for when Senegalese *griots* ('bards') died, their bodies were placed within the shelter of these huge trees.

Nobles et touchantes divagations sous la Lune [Noble and Touching Divagations under the Moon]

1. *Pleurant . . . d'incompris*: the heart of Mary the Mother of God was pierced by seven swords, i.e. seven sorrows. The French here suggests seven degrees of misunderstanding.

2. *impératif catégorique*: Kantian phraseology.

3. *claviers*: keyboards, ranges, spectrums. When Laforgue is at his most philosophical, I have sometimes translated this 'spectrums' or 'frequencies'.

4. *Moloch*: (see 2 Kings XXIII:10) God of the Ammonites, to whom little children were burnt alive. Brewer's Dictionary explains: 'Any ['power'] which demands from us the sacrifice of what we hold most dear.'

5. *kaïns*: this is obscure to me. There seem to be three possibilities: from the Greek *kainoi theoi* ('new-fangled gods'); from the Malay, meaning 'sarongs', or else connected with kaïnite, a hydrous chlorosulphate of magnesium and potassium.

6. *Pan*: see note 26 to 'Locutions des Pierrots' (*N-D*).

7. *Anankès*: from Ancient Greek: need, force, constraint, necessity, suffering, destiny.

8. *Œcuménicité*: Ecumenism is thought of these days as 'A Good Thing'. But Laforgue is thinking of the Ecumenical councils of early Christianity, and objecting to their imposing a uniform orthodoxy. The Bishop of Hippo was St Augustine (354–430), who preached Original Sin and Predestination. As for the Juggernaut, Hindus used to throw themselves under the wheels of this god's enormous ceremonial vehicle. The term is used of institutions which ruthlessly crush individuality.

9. *télescope*: Laforgue sees science as just another ingenious ignorance, with consolatory religious purposes. See Pascal.

10. *lâchons . . . écluses*: also 'to turn on the waterworks', i.e. to howl with grief.

11. *les Muses*: the goddesses of all the (nine) arts and sciences.

12. *Cuver . . . foyers*: *dieu pénate* means 'the god within the house'. In Roman religious practice, the personal god who protected the home. *Cuver*, however, means not only 'to ferment wine', but also 'to sleep it off'.

13. *Inconscience*: a play on the Unconscious and Unconsciousness. The woman is unconscious in the sense of being unaware; the man is aware of the Unconscious.

14. *miroir . . . cætera*: the shapes of the two sexes are controlled by their evolutionary destiny.

Jeux [Pastimes]

1. *D'extase . . . ligne*: literally 'an angler's ecstasy'. But *un pêcheur de lune* means a dreamer or poet, from the old folk-tale of a fool fishing for the Moon's reflection in a pond.

2. *Salve, Regina*: 'Good Health to you, Queen'. The opening words of a prayer used during Mass, seeking the Virgin Mary's merciful intercession.

3. *phalènes*: this image is surely based on the millions of spermatozoa racing for a female ovum, at the moment when a single one succeeds in piercing it – particularly as *phalènes* (moths) has a phallic echo. Cf. note 1 to 'Clair de lune' (*N-D*).

4. *patène*: dish carrying the bread of the Eucharist.

5. *lied*: a German (classical) song. The word is cognate with the English 'lay', a ballad, and therefore similar in meaning to *complainte*.

Avis, je vous prie [Please Permit Me to Announce]

1. *en bonne fortune*: *aller en bonne fortune* means 'to be off to an amorous assignation'; *de bonne fortune* means 'picked up by luck'.

2. *Isis*: the lily is the virginal white Moon, with which he is annoying the Great Goddess of Fertility (Isis being her Egyptian name).

3. *encéphale anomaliflore*: encephalon means 'brain'. Pun on 'anomaly' and 'animal'. Laforgue is thinking of photographs of the human brain, which make it resemble a cauliflower, or some primitive form of life like the sponge, seemingly halfway between flower and animal.

4. *Phryné*: fifth-century BC Athenian *hetaira* who, at the death of her protector Pericles, was arraigned for sacrilege, since she had been the sculptor Pheidias's model for the superhuman statue of Athene in the Parthenon. When the trial seemed to be going against her, Phryne bared her breasts, thus *unmistakably* proving to the male jury that she was under the protection of Aphrodite. It would therefore have been equally sacrilegious to condemn her, and the trial was stopped.

DES FLEURS DE BONNE VOLONTÉ

Title

1. Named in deliberate contrast to Baudelaire's *Fleurs du mal* (*Flowers of Evil*).

Avertissement [Warning]

1. *Ilote*: Helot, a subject race enslaved for centuries by the Spartans. Plutarch relates how they were sometimes fed liquor so as to show young Spartans the demeaning effects of intoxication.

Mettons le doigt sur la plaie [Let's Get Down to Brass Tacks]

1. *Ariel*: in Shakespeare's *Tempest*, Ariel is a spirit of the air, a poetic and sensitive supernatural being, a symbol of the will of the creator-magician Prospero. Also a rebel angel in Milton's *Paradise Lost*.
2. *Danaïdes*: see note 29 to 'Préludes autobiographiques' (*Complaintes*).

Maniaque [Too Pernickety]

1. *dater*: the French *dater* can't mean 'to date someone' in our sense, but 'to mark an important date'.
2. *Protées*: Proteus was a supernatural being from Ancient Greek mythology who, when cornered, would transform himself into animals, trees and even running water. His name seems to mean 'Primal nature of matter', for this is transformational.
3. *valseurs*: *valseur* here means someone who doesn't waltz herself, but keeps a suitor waltzing, i.e. on the hop.
4. *Antigones*: see note 2 to 'Complainte de l'Automne' (*Complaintes*).

Romance [Sentimental Ballad]

1. *lames*: a play on the two meanings of *lame*: 'wave/blade'; *une fine lame* means a sharp blade.
2. *je me r'habille*: literally this means 'I'm putting my clothes back on.' But the (normal) figurative meaning is probably the main one.

Esthétique [Aesthetic Principles]

1. *fous . . . Survivre*: he pretends he's not mad for life after death himself.
2. *Les . . . gêne*: I suspect he's thinking of the self-sacrificial behaviour of the spermatozoon on meeting its ovum.

Dimanches ('O Dimanches bannis . . .') [Sundays: 'O Sundays exiled . . .']

1. *A certains . . . diplômes*: the foreheads in question are important ones, wreathed with official laurel. As for the '*matière bleue*', it is obscure to me. *Bleu* is a colour which carries with it noble, idealistic, naïve or fantastic connotations. But there is also *papier bleu/papier d'huissier* ('the paper used by bailiffs'), and *n'y voir que du bleu* ('to be completely foxed'). As indeed I am.

Dimanches ('Oh! ce piano . . .') [Sundays: 'Oh! that piano . . .']

1. *romances . . . concierge*: the caretakers of blocks of flats (poor things!) have in France a terrible reputation for mawkishness.

Dimanches ('Le ciel pleut . . .') [Sundays: 'The sky rains . . .']

1. *Il pleut . . . bergère*: see note 8 to 'Complainte de Lord Pierrot' (*Complaintes*).

Cythère [Cythera]

1. *Cythère*: Cythera is an island south of the Peloponnese where the goddess Aphrodite had one of her principal temples. In poetry it signifies the mythic domain of sexual love. *Un Voyage à Cythère* is one of Baudelaire's most famous poems, but it ends in cruelty and terror.

2. *toisons*: pubic hair.

3. *concettis*: *concetto* is a conceit, i.e. an over-ingenious turn of phrase, doubtless here an amorous compliment, to which the use of the Italian word adds still more false affectation.

Dimanches ('Je m'ennuie, natal . . .') [Sundays: 'Earth-born, I'm bored . . .']

1. *prêtre . . . messes*: the priest without masses is himself, for he has a message but no rituals.

2. *Danaïdes*: Ixion's 'barrel' was actually a fiery wheel, to which he was bound by Zeus, and which revolved for ever through the skies. Evidently this is the Sun, and his punishment is endless like those of Sisyphus and the Danaids. See note 29 to 'Préludes autobiographiques' and note 2 to 'Complainte des Complaintes' (*Complaintes*).

Le bon apôtre [The Sanctimonious Fraud]

1. *ciboires*: see note 1 to 'Complainte de la fin des Journées' (*Complaintes*).
2. *sans Père*: there is no God, so there is no Father, and we are all orphans; and if we are martyred, it is by our sisters and brothers, and to a Father-God who does not exist.

Petites misères d'octobre [Small October Miseries]

1. *Lares*: *Lares et Penates*, in Ancient Rome, the protective and ancestral gods of the household. They require offspring to continue their worship.

Gare au bord de la mer [Station by the Seaside]

1. *milieux détraquants*: i.e. the social milieux, often dubious, in which we are doomed to find ourselves.
2. *madrépores*: see note 4 to 'Complainte d'un certain Dimanche' (*Complaintes*).

Impossibilité de l'infini en hosties [The Impossibility of Tasting the Infinite in Wafers]

1. *Saint-Graal*: according to some, the chalice used by Christ at the Last Supper, this was the object of the great Quest famous in many Medieval romances. It symbolizes salvation, and the secret of the Universe, which – most people hope – are the same thing.

Ballade [Ballade]

1. *Oyez*: the stagey old 'Hear me!' of public announcements, as loudly uttered by English as well as French town criers.
2. *védique*: see note 12 to 'Locutions des Pierrots' (*N-D*).

Petites Misères d'hiver [Small Miseries of Winter]

1. *Le Cygne*: Lohengrin was the Knight of the Swan, vowed to the Holy Grail. He arrives to rescue Princess Elsa, in a boat towed by a swan. The subject was treated with disheartening solemnity by Wagner in his opera, and with wearying frivolity by Laforgue in *Les Moralités Légendaires*.
2. *pachas*: *mener une vie de pacha* means to live the life of Riley. 'White nabobs' live on the proverbial 'Easy Street'.

Le brave, brave automne! [The Oh So Wonderful Autumn!]

1. *insulaires*: literally 'insular', i.e. isolated. For each individual droplet is its own island of gloom.

Petites misères d'août [Small August Miseries]

1. *saturnales*: wild and joyous ancient Roman yearly festival, lasting seven days, during which (allegedly) slaves ordered their masters about, and great licence reigned.

2. *huit ressorts*: *un huit-ressorts* is a horse-drawn carriage with eight springs, e.g. a *coupé*.

Dimanches ('N'achevez pas la ritournelle . . .') [Sundays: 'Break off the refrain . . .']

1. *chlorose*: see note 1 to 'La Première nuit' (*Sanglot*).

2. *Roland*: see note 3 to 'Complainte des pianos' (*Complaintes*).

3. *arrière-train*: the bustle of the period was tucked up behind in masses of flounces, giving the impression of an enormous backside.

L'Aurore-promise [The Affianced Dawn]

1. *Sulamite*: see note 4 to 'Complainte des pianos' (*Complaintes*).

2. *Poigne*: His Grip, i.e. His Mastery of all the problems of life. But as we shall see in a moment, nobody reaches down from the sky to shake this human hand.

3. *O fille . . . bouche*: this is so elliptical it is frankly obscure, but others have interpreted it this way before me.

4. *Déva*: see note 8 to 'Un mot au Soleil' (*N-D*).

Dimanches ('J'aurai passé ma vie . . .') [Sundays: 'I'll have spent my life . . .']

1. *l'amour . . . Gloire*: 'My heart's love of love', a reminiscence of Petrarch's phrase 'the glory of love'.

2. *holocaustes*: cf. note 4 to 'Complainte du Roi de Thulé' (*Complaintes*).

La vie qu'elles me font mener [The Life They Make Me Lead]

1. *Lotus Du Mal*: a reference to *Les Fleurs du mal*, i.e. his view of women is not Baudelaire's.

2. *coiffées . . . Titus*: a hairstyle in which massed curls fringe the forehead, as in the portrait of Titus, Roman Emperor AD 79–81.

3. *Circées*: see note 5 to 'Guitare' (*N-D*).

4. *Papesses*: legend mentions a Pope Joan (855–7), but the reference here is to Hugo's *Notre-Dame de Paris*, 1832, p. 57, where a pope or popess of the mad is to be elected. Laforgue is often obscure, but he is most so about philosophical, medical, or sexual things. I suggest that the popesses are madams and/or prostitutes, the 'musics' and 'techniques' are sexual, and the domestic sacrileges are the visits of roaming husbands. These sacrileges are passed from hand to hand as these husbands visit now this brothel, now that one, seeking a variety of amusements. Laforgue speaks of a 'calvary', because sexual techniques resemble the Stations of the Cross (one of the main meanings of *Calvaire*), in that there is one after another. It seems therefore likely that *biniou* (bagpipes) already in the nineteenth century had some slang sexual connotation, as it does in modern French – either the male or the female sexual organs (if the former, in the context of fellatio).

5. *Champs-Élysées*: famous (and very expensive) street in Paris, of course, but also the Paradise of the Ancient Greeks. Here it is a sexual paradise, and the Champs-Élysées are 'white' because the activity there goes on all night, and the French for a sleepless night is *une nuit blanche*.

6. *Rosace*: see note 4 to 'Un mot au Soleil' (*N-D*).

7. *remuer . . . sommes*: a pun impossible to translate. Putting one's money (*sommes*) to work/disturbing (with love-making) her afternoon naps (*sommes*).

Sancta Simplicitas [Sancta Simplicitas]

1. *Sancta Simplicitas*: Sacred Simplicity.

Notre petite compagne [Our Little Companion]

1. *Isis*: see note 3 to 'Complainte des noces' (*Complaintes*).

Complainte des crépuscules célibataires [Complaint of Bachelor Twilights]

1. *j'ai-t-y*: a dialect way of expressing the question *ai-je*, standing here for the exclamation *que j'ai!*

2. *douces semblables*: i.e. his sweet *female* fellow-creatures.

3. *claquera*: *claquer* mimics the sound of dripping, but it also means 'to kick the bucket'. The dripping of the rain is the approach of death.

Ève, sans trève [Eve As Ever]

1. *bacchante*: a wild female devotee of the god Dionysus. Drunk on wine, they had the nasty habit of tearing men to pieces.

2. *Protées*: see note 2 to 'Maniaque' (*FBV*).

3. *purgatif*: critics have speculated whether Laforgue's disgust at procreation is in part due to his mother's death, soon after childbirth, at the age of thirty-nine (her twelfth child).

Cas rédhibitoire [A Case of Returning a Faulty Article]

1. *sept facultés*: presumably these are not Aristotle's Five Faculties, but the Seven Gifts of the Holy Ghost, six of which are mentioned in Isaiah XI:2–3. Piety was later added, and the Seven then became Understanding, Knowledge, Wisdom, Counsel, Piety, Fortitude, Fear of God.

2. *vivre . . . traits*: to live by long gulps or draughts of – what for a Frenchman could it be but wine?

Les chauves-souris [The Bats]

1. *battoirs*: the washerwoman's pestle or beetle. The ancient way of washing clothes has only recently vanished. Women took them to the river, where they beat the clothes and laid them to dry in the sun.

2. *Védas*: see note 12 to 'Locutions des Pierrots' (*N-D*).

Signalement [Descriptive Particulars]

1. *Damas*: it was on the road to Damascus that St Paul had his vision of Jesus, and was converted from his principal persecutor into his most powerful adherent (Acts IX).

DERNIERS VERS

L'hiver qui vient [The Onset of Winter]

1. *Blocus sentimental*: a pun on *blocus continental* ('continental blockade').

2. *Messageries du Levant*: Hiddleston suggests these are cold winds from the East. But the image is self-contradictory: these 'packet-boats' suggest also the hope of breaking the blockade.

3. *Oh, dans . . . D'usines*: I see no way of producing this effect in translation. By the addition of '*d'usines!*', the *cheminées* (comforting hearthfires) suddenly turn into grim factory chimneys standing in the rain!

4. *Pactoles*: the Pactolus was the historical Croesus's and the legendary Midas's river – it ran with gold owing to the latter having bathed in it.

5. *masses*: an artist's term referring to the different blocks or areas of which a painting is made up.

6. *paniers*: baskets (for harvesting grapes), and also crinolines as painted by Watteau (1684–1721).

7. *caoutchoucs*: may mean either waterproof clothing or galoshes.

Le mystère des trois cors [The Mystery of the Three Horns]

1. *Roncevaux*: a pass between Spain and France, the legendary scene of the death of Roland. Ambushed by the foe, he blew his horn to warn the Emperor Charlemagne – and died fighting.

2. *Grand-Collecteur*: i.e. the Main Drain.

3. *Pactoles*: see note 4 to 'L'hiver qui vient' (*DV*).

4. *quadrige*: see note 1 to 'Complainte d'un certain Dimanche' (*Complaintes*).

5. *Ton . . . gloires*: see note 1 to 'Dimanches' ('J'aurai passé . . .') (*FBV*).

6. *Saint-Hubert*: the patron saint of hunters.

Dimanches ('Bref, j'allais me donner . . .') [Sundays: 'In short, I was going . . .']

1. *Galathée*: an ivory statue with which Pygmalion, its sculptor, fell in love, and which then came to life. Laforgue spells her Galathea ('Milk-White Goddess'). Entrapment in a hall of mirrors is beautifully expressed by this myth.

2. *Walkyries*: mythical Nordic warrior-maids, famed in Wagnerian opera,

who after a battle would carry dead heroes to bliss in Valhalla. But here they seem more like the Eumenides, who in Ancient Greek myth avenged betrayals of the feminine principle.

3. *Væ soli*: see note 1 to 'Pierrots' (Scène courte) (*N-D*).

4. *ritournelles*: see note 1 to 'Ballade de Retour' (*Sanglot*).

5. *ellébore*: hellebore was traditionally a cure for madness.

Dimanches ('C'est l'automne . . .') [Sundays: 'It's autumn . . .']

1. *Antigones . . . Philomèles*: for Antigone, see note 2 to 'Complainte de l'Automne' (*Complaintes*). In another even nastier Greek myth, Tereus marries Procne, then, preferring her sister Philomela, cuts out Procne's tongue and makes her a slave. When Philomela finds all this out, she releases Procne, who kills her son Itys and feeds his body to her husband. Tereus pursues the two women, but all three are turned into birds, Philomela becoming the nightingale, for her name means 'Loving Melody'.

2. *Alas . . . Yorick*: the dead friend who had been such good company, says Hamlet, as he and the gravedigger contemplate his skull.

3. *feux de paille*: (flashes in the pan, but literally bonfires of straw) are an image for the autumn bonfires of leaves, reminding us of the death of time.

4. *Ours Blanc*: a 'bear' is a surly, unconformable person. He's 'polar', because he seems so cold, and so are the girls and the coming winter!

5. *que . . . sacré*: i.e. the sacred and untouchable sexuality of young women of Laforgue's time.

6. *relevailles*: the Churching of Women is undergone after childbirth, in gratitude for God's preserving them from death – when He has done so. The rite seeks to reconcile the traditionally sacred 'uncleanness' of the female body with the realities of birth and the danger of death.

7. *couleur de pensée*: i.e. pansy-coloured, for *pensée* means pansy and/or thought. Thus, the woman's eyes are unconscious, but the colour of thought.

Pétition [Petition]

1. *divine Rosace*: i.e. the Virgin Mary.

2. *Circés*: see note 5 to 'Guitare' (*N-D*).

3. *Titus*: see note 2 to 'La vie qu'elles me font mener' (*FBV*).

4. *De quoi?*: an expression indicating combativeness and defiance.

Simple agonie [Simple Agony]

1. *RAISON*: an echo of the Marseillaise, the great revolutionary song of 1789. Reason was worshipped as a goddess during the Revolution, but is here denied, as indeed she is in violent revolutions.

2. *O . . . chez vous*: the poet reverts to his 'Oyez!' voice, as if announcing a curfew.

Solo de lune [Moonlight Aria]

1. *l'impériale*: the open platform on the top of a coach.

2. *Ariel*: see note 1 to 'Mettons le doigt' (*FBV*).

3. *Sans miel*: concealed inside the imagery of this poem is the term *lune de miel* – the honeymoon which didn't happen, and which the poet is regretting.

4. *Y . . . port*: deliberately slangy. The allusion is to Lamartine's romantic poem *Le Lac*, but Laforgue either guys such romantic language, or takes it 'down-market'.

5. *Léthé*: in Greek myth, the river of which the dead were obliged to drink, so as to forget they had ever lived.

Légende [Legend]

1. *ciboire*: see note 1 to 'Complainte de la fin des Journées' (*Complaintes*).

2. *sans façon*: without more ado, directly, without ceremony.

3. *Antigone*: Antigone is not a gentle legend at all! See note 2 to 'Complainte de l'Automne' (*Complaintes*).

4. *Cybèle*: Cybele was the Great Goddess of rampant fertility, but her priests castrated themselves in her honour. The violent image is added to by Laforgue's immediately referring to his usual blood-red sunset.

X (O géraniums diaphanes . . .) [X: 'O diaphanous geraniums . . .']

1. *Sacrilèges monomanes*: 'obsessive blasphemies'. Or, alternatively, 'blasphemous monomaniacs' – for one cannot tell which is the adjective, and which the noun.

2. *Emballages*: usually translated 'wrapping-paper'. But it is also a cycling term – the spurt leading to the final sprint (attested at least as early as 1884).

3. *Thyrses*: the thyrsus was a phallic ritual object carried by Dionysus and

his worshippers. It was a spear-shaft wreathed with ivy or vine-leaves and tipped with a fir-cone.

Sur une défunte [On a Dead Woman]

1. *Vous . . . pas*: the conditional tense indicates his incredulity.
2. *Cette . . . destinée*: in Laforgue love is the result of chance and the Unconscious. The One Perfect Love is pure wishful thinking.

XII ('Noire bise . . .') [XII: 'Black North Wind . . .']

1. *l'âme . . . tournée*: normally 'one's head is turned'. Here, the soul is turned.
2. *O . . . courage*: quoted from Baudelaire's *Un Voyage à Cythère* (though there the poem ends in a vision of horror).

INDEX OF TITLES

INDEX OF FIRST LINES

READ MORE IN PENGUIN

In every corner of the world, on every subject under the sun, Penguin represents quality and variety – the very best in publishing today.

For complete information about books available from Penguin – including Puffins, Penguin Classics and Arkana – and how to order them, write to us at the appropriate address below. Please note that for copyright reasons the selection of books varies from country to country.

In the United Kingdom: Please write to *Dept. EP, Penguin Books Ltd, Bath Road, Harmondsworth, West Drayton, Middlesex UB7 ODA*

In the United States: Please write to *Consumer Sales, Penguin Putnam Inc., P.O. Box 999, Dept. 17109, Bergenfield, New Jersey 07621-0120.* VISA and MasterCard holders call 1-800-253-6476 to order Penguin titles

In Canada: Please write to *Penguin Books Canada Ltd, 10 Alcorn Avenue, Suite 300, Toronto, Ontario M4V 3B2*

In Australia: Please write to *Penguin Books Australia Ltd, P.O. Box 257, Ringwood, Victoria 3134*

In New Zealand: Please write to *Penguin Books (NZ) Ltd, Private Bag 102902, North Shore Mail Centre, Auckland 10*

In India: Please write to *Penguin Books India Pvt Ltd, 210 Chiranjiv Tower, 43 Nehru Place, New Delhi 110 019*

In the Netherlands: Please write to *Penguin Books Netherlands bv, Postbus 3507, NL-1001 AH Amsterdam*

In Germany: Please write to *Penguin Books Deutschland GmbH, Metzlerstrasse 26, 60594 Frankfurt am Main*

In Spain: Please write to *Penguin Books S. A., Bravo Murillo 19, 1° B, 28015 Madrid*

In Italy: Please write to *Penguin Italia s.r.l., Via Benedetto Croce 2, 20094 Corsico, Milano*

In France: Please write to *Penguin France, Le Carré Wilson, 62 rue Benjamin Baillaud, 31500 Toulouse*

In Japan: Please write to *Penguin Books Japan Ltd, Kaneko Building, 2-3-25 Koraku, Bunkyo-Ku, Tokyo 112*

In South Africa: Please write to *Penguin Books South Africa (Pty) Ltd, Private Bag X14, Parkview, 2122 Johannesburg*

READ MORE IN PENGUIN

POETRY LIBRARY

Blake	Selected by W. H. Stevenson
Browning	Selected by Daniel Karlin
Burns	Selected by Angus Calder and William Donnelly
Byron	Selected by A. S. B. Glover
Clare	Selected by Geoffrey Summerfield
Coleridge	Selected by Richard Holmes
Donne	Selected by John Hayward
Dryden	Selected by Douglas Grant
Hardy	Selected by David Wright
Housman	Introduced by John Sparrow
Keats	Selected by John Barnard
Kipling	Selected by Craig Raine
Lawrence	Selected by Keith Sagar
Milton	Selected by Laurence D. Lerner
Pope	Selected by Douglas Grant
Rubáiyát of Omar Khayyám	Translated by Edward FitzGerald
Shelley	Selected by Isabel Quigly
Tennyson	Selected by W. E. Williams
Wordsworth	Selected by Nicholas Roe
Yeats	Selected by Timothy Webb

READ MORE IN PENGUIN

A CHOICE OF CLASSICS

READ MORE IN PENGUIN

A SELECTION OF POETRY

American Verse
British Poetry since 1945
Caribbean Verse in English
Chinese Love Poetry
A Choice of Comic and Curious Verse
Contemporary American Poetry
Contemporary British Poetry
Contemporary Irish Poetry
English Poetry 1918–60
English Romantic Verse
English Verse
First World War Poetry
German Verse
Greek Verse
Homosexual Verse
Imagist Poetry
Irish Verse
Japanese Verse
The Metaphysical Poets
Modern African Poetry
New Poetry
Poetry of the Thirties
Scottish Verse
Surrealist Poetry in English
Spanish Verse
Victorian Verse
Women Poets
Zen Poetry